ONE
YOUR WELLNESS GUIDE TO BODY, MIND & SOUL

Mirav Tarkka
&

Parul Agrawal, Olja Aleksic, Shalini Arora Kochhar,
Carina Bernardino, James & Claire Davis, Martine de Petter,
Cristina Drannikow, Udi Gon-Paz, Amy Gyles, Nikki H.,
Klana, Sarah Lines, Rene Murata, Tatjana Obradovic Tosic,
Jola Pypno-Crapanzano, Jasjit Rai, Mike Senior,
Elena Berezina Velema, Juanita Viale, Natalia Volchkova,
Martina Wojtylova Opava

Edited by Heidi De Love

Copyrights
←—∞—→

LEGAL DISCLAIMER

The entire content of ("ONE"), must be considered as exclusively informative and cannot in any way be understood as a substitute, alternative or supplementary of professional opinions or medical consultations, nor refer to specific individual cases, for which we invite you to consult your own attending physician and / or recognized specialists. The contents of ("ONE") are for informational purposes only and should not be intended to treat, diagnose, prevent or treat any ailment or disease. The authors of this work decline any responsibility for any consequences deriving from a use of its contents other than merely informative.

Nothing contained in this work constitutes or intends to constitute a suggestion of any nature. If the user of ("ONE") if you feel the need for advice in relation to any topic, you are invited to contact a qualified professional in the specific field.

If the user ("ONE") suspects or is aware of having or having had or being exposed to problems, disturbances and / or physical or psychological illnesses and in any case in any case, must rely on appropriate medical treatment recommended by a professional of their own trust.

Despite the scrupulous care used in the preparation of ("ONE"), drawn up with the utmost accuracy and diligence, it is not possible ensure that the information contained within it is free from errors, omissions or inaccuracies.

(MIRAV TARKKA, HEIDI DE LOVE & THE "ONE" AUTHORS) disclaim any liability, direct and indirect, towards readers, regarding inaccuracies, errors, omissions, damages, deriving from the aforementioned contents.

The authors of ("ONE") cannot guarantee the users of the book to obtain the same results of personal, character growth, psychological, motivational, physical or any other nature or denomination on a par with as set out in this work.

Within ("ONE") the ideas of consultants and experts are cited and hosted which in an absolutely free form, not constituting what they affirmed an opinion of a professional or similar nature, offered their contribution for information purposes only, without any presumption or willingness to place oneself above the recognized traditional medical system. It is at the free discretion of the user of ("ONE") and its absolute responsibility for any willingness to follow or replicate some of the advice proposed therein or to contact other competent personnel, according to your own beliefs, knowledge, habits and wills.

Everything included within ("ONE") must always be understood as the subjective opinion of the author, given that these considerations can also run counter to the precepts of knowledge taught in universities and / or in the scientific world and therefore go there considered as simple expressions or controversies of a personal and in any case non-professional nature, having to make exclusive reference to/and reliance solely on traditional and recognized fields of knowledge.

What People Say...

"This book is the perfect gift to yourself. It is an inspirational learning guide on how to open your heart, mind and body and awaken to your true potential"

Rosie Nolan - Mind, Body and Soul Academie, Mougins.

"Kudos to The Team "One" for the concept and the Book. This truly is the one stop shop for wellness of Mind, Body and Soul! A definite Read. Read u must!"

Eric Brundage- Publisher Monaco Life

"A marvellous collection that samples some of the best advice woven into an intimate tapestry of stories from women who found the tools to take them to where they wanted to be. Each chapter provides a journey of self-discovery as the authors share their journey with you, the tools they found, how they applied them, and the results they achieved. Practical exercises and meditations are sprinkled throughout. A joy to read!"

Janet Benaquisto- Marketing Director, RISK, Inc.

"As a creative, I rather follow my instinct, I welcome surprises and I like to give up or leave any planning and organization at the last minute. But I have to say that this book's tools have started to inspire me immensely and they disturb my procrastination. Everything is very close to my heart and I am surprised how easy, naturally and clearly it is defined. These tools show me the way to happily go where I want. And also, how I can achieve a targeted surplus more efficiently and faster, which I can then put into a meaningful project and action."

Mrs.Katerina Geislerova

"I read it in one breath. Made me realise there is more behind the things I do intuitively and inspires me to try out all the stated steps."

Zorana Josic, Advisor at Deutsche Gesellschaft fur Internationale Zusammenarbeit (GIZ) GmbH

"A life changing book! When you start to live your life orgasmically, find your inner strength, learn how to treat your body and mind as ONE, you will become unstoppable and life becomes magical. This book will make all of that happen".

Princess of Seborga, Nina Menegatto

"I love all the advice given! I love how it ends on such a positive and encouraging note. Giving people hope that they have much more control than they might believe over their mental and physical state.

Dr. Lina- Pure Life Team

TABLE OF CONTENTS

DEDICATION

←—∞—→

Dedicated to those we love,

And those who are passionately seeking more from life.

With love and gratitude

The ONE-Team

FOREWORD

←∞→

When I was asked to edit ONE, I immediately accepted not really knowing what I was letting myself in for. I have edited many wellness articles and books so naturally I expected something similar. It turned out I was very wrong. Editing this book has been an extraordinary journey, it was in fact emotional and at times extremely confronting. Each author has an incredibly strong story, they have written from the heart and have shared their most difficult moments with you, the reader. It takes courage to stand up and admit to the world that your life is, or in this instance was, far from perfect and yet all of them have grown from their experiences.

I am no stranger to challenges, parenting a child that has a lot of trauma, balancing work with being a mom and wife, it takes its toll. We all get lost in our day to day lives until we realise that there is more to life. But often we are unsure where to start, there are so many books, blogs, podcasts and therapies out there. It is a sure sign that there is a need for the information. ONE has managed to capture 22 different ways of bringing more balance to your life.

Every chapter gave me practical tools to improve my way of living, easy and accessible. After each chapter, I felt inspired, encouraged that yes, I too can get more out of life but even more importantly, I felt I deserved it.

I am convinced this book can change people, change their way of living but most of all it can teach people to love themselves. I am very grateful I was asked to work on this project, I have edited the book in such a way that each author kept their voice and their message and the result is as extraordinary as it gets.

I hope you will enjoy reading this book as much as I enjoyed editing it.

Read it, pass it on to your friends and family or give it as a gift because truly, there is no better gift than the book that keeps on giving.

ONE is unique in every single way!

With love and gratitude
Heidi

To our readers
with Love ♥

Confession From The Publisher

←∞→

"ONE" was born in my head just like my younger daughter's name came to me; a gentle, yet certain whisper in my head, telling me to listen to it. I must do it.

That gentle voice arrived while I was showering, and I remember literally jumping out of the shower, rushing over to my computer and starting the process of creating something which simply had to be created.

As I am writing this, I have goose bumps all over my body. I still don't fully grasp what has happened; I was led to this journey; I was an instrument in the hands of the universe. And, as always, I obeyed.

"you must do it now" the voice repeated. And so, I rearranged my priorities and my schedule, and let "ONE" lead the way. As the days passed, ONE was created, marvelous people came into my life, people I know will stay in my life forever, as our souls are united with the mission ONE has created.

We worked hard. Stealing time from our loved ones, sacrificing our sleep and ourselves. We created ONE, just as life is created; with unconditional love, with patience, with dedication.

It is hard to describe the feeling, the euphoria of bringing ONE to the world. It was something I couldn't wait to do; I don't really want it to end.

You will feel the love in the lines of this book. You will embrace the energy and accept it as yours, it is inevitable. That is, on top of the transformation this book will bring to your life and the lives of your loved ones.

To me, ONE represents a new family, a global family, people uniting together, as ONE.

Thank you for choosing me, as your author, your publisher, your "pachamamma".

I am truly honoured.
Mirav

Message From The Book Launch Team
←—∞—→

"ONE"- the book is purely a labor of LOVE!

I have had the honour of helping hundreds of authors publish their books and I have to say that the way "ONE"- the book came into existence is nothing less than a miracle.

From idea to concept to having all the contributors, chapters, cover and the manuscript ready in less than three months shows the commitment, dedication, strength and unity of everyone working hard behind the scenes.

I applaud Mirav Tarkka, the compiler of "ONE"- the book, the soul behind this project for her innovative idea and for infusing enthusiasm among all its contributors. Heidi De Love, editor and the mind behind the book beautifully brought all the stories to life. All the contributors worked together in synergy just like different parts of the body for the creation of "ONE" the book.

In today's day and age when we are inundated with outside influences, environmental pollutants and voices screaming at us from multiple directions and devices, "ONE"- the book will help you to be in-sync with your inner self and live the life of your dreams.

"ONE"- the book is your ultimate guide to optimum mind, body and soul wellness. I invite you to find your perfect health between the pages of this book.

Parul Agrawal
Author, TEDx Speaker, Bestseller Book Launch Expert
www.parulagrawal.com

Power Of Warrior

By Mirav Tarkka

"COMMONNNNN!!! GIVE IT TO ME!!!! I WANNA SEE THE ANIMAL IN YOU!!" I screamed from the top of my lungs, while hitting the boxing pads one with the other, making a very loud slapping sound, and I was running, jumping, punching and screaming, my eyes blazing with fire , drops of sweat forming on my forehead, I could feel I was running out of breath, but I didn't stop.

I never stop. And neither should they.

Looking around me I felt so proud of my trainees. They were working as hard as they could, no one was giving up. No one. And I know, I was mainly responsible for that. Some of them were tired after a long day of work, hungry, worried about their own personal problems. But they came all the way to my crazy training class, and the loud music and screaming fuelled their bodies and doubled their energy.

I admired them as much as they admired me. And they were changing in front of my eyes, becoming a version of them they didn't know existed, a version of them which was buried and covered by layers of routine, work, worries, and everyday life.

Satisfied, I went back to my stand. "60 seconds as fast as you can, only 60 seconds!!! that's nothing! Common you can do it, and then you can rest" I ordered. Meanwhile, as I was preparing the calmer music to follow, I got a glimpse of Gianfranco. He always amazed me.

Gianfranco was the sweetest, shyest guy I had ever met. He was good looking, athletic, smart and good hearted, but so introverted and so unaware of himself, he kept his eyes down at all times. As a result, he was lonely, had a boring job and was clearly not aware of his potential. He lived a compromised life, not believing he could do more.

He had a huge crush on me, and every time he walked into the gym he started blushing and looking down shyly.

I smiled to myself. Look at him now! As the music was pumping loud, Gianfranco was the fastest of them all, he was looking straight forward, focused, fierce, certain, strong, determined. Nothing remained of the shy, introverted man from before. There was no giving up here. This hour had changed him. It was as if he was reborn, or more likely- as if he realized who he really was. His true power. His inner warrior.

He was unstoppable.

And he was not the only one.

Within my 20 years of training I have coached and trained over 700 people around the world, with different backgrounds, ages, circumstances and bodies, I never had one person who was equal to the other, but all of my trainees had one thing in common. Through my training, they found their power. Their inner strength, their raw, undefeatable, true power. The one they were born with, the one we are all born with. That power that keeps us going when it's impossible, the power that saves our lives if needed. The power mothers use to protect their children from their worst enemy, that soldiers use to protect their country. The power of the warrior we all have inside. A power which should be honoured, cherished and nurtured, or it will just get buried and die with us some day.

Acknowledging, recognising and nurturing this power makes the difference between living your life on "auto pilot" (like Gianfranco did before the training), going through your everyday motions, having a job which doesn't excite you, having a partner who doesn't "make your heart skip a beat", having a life without much... taste it in. Boring. Predictable. Unsatisfying. But, yes, "safe". (not really, just feels this way). Or, having some "pepper" in your life, like we say in Israel; live with passion, with "fire", with purpose! Use that power, that warrior, to conquer everything, to create, to astonish, to thrive, time after time.

For me, that is the only way to live.

Now, I was lucky. I had a very challenging life. Abusive relationships, near-rape and near-kidnap-experiences, thrown to the street with nothing a few times, 4 wars, 2 years in the military, change of countries and endless houses, stalking, a broken marriage, motherhood, single motherhood... you get it! Why lucky? Because my warrior got constant training. My warrior couldn't hide, couldn't bury itself in a boring life with a boring job. My warrior had to pull me out of situations, save me, push me and convince me to stay alive. And so, with all this training, my warrior got super strong, challenge after challenge, victory after victory. I learned to train my warrior, while training my mind, my fears, my beliefs, my demons. I learned to use my warrior to serve me everywhere in my life, and that is what I taught my students. When the class finished, I would tell them to not forget how they felt. To write it down, to breathe it in, to live in it as much as they could, and take it to their "outside" life. Use it there.

And most of them, did.

Your warrior is either waiting for you to discover it and unleash it, or it is already unleashed and you are ready for the next level of training.

In any case, let's start from the beginning.

How to acknowledge, recognize, unleash, train and protect your POW (power of warrior).

Step 1: Acknowledging your POW

Let me ask you a question. When was the last time you felt truly unstoppable, as if there is nothing you can't conquer? It could have been after a real good workout, or a day you reached a goal you were working towards, accomplished something important, or even after a very satisfying sexual episode :)

That feeling, of the world being yours and you having control over everything, that is when your POW was sticking out its neck and showing you a glimpse of its existence.

Since we were born with that power, the power of life, the vital energy, it is always in our bodies and minds and is there to serve us in cases of "emergency". But, like everything in life, if it doesn't grow it goes. What doesn't get used, loses its sharpness and strength, and since most of us don't have emergencies happening very often, our warrior doesn't get trained.

Without training, our warrior weakens, A weak POW leads to the "autopilot" life we spoke about earlier, as it is comfortable, "safe", and undemanding from the weak warrior... the snow ball grows and grows, as the autopilot life weakens it even more.

Until you force it out, and force it to train.

So, the first step is to acknowledge you have your POW inside of you, realise it has been sleeping for a while, and be willing to wake it up. Asking yourself when was the last time you felt powerful, will help you indicate what has happened and when, what has weakened your POW so much. It is important to understand the source of the weakening, to be able to protect your warrior and yourself and live a truly empowered life. Understand your life can be lived much more powerfully, much more passionately, and that the time has come to make a change and wake up your warrior. That time is NOW. This is the most important step towards your true empowerment, the moment of clarity and decision.

Step 2 Training your POW

Your inner warrior needs a war in order to "show its colours" and start training. That is because a situation of extreme danger, stress, surprise and pain releases one of the most important hormones in our body- Adrenalin.

If you place a little kitten (don't worry! I am a great animal lover and Vegan! :) in front of an angry lion, the kitten will run away as fast as it can, faster than ever, as the Adrenalin kicks in. But, if you place the kitten in a closed space with no exits, the kitten – small and helpless as it is- will fight with all it has. The Adrenalin serves for those 2 situations; Flight or Fight.

Then comes the third F, the dangerous one.

Let's say our kitten was going to run, then fight (as it found no exits), then it remembered that it is only a kitten and has no chance of survival (belief & mindset), and so hesitation kicked in too. All this happened within the first 5 seconds of the lion's potential attack. After 5 seconds, Cortisol is released to the blood stream. The mind realises the body is too slow for a fight or flight, and the goal now is to defend the heart as much as possible from the attack. So the body releases Cortisol which "freezes" the muscles. It numbs the mind to protect it from trauma.

The "freeze" situation is the number one reason for failing to defend yourself. The kitten has accepted its faith and is waiting for its verdict by the lion. Its warrior has surrendered. It is over.

This is why it is so important to act fast on your decision. Action, whether it is physical or mental, in the first 5 seconds produces more Adrenalin, prevents the freeze mechanism and allows your warrior to do its job.

People live in the "freeze" state all their lives. Numb, unwilling, blocked, frozen. The warrior is buried so deep inside it has lost all hope to shine again. But you, who are reading this, are not like that. You want to break that cycle, or maybe you already have and want to keep it going.

So, how do you train your warrior, without putting yourself in danger?

Simple.

What can produce Adrenalin, other than danger?

You've got it! Exercise!

To release Adrenalin in your body you must train. You must move! You can choose high Adrenalin activities like extreme sports, or set yourself goals and challenges that would fill you with Adrenalin and passion, or just do some aerobic activity.

There you go!

The more intense the activity, the more Adrenalin will be released, the better training your POW gets. This is why Gianfranco has changed so much during the training- as all my students have. My training was hardcore, I was scary :) the shouting, loud music, crazy ideas, high intensity were magic for their POWs. And once your warrior is out- you will not want to bury him in again.

Step 3. The principle of never giving up

There is always a point where you feel that you can turn back or stop what you are doing- in other words: give up. There is a magical power that either pushes you beyond your limits, or keeps you in them. Most people give up. It is easier. It is more comfortable. It feels safer, and this is what keeps your power, your warrior, buried.

But if you push through, if you keep on going, no matter how hard, no matter the pain, no matter what! - you will discover the delicious taste of victory, of achievement, of pride.

Determination will save your life. And it will also, create your life.

You know, every time I talk about my personal story and challenges, people ask me; "how come you never gave up? You are so strong!" but I never really saw it that way. I would answer that I simply don't know another option. I was born into war, into conflict, into blood and sweat and tears. All I have achieved in my life has been achieved by blood sweat and tears, and so my warrior is so trained, so connected, so alert! That "giving-up" was- and still is- never really an option.

This is exactly what I want for you.

Step 4. Nurture & Protect your POW

Once you have unleashed your POW and have realised its power and effect on your life, you will never want to live without it, trust me. But life being life, challenges, problems, routine, other people can deflate your strongest will and drag you back into the "auto pilot" comfort zone, where your warrior is buried and forgotten.

You need your warrior, as it is your will to survive, your saviour at times of crisis, but it is also your fighter's spirit, your extra motivation, your determination, your willpower, your passion. And your warrior needs you. It is a symbiosis, one can't live without the other, one "feeds" on the other. You must treat your POW with respect, nurture it and protect it, even when you feel you don't "need" it.

How do you do that? Easy.

First, be aware of the slippery slope of "auto-pilot" living. Ask yourself constantly if you feel too comfortable, too monotonic, even bored. If so- time to change something in your life. Time for an environmental, mental and emotional detox, time for new challenges, new stimulations, new habits.

I know, life can get too comfortable and you might feel absolutely no need to change anything, why should you...?

Because in life, the rule of "grow or go" works each and every time. With your body, with your brain, with your relationships and so on. We need to freshen up, we need stimulations, we need change! Change is good. Even when it is difficult. And your warrior will thrive on challenges, passion, excitement, Adrenalin.

So excite it! Live your life every single moment! Feel the fear of change- and do it anyway! And it can be in many ways.

My favourite, daily way to keep my POW alert is exercise, and I strongly believe it is the best, and safest way, to inject energy and stimulation to your life. With exercise you face difficulties, you create challenges, you push your body to its limits, you release Adrenalin, and Dopamine , and other great hormones, you deal with suppressed emotions, and you get stronger physically and look better too :) It's a win-win situation :)

Train your POW, protect your POW from defeat, it will protect you for the rest of your life.

Step 5. Use your POW to create an unstoppable life

Your warrior will thrive with stimulation, excitement, Adrenalin and challenge, it will give you more power than you have ever dreamt of and will help you to accomplish more than you think is possible. You will push your limits always further and your results will surprise you time after time. With time the feeling won't leave you and you will feel certain that nothing is impossible.

But the magic isn't just in the destination, it is also in the journey itself.

Training your warrior will increase your determination level, your self-discipline and your drive.

It will open you up to an awareness you didn't have before; you will become "jealous" of your Adrenalin and stimulation, alert to opportunities and open to challenges. You will also be able to detect potential dangers which can put your POW into sleep.

Your decision-making skills will improve tremendously; as you will learn to face fear and chose to see "problems" as challenges and opportunities to grow, you will also learn to seize the moment, live the now, enjoy the process more. Decision making will become fun, you will become more decisive and, some might say, impulsive, as the connection with your inner warrior increases that. The feeling that you are safe and protected will give you courage and will push you away from fear.

Imagine what your life would look like without fear of failure. That my friend, is true freedom.

Your warrior will encourage you to take action upon taking your decisions. Action generates Adrenalin, and that feeling is drunkening :) You will no longer take forever to do things, you will become a go getter.

You won't even consider giving up. True warriors never give up, there is no mercy, you take no prisoners. You go get what you want, you accomplish the mission, you follow your decision by action and you never, ever, give up.

No matter what.

In other words: Your warrior's characteristics will rub off on you; you will feel fearless, strong, unstoppable, confident. You will conquer what you wish for, and you will be taking pride of your accomplishments.

But, the greatest quality of the warrior (this might surprise you!) is not the fighting spirit, the strength, the power and the no mercy approach.... The greatest quality of a good warrior, is the ability to keep one part of it sensible, merciful, kind, generous, loving. No warrior can truly defend itself if it doesn't love itself, self-defence always begins from self-love. Being a warrior doesn't mean you are in a constant conflict and willing to fight all the time. Being a warrior can mean living in peace and harmony, and just having the physical ability to defend yourself, this is why you must train yourself and the warrior. Being a warrior means "*si vis pacem para bellum*" - if you want peace, prepare for the war. A warrior is always ready, always trained, always alert, therefore safe, secure, protected, and strong. Your inner warrior is no different. If you keep it trained, if you keep your life exciting, you live with passion, you increase your energy and you work towards your goals with enthusiasm... your warrior will remain trained and happy, you will live an extraordinary, energetic, powerful life, and "war" (boredom, "autopilot", lack of action and so on) will not be part of your life. Instead your life will blossom with the simplicity, beauty and joy which real peace contains.

Before I end this chapter, I would like to give you a short example of my story, to help you understand the big picture of the POW and how it serves you.

The first time I remember myself feeling my warrior was when I started Muay Thai. Kick after kick, as the bruises filled my legs and body my warrior was the happiest ever. Before Muay Thai, I was a plain, normal girl. I had no stamina, no passion, no power. And I was scared of so many things. Muay Thai was aggressive, rough, merciless. I trained with men, all older than me, and my warrior was forced to play with the big sharks. At the time, I didn't know that my warrior, now being trained, would literally save my life.

The years which came later have tested my will to live, my will to survive. I went through living in the streets, wars, pain, loneliness, being nearly raped, being abused and rejected time after time, suffering from hunger and poverty, provoked, humiliated and pushed to the corner many times. My warrior, now strong and trained, wouldn't let me give up. In the worst of my moments, the worst of my despair, I still didn't give up. I still didn't lose my fighting spirit. I would wipe my tears, take a deep breath, go hit the bag to feel my POW again. Punch after punch, tears became screams, pain became relief, the lump in my throat cleared and I would breathe again.

I wouldn't be here today without my warrior.

Today, years later, my warrior remains strong, stable, ready to fight, although my life is nothing as it used to be.

I truly hope you have found value and inspiration in my words, and wish you a life where you conquer all you have ever wanted, a life which is interesting, exciting, breathtaking, and definitely worth living.

Remember; ONE LIFE. LIVE IT WELL.

Love,
Mirav

ABOUT MIRAV TARKKA

Mirav is a Power Coach, a bestselling author, a publisher, an online TV show creator and host, an International Self-Defence Expert, a former IDF Operational Sergeant and mother of 2 little women.

Through her life, Mirav has had her fair share of breakdown moments. She had to rebuild her life from scratch many times while dealing with a roller coaster of emotions, wars, challenges and pain, but she kept going - no matter what.

Throughout the difficulties and loneliness, following her experiences with martial arts, military service and her love for weight lifting, she always found her power in the physical world, and used it to help her push through and accomplish her goals. She transmitted that knowledge to hundreds of students who came to her courses from all over the world.

Going through a profound personal journey, she discovered the power of the mind not to be less important than that of the body. Mirav then created a method which combines strengthening the body while sharpening the mind, in order to help people around the world use their true, raw, authentic power, unleash their inner strength while working on their mind muscles so that they can enjoy every aspect of life to their fullest potential.

"I believe all of us should feel the fire and taste the spice life has to offer. If you live your life using your true power, the POW (Power Of Warrior, ™) in you, there is nothing you can't accomplish"

"Imagine what your life would look like without fear of failure. That my friend, is true freedom."

CAN GREEN JUICING HELP YOU EVOLVE SPIRITUALLY?

By Parul Agrawal

←∞→

"Each of us is here to discover our true selves; that essentially we are spiritual beings who have taken manifestation in physical form; that we're not human beings that have occasional spiritual experiences, that we're spiritual beings that have occasional human experiences" ~ Dr. Deepak Chopra

We all originate from an infinite source; eventually go back to that source and throughout our journey on this planet we are seeking to find this ultimate infinite source. What is this source for you; God, divine power, a sacred-spiritual realization or is it a sense of aliveness and connectedness to the self, soul and the universe? Have you ever struggled to seek the deeper meaning of life? What are your ideologies to get closer to this infinite power or in other words to gain spiritual fulfilment?

Do you find your connection to the divine by your association with a church, temple, mosque, or synagogue? Or do you pray, chant and meditate to strengthen your relationship with this higher power? Does yoga, journaling, or your love for a particular hobby, music, dance, arts and nature help you become more aware of your inner self while staying connected to your outside Worldly experiences? Whatever be your path, the ultimate goal of every seeker is to discover their true selves.

For some of us this discovery comes from clean eating and specifically Green Juicing. Clean eating not only purifies the physical body but it also creates an increased awareness of the subtle spiritual force. Raw fruits and vegetables are full of vital live enzymes and when consumed in the form of green juices, these enzymes rejuvenate our body at the cellular level increasing the life-essence streaming within us. This increased life force brings a feeling of great bliss, happiness, and connection to the sacred source.

Every stimulus including what we drink and eat affects the activity of spiritual energy centres or "Chakras" in our body. We are surrounded by negative energy in all aspects of our life. The food we eat, the water we drink, the air we breathe is highly polluted and these tend to increase the negative energy in our chakras. Research conducted by Spiritual Science Research Foundation suggests that the negative energy of the chakras was decreased and subtle spiritual state was enhanced after consuming fruit juice. The research also points out that the positive vibrations from the juice are also emitted into the surrounding environment; thus, spiritually purifying our internal body as well as our external environment.

Juicing can help us get rid of all the garbage we put into our systems not only physically but also mentally, emotionally and spiritually. "With juicing, Garbage In=Garbage Out," says Shay Vasudeva, Goju Instructor who utilizes the power of green juices for both her physical and spiritual growth. Raw food chef, Janet Lee juices for the ease and the convenience of 'eating' soon. She loves to juice when she has a busy day and planning a meal is difficult. She also enjoys juice cleansing on a regular basis and believes that her connection to Spirit has increased as her diet has gotten cleaner and closer to nature. She now lives on a high vibration of raw plants through the power of green juicing.

People juice or do a juice fast for many reasons, weight loss being one of the main motivators. I personally started juicing for this very reason. I felt light in my body as well as my heart with the release of my excess weight. A new sense of joy, satisfaction and fulfilment engulfed my entire existence. Even without trying for it, I created a new opening and awareness to everything around me. We were all born with incredible intuition, but our unclean eating habits and lifestyle puts a mask on our innate intuitive abilities. With green juicing I was able to unmask my deep state of intuition and tap into the World of miraculous possibilities by listening to my inner voice.

Dr. Deepak Chopra in his book Synchrodestiny talks about the two symptoms that point out a transformation is taking place within an individual towards a higher consciousness. "The first symptom is that you stop worrying. Things don't bother you anymore. You become light-hearted and full of joy. The second symptom is that you encounter more and more meaningful coincidences in your life, more and more synchronicities. And this accelerates to the point where you actually experience the miraculous." I truly started my transformation and discovered my path towards enlightenment through the power of Green Juicing.

I invite you to try a glass of fresh green juice with one of my favourite recipes "Wellness Mantra" and embark on your own spiritual journey today.

Love,
Parul

Wellness Mantra: Wheatgrass + Apple + Turmeric (Servings: 1)

Ingredients:

- Handful of Wheatgrass
- 1 Apple
- 1/2 inch Ginger
- 1/2 inch Turmeric
- 1/2 Lemon

Method:

- Wash Wheatgrass
- Wash, core & cut apples into wedges

- Clean and scrub ginger and turmeric
- Take few strands of wheatgrass along with apple and juice together to avoid wheatgrass blades clogging the juicer.
- Juice ginger, turmeric and lemon & Enjoy!

References:

"Spiritual Health Effect of Drinking Fruit Juice", Spiritual Science Research Foundation, Sep 2014

ABOUT PARUL AGRAWAL

Parul Agrawal is an International Bestselling Author, Speaker, Bestseller Book Launch Expert and contributor for publications like Forbes and Thrive Global. She holds two Master degrees in Engineering from Arizona State University (ASU), worked as a Research Scientist at ASU and Engineer for Intel Corporation. However, her entrepreneurial spirit called her to venture onto the risky path of online business. Her passion for family well-being, inspired her to write a book on green juicing which became an Amazon International Bestseller. Parul has not only continued her success as an author and businesswoman, but she has paid-it- forward, by helping over 300 writers become bestselling authors, too. She is the founder of an International Digital Marketing and Publishing Platform where she helps thought leaders write their books, build their platform, achieve bestseller authority status, and land in mainstream media. Learn more at parulagrawal.com and follow on social space @authorparul.

1 In A Million. My Untold Story.

By Olja Aleksic

←—∞—→

For the most part of my life I was told how emotional, sensitive, even vulnerable I was, how I should toughen up. At the same time, I was too much of a pain in the ass. Too needy, asked too many questions, wanted so many things. Too brave, too reckless, adventurous, too much of a dream. STOP CRYING is one of the phrases I was hearing throughout most of my childhood. From my father in particular, his parents and my grandparents, especially from grandfather.

Another favourite was; IF YOU CONTINUE TO BEHAVE LIKE THIS, YOU WILL NOT AMOUNT TO ANYTHING.

I cried and was heartbroken because there were so many things I couldn't understand. I was a dreamer, in my mind, I had a world that was so different, it was fun, it was full of love. That world was like a sunny day on a beach, when you close your eyes and feel the warmth. And when you open them and you see the sparkly sea and you just know that in the evening there will be some wonderful lover who'll make you feel so damn good.

Back to reality. By the time I was 10, the year my parents divorced, my soul was so heavily bruised that, to this day, it is hard to connect all the dots. During the first ten years of my life, my country Serbia was still recovering from civil wars that had raged in the nineties. Many of us were dealing with poverty and loss. That same year my parents divorced and our country was bombarded heavily for months. So, I guess I do not have to go into detail about my family's mental state.

My sister, who was 4 at the time, left to live with our grandparents (from my mother's side) and my mom had to take two full time jobs in order to support her and me. So, at 10, all alone, thinking that I was too much of everything because everyone said so all the time, I started to read, and read and read some more. Everything.

I also started playing professional basketball. So, school, basketball and books. Two sides of me, the introvert and the extrovert were growing up in parallel. We were moving around a lot, I think 16 times or so, I was switching schools and friends continuously. I had zero constants in my life.

Or, actually, come to think of it, I did have two. One was that my father and his parents never stopped bullying me and my mother. Nothing was ever good enough. The other constant was my mothers' unconditional love. Her love as huge as the universe itself, but nothing could shield us from all the hurt and pain.

I felt everything so deep, like all the pain of the world was on my shoulders and I was supposed to fix it somehow. I had been always feeling that.

Deep down I knew I was different. Somehow, I was always in the spotlight, people loved me. I loved books. Being a girl and a teenager in those years was challenging so I kept seeking comfort in books, stories, poems. Later on, it was ancient Greek literature and mythology. When I was 15, I decided to enrol into the Philological Gymnasium and study ancient Greek and Roman mythology, languages and literature.

It was the first time I realised that, in the past, people had their own ways of explaining things that they did not understand. And, oh boy, I had so many things I did not understand. Myself, emotions, the world. We just had to be clear about everything, life was happening, nobody had the time nor the capacity or awareness that we should deal with our emotions, empathy, sensitivity, etc. Our parents and their parents were trying to survive in a post war country so we all did our best. They as our teachers and we as kids.

But the thing is, until the moment I enrolled in college I was full of anger, and after a few years I ended up in therapy for depression. Talking to the therapist did not help, medications did or did not, I have no idea. What helped the most was adopting a dog. At that time, I was in a relationship with my husband to be, but the relationship was a real struggle. I was barely dealing with my own life challenges, and his story is even crazier. So, two broken pieces.

Even though I can tell you now that my healing process started with that first dog, the darkest days were yet to come. The paradox was that I was thriving in business. After college, I started climbing the corporate success ladder. I found my passion, working with people, personal development, leadership, creating and supporting top talents, high achievers. But, the more successful I was, the less energy I had in me. Less sparkle, more pain. One day, like a tower of cards, I collapsed. I found myself in a medical vortex of hell. 12 different specialists couldn't figure out what was going on with my body. I had a biopsy, 1 in a million super rare form of sarcoma, my whole body was destroyed, I couldn't talk or walk. 9 months later, with no proper therapy treatment, but being tired from going from one to another alternative approach, I stumbled on quantum medicine. They explained that it is about shifting the vibration of every cell and organ and aligning it in accordance with my DNA. Yeah, well, I was like "OK, now I am in Star Wars". But I tried and it changed my life. So, this machine started to treat my body and my healing process officially began. I was told it would take me about a year to recover sufficiently to be able to start with normal life activities. But, in less than 6 months I was pronounced a medical miracle. What nobody knew was that as my body started to heal, my mind too was ready for a healing transformation. For me it was a parallel process. I needed to heal from self-abusive emotions and behavioural patterns, from toxic relationship, from anger. And from the damage that all those emotions had done. But what I discovered much later was that since I was 10 there was some kind of bacteria in my lungs that was messing up my body and this was why my immune system couldn't cope. So, the thing is, there was an external "enemy", but I was the one that was nurturing it and feeding it.

In the end it was my career that broke me, but also the choices I made. Because my upward trajectory was so fast and furious, my downward trajectory was no different. It seemed I was left with no choice but in the end, I chose to become the person I am today. I found my purpose and destiny in helping others to become authentic leaders of their lives and careers.

So, there you have it, the parts of my life story that are relevant to what was crucial to my complete recovery and healing on all levels. Treatment by the quantum machine was one side of the story and the other was my ability to go back to basics. And the most important lesson was learning how to detach from the outcome. To have the ability to be grateful, mindful, present, to be compassionate and loving. To create healthy relationships and build a healthy business.

The ability to detach from the outcome is the #1 skill that helped in those make me or break me moments. But the most powerful discovery for me was the fact that this ability can be mastered by mindfully practicing simple activities. So, I went to basics, again.

When it comes to achieving mind and body balance, detaching from the outcome became my top leverage. Attachment literally means giving up your power. And detachment is like the antidote for this, the opposite, it means having faith, being able to trust yourself, trust the process, trust the universe.

The trick is to utilize all three brains that human beings have – in the head, the heart and the gut. By balancing them out, the healing process starts from within. Use your head brain to create structure, plan and process. Your heart brain for encouragement and passion. And gut brain for actual decision making.

STEP ONE – UNDERSTANDING

MASTER THE POWER OF LISTENING

I will share one of my more difficult moments in life with you.
So, I previously worked as a corporate team leader and during that

period one of the greatest lessons I learned was the importance of and the difference between feedback and coaching when it comes to people management. So, what's wrong with feedback? Well it has become something of an unsolicited advice in a working environment. It is something that demands you to change, it implies that you are bad at something and that you need to change something in a way that you are being told to.

On the other hand, with coaching, we have sessions of asking questions and listening, and this doesn't even need to be done in the form of sessions, it's an all-day everyday interaction with our people, and what happens then? We are building relationships organically and people actually want to change, to have better productivity, to be more efficient, to scale their sales or other results, whatever is important at the time.

That is exactly why there's so much science about people management. So, the effect is so much greater when you're listening and at the same time showing empathy instead of judgement. This is super important because with feedback you have judgement, people feel it, but listening without judgement really awakens their desire to shift and to transform themselves.

And why is this relevant for this topic? Well, all of this was about external listening. I had been listening to those external voices for a long time and I considered myself to be super good at that, I considered myself to be the master of listening. I had top engagement and top empowerment results in my department, I was feeling good about working with people, and driving that necessary change. But there was still this one thing, I felt I missed out on something. I had forgotten to listen to myself - to my inner voice, my intuition, my inner intelligence.

And what happened? Year after year I was having health issues. My health was deteriorating more and more and I hadn't been feeling well for a long time but when I would go to my doctor she would always say "Oh you're working in the corporate world, you must be stressed out, it's burnout, just lay down and get some rest. "

So, I thought that that was it after the first couple of visits but then after a while, I was pretty sure that something was not right. My inner voice was speaking to me again but I wasn't listening and I ignored it completely. And of course, to keep this long story short, it was really tough at the end, as I mentioned previously and it took me almost a year to recover once they finally managed to discover what was wrong on a physical level.

I was so mad at myself afterwards, I was absolutely furious because, come on - all that listening and I knew the statistics, 80% of all creativity, ideas, information, everything comes from listening.

But why did I ignore this, my inner voice? I wasn't aware of this at the time but I was ignoring my inner voice because I was too attached to the outcome. I was so focused on being this thriving, successful leader, and I was enjoying it too much and that voice inside me which was telling me that maybe things are not the way they seem or maybe I'm living a lie, that voice was telling the truth.

I was too attached to my burning desire to succeed, I wanted to prove everybody wrong about me being too sensitive and too emotional, and that's why I completely ignored these signs that were telling me that I was wasting my listening skills and my voice somewhere where they didn't matter, where they weren't as important.

I was powerful and loud when doing my job but then I would go to the doctor's office and I would be silent and agree with the doctor that work stress was the cause of everything when deep down I knew that that wasn't the whole story. So, I wasn't fighting for myself, I wasn't listening to my voice. And this is my main point and the recommendation is this:

Practice listening and start with external voices, be skilled with this, but don't forget the internal voice because there is a chance that you are ignoring something, something that needs to be attended to properly.

It doesn't have to be a health issue but if it is something important that you are ignoring because you don't have time to deal with it, you don't want to do that, what's likely to happen is that you will reach your outcome, your goal, have that burning desire fulfilled but in reality if your entire energy and vibration are not at the same level, everything will collapse.

But, by listening, the same as people on a coaching session, your mind and body's response will actually want to shift from self-destructive to healing and powerful, it will change in order to have better productivity, to be more efficient.

STEP TWO – NURTURING, BEING AWARE OF EMOTIONAL MIRRORING

Emotional mirroring is exactly what the name says. Our bodies have a mirror neuron system that is responsible for our social cognition. This means that these mirror neurons enable emotional reflections. This is pretty cool when it comes to social and emotional intelligence.

It allows you to have a greater impact and adapt better. But on the other hand, if you're a highly sensitive person or an empath, both of which I am, you are probably mirroring, reflecting other people's feelings more often than you'd like. So, what does this look like in real life?

It usually starts with a good relationship with a friend or co-worker. Why am I mentioning this? In my case I had both these situations. When I was going through a toxic phase in my relationship with my partner and when I was having a hard time due to a demanding boss at my previous job, I had one co-worker and one friend going through a similar situation. And it was a relief knowing I wasn't the only one, I had some support, someone to talk to, someone who understood me and what I was going through and how I might have been feeling. These encounters allowed me to vent and for a while this was really good for me. But then I began feeling a little drained, exhausted, I would have headaches after these encounters, and I wasn't really feeling so good after venting out.

So why was this happening? Well, we all have different belief systems, different standards, desires, experiences. We're all coming from different perspectives. I found myself mirroring the other person's emotions.

So, what happened next? Well in the demanding boss situation, it wasn't that stressful for me as it was for the other person, my co-worker, but while talking to her I would start to feel her pain, feel the same way even though my reality wasn't nearly as bad. The same in terms of my relationship, I wasn't really feeling as terrible in my relationship as my friend was in hers. And after a while, my body started to manifest this disbalance. So how can you recognize that something that was your strong support system and was really beneficial for you has started becoming something that in fact is adding more stress to you? Well, your body is showing you what you and your inner intelligence are trying to tell you, and it's as simple as that. It's really important for you to try to distance yourself, to set some healthy boundaries around you, particularly if you're going through a rough time at the moment.

SELF COMPASSION. LET THE BURDEN GO.

It is widely known how important self-compassion is and the big changes that it brings. Yet we're all still regularly overlooking it. It is especially important when you're a perfectionist, self-critical, self-judgmental, when there is something, you're blaming yourself for, a decision or something we did or didn't do.

The opposite of self-compassion is all this negative self-talk that emerges when we aren't expecting it. So why do we do this? Well, fear of failure lies behind all of this, fear of making mistakes, of making bad decisions.

And on the other hand, we believe that if we are tough on ourselves, if we tell ourselves that we are not good at something, that this is going to motivate us more to do it better. This is not how things work.

I had been blaming myself for a long, long time for something. And then recently, I just got up one morning and started to go through my morning routine, but somehow, I was feeling a little lighter (yes, I was eating as I normally do every day). I was feeling really good but I wasn't sure what it was. Days went by, I was feeling great day after day, and I started to feel that somewhere along the way I had left something behind that I had been carrying around for a long, long time. And after a while I began to recognize exactly what had happened.

Five years ago, my father passed away. But a few years before I stopped communicating with him and when he passed away, I blamed myself for this decision. Years passed and this was something that I carried around with me, like a backpack. From all of the things that I was blaming myself for this was the biggest one. But I wasn't paying attention to it.

Now, to go back to that particular morning when I had gotten up feeling so good. I realised after a while that I wasn't carrying around that backpack anymore. And I wasn't sure where it had gone or when exactly this had happened but after a while, I could connect the dots and see clearly what actions had led me to becoming free of this burden.

And again, it was pretty easy, you just have to be consistent, that's the main point. For such a long time I had been telling myself that I shouldn't have done this, this was the wrong decision, I was judging myself, blaming myself, feeling so bad, going through that situation over and over again, what could I have done differently, would it somehow have affected the outcome…

Until I understood we're all doing our best. At that very moment when we do something we are choosing something, we're deciding something, we are making our decisions based on the information that we have, the opportunity that we have, the knowledge that we have at that time and our capacity, our current emotional state, health and well-being in general.

So, if we had known better, we would have done it differently, better, right? The point is we're doing our best and this is the first thing that we should repeat to ourselves – that we shouldn't be so hard on ourselves, we're doing good, we're trying. Another thing is – we all suffer. Everybody suffers, everybody. So, it's not just about you, it's not about you doing something wrong and feeling bad because of it – everybody suffers. This was something that I was repeating like a mantra, reminding myself, for a long time. And it didn't work instantly but then after a while it did. I had previously said that our motivation for judgement and self-blame is driven by this belief that we're going to be better if we're constantly telling ourselves that were not doing something right.

In my previous, corporate job there was this legendary manager who was famous for his specific managerial style. He was known for his positivity. When his employees would come to him with some presentation or analysis, even if it was totally shitty and they expected to be told as much, he would say something like "oh, this is good, this is interesting, very nice. Listen I'm looking at this and I'm thinking maybe we could try to work on this or that, from this angle, what do you think?" so his employees would always acknowledge that great idea of his and come back to him later. He was a kind of a celebrity because of his style, and he was not only like this at work, this was his lifestyle.

And what's the moral of this story? Well, this is the way that you should speak to yourself. This is the way you would speak to a friend, a family member, so why are we so hard on ourselves? Why do we say things like Oh you're so stupid, why did you do this, how can this be happening again, you're doing it wrong again, etc. Don't micromanage yourself, be the leader, be the one that inspires and motivates and drives the change in a positive way and looks at everything from the positive side. Be that kind of leader to yourself as well. For me, self-compassion is all about this. Leave that backpack, put it down and lead yourself. You know that leadership is not just a job title, it's not something that has to be written in a contract to be applied, it's a lifestyle. So be the leader!

Things that were directly related to my ability to ditch that backpack were the following:

1. Firstly, everyday guided meditation or hypnotherapy. I have some really good audios, and you can google whatever works for you, there is good stuff out there you can use to rewire your brain, even if this is not your usual thing. It wasn't mine, I thought that I wouldn't have the patience to sit still and listen to someone's voice for 20 or 30 minutes, but you can practice it and you'll be seeing the benefits pretty quickly.

2. Another thing for me was yoga because it connected me on a mind and body level, I was able to ground myself and be more in tune, and my heart, my gut and my brain became more in sync.

3. The third thing is mindfulness – be present, stay present. What

helped me was paying attention to my dogs. They are so fully present and so fully in this moment now that they were teaching me how to stay present, I was their student, and I was learning from them found it to be very helpful.

4. There is additional stuff that I do like intentional laughing, and dancing, I dance every morning a little bit by myself.

I do these things in addition to repeating my mantra that everybody suffers and that things are not my fault.

So this was the part about self- compassion, it's something that takes practice, something that you can easily do for yourself. So, decide – decide to be a leader and not a micromanager, and I'm really looking forward to seeing you on this side. Here, the air is light, no tachycardia, no stomach pain, no headaches, no joint pain.

STEP THREE- ATTRACTING ENERGY IN MOTION

Emotions are in fact energy in motion. In motion means that these emotions are not constant, which we already know, because for example, early in the morning we're grumpy, then we start having fun, then we're in love, then we're feeling angry and so on.

Further, non-constant means that we're not defined by our emotions. This means that all these emotions are not who we are. And I really like this particular explanation from Osho and I like the comparison to a flower arrangement that he makes.

> *"Imagine a flower arrangement and all those different flowers. The flowers are our emotions. One is anger, another is passion, the third one is grumpiness etc. And what keeps everything together in one arrangement is this string, this thread that we cannot see. "*

When we're looking at this arrangement that thread is invisible to us, but that's what keeps it together. I like the picture this paints because it makes it easy to understand how emotions are there, that they are the most visible part of any situation, but it also shows us that there is something behind it all that's keeping it together.

And naturally you're wondering what this string is, what is this thread when it comes to us humans. I'll try to explain something that was really hard for me to understand at first and now that I'm able to understand it well enough, I discovered that there was really no need at all for me to understand it in a logical state of mind. All I needed was for my inner self to grasp it. But perhaps you need to understand it on a logical level, just like I did ten years ago. This thread, this string that is holding everything together, is something that some authors are calling our higher mind, some refer to it as higher consciousness, and I will for today's purpose refer to it as our essence, as our self. When I say our essence, this is directly linked to our heart and of course these flowers, these emotions that we have, are coming from our heart. And for centuries we have been taught, from generation to generation, to suppress these feelings, these emotions.

Now, a little bit more about my story. Ever since I was little, I'd been trying to figure out why I felt this kind of mismatch, misalignment, I was always feeling like something was off. What I mean by that is that from a young age I was asking my mother – sorry mum, I know it hasn't always been easy with me – these kinds of questions: why do we humans organize ourselves in a particular way, why do we have borders, why do we have money, why are some people wealthy and some are poor, and I know that these are all naive questions but I'm sure that you can understand how a child might be confused by all that. So, when I was old enough, I started studying more about philosophy and psychology, I was reading and listening all the time.

And over the past decade I can say that I've finally managed to make some sense of it all, but I needed 10 years of active involvement and digging up these different theories, on who we are, where are we heading, what is the point and so on. And now I find myself here, and I would like to welcome you all to be here with me. I am now in a place where I'm finally connected to this thread. I am seeing it, I am seeing this string, I am connected to my essence, I am connected to my true authentic self and I'm finally understanding what these emotional patterns and this flow are meant to look like for us. I am here. But of course, this is not a destination, it's a journey, and this is only one part of it, one checkpoint, that's how we should be thinking about it.

Now, to go back to energy in motion, and me trying to figure it all out. While at my previous company, I was working as a contact centre team leader at one point and I conducted a case study. I had been observing 15 people in their emotional intelligence, their behaviour over a 12- month period. What I was seeing in practice was that there were individuals who were able to understand how emotions affect their performance and how they can manage and handle them, and how they can use them to attract what they need. So, they weren't running around like crazy trying to reach their targets, no, they were handling their emotions, they were present, they worked focused, and achieved results. This was astonishing and ground-breaking for me because I was finally able to see in practice, in real life, those things that I had only been reading about in books.

And I also finally understood how this should be working for me. But what I was struggling with was the question of what I was supposed to do, to be that person who knows how to handle and manage emotions, how to use these them, this energy in motion, to obtain what I want. I had been struggling with this for a while and I told you at the beginning that my number one mistake was struggling to comprehend all of this. There was no need for my brain and logic and mind to understand it because, luckily, my inner self had already understood it.

After some time, I finally reached that point where I was starting to feel like myself. And the more I was feeling like myself, the less I was asking those questions that I had mentioned earlier: why we as humans did this or that, why we organize ourselves in the way that we did, I finally understood and recognized that behind all this reality was the fact that humans, for generations, had been suppressing their own feelings and emotions, that they had been building their worlds based on logic and completely ignoring all the rest of it and that this is why we have what we have. But there is a minority, those people that we consider to be wise, so full of wisdom. We can see this light inside of them and that is because they managed to tap into that part of themselves, because they were able to see that thread, they were able to start that inner flame and from that they were able to manage and arrange their own emotions, their own flowers.

The very first step is just observing your emotions, don't suppress them. It's going to be alright, nothing bad is going to happen because as long as you aren't suppressing them, you're encouraging your inner self, your essence to be awake and to be in charge. And that's it. It is not essential that you understand this on a logical level, but it's important for your essence that you start opening yourself up to these ideas because, as I've already pointed out, being on this side is really incredible and I truly don't have the right words to express myself, not even in my native language, because this feeling of freedom and weightlessness is inexplicable. All that I can say is that I would really like to encourage you to awaken that part of you, to be in charge – you, not your higher mind, not your brain, not your logic, because all of these are just mechanisms that your inner self, your essence should be managing, it is something that should come from within. The current state for most people is a reaction to external situations, like someone has a remote control and is pressing buttons and you are reacting, feeling this, that and the other. In order for you to be the one who is in charge you need to tap into that inner self.

LOVE

Love is the most powerful emotion of all and as we said emotion is actually energy in motion, so if we're talking about love as the most powerful energy that there is, it's natural that we want to attract more of this power into our lives, into ourselves, it has magical healing power.

To go back to my early age life, reality was that I was always feeling so damn stressed out because of all different kinds of physical discomfort that I was experiencing, all kinds of pain. And I've always had a really rich inner imagination and creativity and I was so angry with myself because my body wasn't able to follow me in that. So basically, I thought of myself as being too weak and I was mad at myself and frustrated because I had all these ideas and I was unable to bring them to life because my body simply couldn't cope. So, all this stress and anger had been accumulating as I was growing up and the discomfort was getting bigger and bigger and of course this was really painful.

I realised later on, what I see now clearly, is that I had no self-love. I was angry and I considered myself cursed and the people around me could easily hurt my feelings, with some misplaced sentence or something futile, they weren't able to see how this was a real struggle for me. In their eyes I was just this child, and later this young adult, that has and gets everything that she wants. But I was never satisfied because as successful as I was becoming, I was always aware that I wanted more and that I could achieve more but that my body was stopping me. But I was missing the point, I didn't understand that my body and my soul and my inner self and my mind and my heart - that they are all one, one organism. What I really needed was to attract more love – first self- love and then to find out and experience and feel how this works in other relationships and other areas of my life. So, even though nobody taught us that we should practise self-love, the first thing that you should do is to look closely inside yourself and into your life and you will find for sure some areas where you don't like yourself. It doesn't matter whether it's your teeth, your skin, your weight, being too shy or whatever it is about you that you don't like. Find those areas, detect them, and you will see how you can turn this around. But it really is super important that you practice self-love, that you attract this self-love so that you can detach from the outcome. We want to detach ourselves from that depressing angry state.

These are few things that work well, and not just for me but also for so many other people that I know.

1. The first thing is something that I have been doing for so long without even realising that there was somebody, in this case Osho, who recommends it. I had been doing it intuitively. And this is yet more proof that we have all the answers within ourselves and that we just need to listen. So Osho recommends that you do 20 minutes of intentional laughing, laughing with intention creates the feeling of happiness inside your body even if there is nothing funny, then 20 minutes of lying on the ground, so you should lie down and connect with nature, and 20 minutes of dancing – this is my favourite, and he says that if you practice this between 6 to

8 months you will feel this incredible transformation. As for me, I'm not doing it in that specific order and I don't do it in one hour bulk per day, but I do all three things every single day, and in my case I only needed three months to start feeling a huge healing transformation, a big shift happened to me after that period. For the nature connection, it would be good if you could be outdoors, but for me it works from home. I would lay down on my wooden floor and just cuddle my dogs and this would be that connection and grounding for me. And if you don't like dancing just move, do something with your body, and you will see the change.

2. The second thing is simply slowing down. Whatever it is that you're doing try doing it with less intensity, when you walk - walk more calmly and be more present and pay more attention to your walk, just slow down. When you're in the shower don't just scrub yourself and run out, slow down, take it easy. And why is this important? If you do this for three weeks you will see that everything else, your anger, your depression, your anxiety, everything will decrease. As I said, it's all one organism, so if you slow down physically, the things that you are doing, you will calm down your emotions as well. This is important so that you can reduce that intensity and this is how you open yourself up to attracting more love.

3. And the third recommendation, straight from Osho, it's a radical one so I'm just going to tell you about my experience: one day I was sitting in my room and I could hear my husband from the terrace - he had at one point started barking with or at the neighbour's dog, so our two dogs just joined him and this had become one barking crowd. And I was completely astonished, thinking to myself is this really happening, what's going on? But what I didn't know at that time is that there was somebody who recommends practicing some type of animal behaviour. So, if you like dogs or feel that you could mimic a dog, close yourself inside a room and jump around or bark or whatever that animal of yours would do for fifteen minutes. This is really going to awaken that wild side of you and when you awaken that wild, animalistic part of you, it will in fact neutralize your problems. If you're currently finding yourself stuck in some

kind of a negative loop, this is the number one thing that can help you. This is especially good for you if you find yourself lacking energy and are in a moody state, and you need to level up this animal instinct. To be honest, I don't bark around but what I often do and what most dog owners that I know do, is that I communicate with them and mimic some of their sounds. Also, cuddling and petting animals can really shift your energy and help you be more resilient at that moment when you need it. Yes, I am dead serious.

THE FLOW

Being in a state of flow or in the zone is the complete opposite from feeling continuously stressed or even temporarily stressed or experiencing any kind of anxiety.

Ever since I was 15 years old, I've been fascinated and amazed by the ancient Greek civilization and I found one aspect of Greek civilization particularly mesmerising. The oracles. Why oracles? Well it sounded completely crazy to me to have a kind of temple or oracle, and this one prophet, and a lot of people coming to that secret place in order to get life-changing answers. The impact of these places was enormous at that time. And what I found most interesting was that this prophet would always have to enter an ecstatic state, a kind of a trance, in order to receive the message from God and pass it on to the commoners who were coming. Basically, this involved some mythology, but it also explained quite a lot. This was my first encounter with this kind of an ecstatic moment that I was attracted to.

Later on, playing basketball professionally, I had the opportunity of experiencing this myself and a few times I really entered that strange mind and body state where you're basically unaware of time and your surroundings and you're simply in that action and movement and you're reaching and going far beyond your initial goals and you're achieving some really extraordinary results. So this is one example, and you're surely familiar with this kind of zone or flow existing in different areas of life, hearing for example poets, creators, all kinds of artists explain how they're not sure of the exact moment when the muse had entered the room and they actually started creating something or when you hear stories of pianists that had no idea how they had managed to play that amazing piece…

So later on when I was in college I began studying Goleman's Emotional Intelligence, which I've already mentioned, but this was the first time that I understood on a logical level that there is some kind of scientific proof behind all this, and that we now know what is happening to us when we enter these different states.

So, the more you are focused on a particular activity which you are enjoying the less intense your cortex activity is. It's not more involved, it's less, and this allows your body and your mind to detach completely from all surrounding sounds and any kind of noise or people, everything around you, which is really interesting. And when you're in that state, this is actually the state of complete inspiration. This is exactly why intentionally tapping into this kind of state helps to detach from any outcome or burning desire.

So how can you do this? Well there are a couple of prerequisites.

1. The first is that this activity that you're doing has to be something that you really love and enjoy, and gives you the feeling no one else exists while you're doing it. Something you're very skilled at. Imagine when you're going to dance class, for the first couple of times you're going to be focused on your steps, on doing them correctly and in the correct order, but then after that you won't have to pay so much attention and put so much focus on your feet or on wondering what to do with your arms, etc. You're enjoying it and you're skilled at it, that's the first step.

2. Now the second step: let's say you're an athlete and you want to run 10 kilometres but your usual run is six or seven. Basically, you know how to run, you don't have to pay attention to how your body is moving. Now in order to tap into that state of flow you should focus on movement and on breathing, you should put a little more effort into your concentration, concentrate totally on what you're doing. It's probably a little odd because we want to detach, but in this initial phase you are completely focused

on what you're doing. For example, if you're writing just try to focus on your pen and on the movement, completely focus, this is step two.

3. And the third, important thing, is that this goal that you set for yourself should be challenging enough for you. Why? Because, and I was able to prove this a couple of times when I was a team leader at the company I previously worked in, people are giving their best and achieving crazy results and creating amazing things when they are properly challenged. So, this goal should definitely be something out of your comfort zone but also shouldn't be too stressful and cause anxiety.

This flow state is widely known as the zone and there are also examples in the animal world. We know that squirrels go nuts for nuts and they go into that zone and nothing can distract them from reaching their goal.

If you don't have anything that is directly related to your job or current outcome that you are trying to reach then do reverse engineering – try to remember during which activities you were able to enter that state of flow in the past, and do that. it's going to help you feel less stress and anxiety. And as we've already mentioned this state of flow is the direct opposite from negative feelings, in this state of flow you are completely free of your ego, so no negative self-talk, no procrastination, no self-criticism, no thinking that something bad is going to happen, no worries at all because you're completely unaware of what is happening to you and you're simply creating something or reaching something extraordinary. And this is the perfect healing process.

To conclude, I have realised that my story is everybody's story. We all suffer, in one way or another. Poverty, bullying, wars, harassment, traumas, bad role models, bad relationships, feeling alone, feeling alienated, having doubt...We all have our stories that make us who we are today.

And there is another universal truth. We all do our best. Our parents, family, friends, everyone does what they truly believe is the best. When I finally realized this, I could finally see another perspective about my father and his family, it painted a completely different picture.

I could see my grandfather as this young boy who lost his father in a war, I could see him walking miles in order to reach the school, I could see him becoming this proud and successful man making a ton of money

I could see my father as a small child that had the impossible task to rise up to his "super-dad's" expectations. And I could see clearly how devastating it all was. But, also, I am finally ready to forgive and to remember the good parts. I am ready to remember only moments when he was my dad, cheering me on at games or cooking his famous fish soup and pancakes.

Forgiveness. It will set you free. I am writing this on a plane, travelling from Belgrade to London. I am on my way to meet people that I thought didn't exist. Likeminded people. Forgiveness gave me the opportunity to go beyond my wildest imagination and to be able to use all the experience, all the good and all the bad and to create this incredible global empowerment movement, to create infrastructure that will support transformation for many women. Because we are all meant to amount to something. And tears are healthy. Tears mean you have what it takes to heal completely. I promise.

So, I guess that I want to say that anything is possible. It is possible to be on a verge of existence in one moment and to have a drink in Noting Hill in another. Just trust.

Oh, and something else, I was never actually alone, so neither are you. Just trust. And you will groove the world.

Love,
Olja

ABOUT OLJA ALEKSIC

I'm Olja Aleksic, Leadership Mentor, on a mission to break taboo topics around women's emotions and business success. That is why in 2019 from being a leader in an international cooperation I became the leader of my business.

I started the Sapfo Groove Initiative through which I globally support women on a similar career path. I help them heal toxic relationships with themselves, to break free from self-maltreatment and step into self-confident authentic leadership roles.

I am the author of the #Authentic Leadership programs, tailor made for high-sensitivity, creative women who have always been somewhat rebellious. Because I believe that these women are destined to be authentic and innovative leaders and drivers of positive change in society.

I am a graduate philologist in Greek language and literature, which continues to be an inexhaustible source of inspiration for me. I am currently undergoing an Art as Therapy certification program, and at Extraordinary Growth Academy I am learning the principles of running a business through aligning personal energy and vibration with vision, practicing yoga, working and living with a good groove, a husband and two super groovy dogs.

"The ability to detach from the outcome is the number 1 skill in life!"

WTF IS "HAPPY-NESS"!!

By Shalini Aroraa Kochhar

Happiness is as a butterfly, which, when pursued, is always just beyond your grasp, but which, if you will sit down quietly, may alight upon you." – Thoreau"

Empathy comes with its own hang-ups. Humans don't usually give a spiel about the importance of change, until adversity takes them back to negativity, then they care! The real courage, having the balls, comes from smiling through the shit and flowing with the winds of change. The question, though, stagnates at the fundamental "do you have the balls?"

We grew up on the "once upon a time" stories so let me tell you one about one of my clients'. It involves identical twin girls (in nothing but their appearances). Same home, same upbringing but divergent personalities. Charlize 'n Reese were two beautiful sisters.

Charlize was the early riser, the go getter. Before Reese even opened her eyes, Charlize was already done with a rigorous workout at the gym, few laps in the pool and been through the unending supply of newspapers. And of course, woke her sister up just as she needed. Reese was the smart ass - a late riser, instant coffee drinker (nothing else worked with her time management skills), only to be stumbling an hour late into work…

Her trick though, lay in reciting her Charlize's morning routine as her own to inspire all the people that worked with her... They loved her!!! She had them enthralled by her positive vibes and words.

Reese was a brand queen, wanted the Birkin and the Chanel to do the talking, there was no end to her shopping desires and you can only imagine the balance on her "savings account." At least she thought she was living the life of the rich and famous and like most of us, derived all her drive from that and only that.

What Charlize thought was luxury...Reese thought was necessity. Contentment - not for Charlize!

Charlize had a boyfriend that looked like McDreamy and charmed like McSteamy - an idea that did not sit well with Reese! Of course, she believed "what's mine is mine and what's yours is mine too." Reese had everything – but evidently, had significant difficulty seeing the value of it, I doubt she had ever tried!

It was all fun and games, though, until McDreamy and Reese crossed the line, leaving no stone unturned in hurting Charlize. While Charlize lost what she thought was love, Reese was busy winning the "she can have it all" contest.

Surely most of us are familiar with the idea of karma (but more importantly, in the wise words of Alicia Keys) what goes around comes around, Charlize had been heartbroken but she carried on with life and continued to work with her positive demeanour, helping people and changing lives along the way. Some would say, she dealt with what for her had been the unimaginable.

Reese, with her 4 million followers (she had a million likes by time she sneezed), had gone from social validation to a slump of loneliness, resentment and anger. The girl that derived her dopamine high from Instagram followers, had realized somewhere along the way, that the love and support of her sister was incomparable.

It isn't difficult to understand anymore, the girl with the broken heart took it all in her stride and focused on growing from it and Reese with her accomplished mission was left, lonely, in a pool of guilt. Yes!

Relationships do play the biggest role in us being happy!

Hours of gossip and girl talk with Charlize were the root of Reese's positivity. Reese knew she needed some happy inducing to rid herself of the pain, and if not family, then a Happiness Coach!

It was then that she came to me and during these therapy sessions she opened up about all the avenues she had at her disposal because she could have anything money could buy but as the old saying goes "Money can't buy happiness." When asked to describe Charlize, Reese burst into tears but made it known that Charlize is the epitome of "grace and gratitude." She continued to describe "She walks into that gym 'n spreads love and laughter. In fact, the gym instructor who is not so well to do so - she takes care of his daughters' education. "Giving" is the norm for her. She is the only person that accepts me with all my quirks and sometimes because of them, because she's a glass half full person

She's her own person, doesn't believe in "keeping up with the kardashians (Joneses)!"

In fact, she always told me "I got your back", live life on your terms 'n do what makes u happy so u have no regrets in fact it was our tag line "Sleep with George Clooney if u must ". Have no regrets ...and look what I did I slept with her boyfriend, out of resentment and boy, I have nothing but regret.

Shalini, I love my sister, my confidante, my alibi, my go to... she's my happiness I want only her ... turn back the clock ... help me!!" This may have been Reese's first show of empathy and love for another person (feelings she had lost no thanks to the social media revolution that has made human connection redundant) in years!

And with those intense emotions and her breakdown, Reese had a heart attack. When she opened her eyes after a few hours - Charlize was sitting next to her holding her hand. she looked at her firmly but smilingly and said "I forgive u"

Logically Reese should now live happily ever after because all she wanted was Charlize....

But for how long? She certainly had her moment of realization but who is to say just how long that moment of truth will last.

When you think or say "I will be happy when..." what you are really saying to your subconscious mind is "I will not be happy until..." Assuming you reach the until, it's like this - What is the happiest day of a man's life? The day he buys his first golf club and the day he sells his first golf club. What makes u happy today, may not make u happy tomorrow!

Here's what I would like you to take back from my simple story, and in true millennial style, let me say it in hashtags!

#smile - "fake it till you make it"!
#exercise 'n eat right - when your body moves your mind grooves
#positiveaffirmations- positive actions not just positive thinking!
#vanityissanity - I love me!
#besexy- if you look good you feel good!
#primetime is for people we love not for social media!
#passion- add a hobby a "soul stirrer" - Reading, Writing, Running, Swimming.
#forthingstochangewehavetochange
#contentmentnotConsumption!
#selftalk- Stop keeping up with the Joneses or should I say Kardashians!
#Want it Be it! You move that cheese!
#Noregrets is a life well lived! Sleep with George Clooney if u must (wink wink)
#Love is a universal language- and u don't need Duo Lingo to learn it
#progressnotsuccess is the key to happiness - Everybody should get Rich and Famous and do everything they ever dreamed of so they can see that it's not the answer."- said Jim Carrey
#GrowGive&Forgive- it's only by giving that we receive!
#Grace&Gratitude-If you're Happy n u know it clap your hands

And last but not the least

#sarvebhavantusukhina- may everyone be happy

Live your life so that your epitaph could read "She came, she loved and she left a legacy of happiness "

Love,
Shalini Aroraa Kochhar

"No regrets is a life well lived. Sleep with George Clooney if you must (wink wink)"

ABOUT SHALINI ARORAA KOCHHAR

♡ Shalini Aroraa Kochhar Has been a Luxury and Lifestyle Consultant in India for over a couple of decades promoting and launching Luxury Brands. Public Relations and events being her core strengths. She is an author, Blogger and Columnist and a Television Anchor. Having been a Miss India finalist limelight could hardly evade her so Shalini went out there and founded and formed the "Women on Top" forum which brings together women entrepreneurs from different walks of life under one umbrella and creates opportunities for them to brainstorm and grow through interdependence in India and Globally. Shalini launched the Women on Top forum with a book called "ShaliniSays Women on Top of their Game!" Which features inspiring stories of 100 women entrepreneurs, she is now working on her next book which will feature 50 women Globally. This initiative of hers was to raise funds for Breast cancer victims and raising awareness for Breast cancer.

Shalini has been the Ambassador for the "Pink Ribbon" breast cancer foundation creating awareness across India and she is the Ambassador for the Better World Forum Monaco.

A certified Life Coach, a motivational speaker and a Happiness Guru she travels all across the world in her pursuit of Transforming lives one life at a time. She believes if we all do our bit; we can make this world a better place for you and for me and the entire human race. She inspires everyone to "Give Back". She has won many awards by various organizations, such as ALL- All ladies league at the Women's economic forum and The United Nations- ICUNR The Dr Ambedkar National Award, for her efforts to empower women and raised funds for various causes related to women.

She has her own jewellery line Sak's Monaco which retails in Monaco, Milan and Berlin and has been showcased during all of Europe's Fashion weeks.

Her upcoming books other than the "World bestseller Global edition "ShaliniSays women on top of their game!" are:

1. Love you zindagi (love you life) with Gulraj Shahpuri
2. Find your emotional G-spot with Kanika Sethi Babbar Also in the pipeline are the "Women on Top Awards"

She now lives in Monaco and is definitely putting India on the map as she continues to make a mark there through her work. Shalini leads an inspired Life and is an inspiration herself... Her motto - I believe I can Fly. I believe I can touch the sky.... So she will!

Courage To Overcome Emotional Barriers

By Elena Berezina Velema

"Those who flow as life flows know they need no other force"
Lao Tzu

Have you ever found yourself stuck in your own emotions, unable to get out? Swept away by what someone had said or done?

It is easier to be in alignment with ourselves when things are going our way, but what about those other times when things just don't go right? Our natural reaction to painful situations is to shut down and protect ourselves. We become rigid and try to resist whatever it is that life is throwing at us. This rigidness however does not always work for us. We need to stay strong and keep our integrity, but at the same time it is vital to remain flexible to be able to move forward.

Think of the gracious palm trees that stand on the beach by the sea side. These tall lean trees soak up the sun on the bright days and when the storm comes along, they bend under the strong forces of the wind. Staying whole and strong in the tough times and at the same flexible, not trying to fight with the forces of nature. While the trees that are stiffer are broken and uprooted by the passing storm, the gracious palm trees remain whole and untouched. "So, what is the palm trees' secret to staying in one piece? The answer is flexibility".

Often enough on our path to well-being we find ways to be flexible with our body by doing yoga, Pilates or stretching. However, many of us do not extend this notion to our minds. So when a challenge comes along we become stiff and rigid, trying at all cost to protect ourselves from the uncomfortable feeling that the situation is bringing up in us. Forgetting that it is a sure way to get hurt. Instead we can be whole and one, just like the palm trees on the beach. Keeping our core and at the same time going with the forces of life and not fighting against them.

In my practice as a personal development coach in Monaco I have seen so many people struggle with letting go of the negative emotions of anger, resentment, betrayal and feeling completely trapped. Sarah, one of my clients, struggled with the feelings of loss and unfairness. Her husband's company went bankrupt and they had to sell their beautiful home in the hills, their cars and were left to live in a cheap little apartment with their two children. Sarah could not let go of the pain of loss she was feeling and every day spiralled down, locking herself away from the world. She felt so alone.

We started a coaching journey together and she soon found ways to accept the situation she was in and acknowledge her feelings. Sarah found the courage within herself to start letting go of the pain and to relax into it. Instead of being stiff and holding on to old baggage, she found a way to invite flexibility in her life.

The key for Sarah was the technique I am going to reveal to you in this chapter. A technique which helped her realise that she is not alone. There are people on this planet that are experiencing exactly what she feels this very moment. The pain that she felt was felt by men, women and children all over the globe. This awareness awakened compassion in her and an openness to the world. And that was just what she needed to start her journey of letting go. Feeling one with all of the people that are going through a loss like she does, Sarah opened her heart and allowed the first glimpse of light to start flowing in her own little world, where she had locked herself up in the dark. By losing her house Sarah has found a path to her true self. By losing her attachments she came much closer to her inner values and to what truly makes her feel alive. Today Sarah has much less possessions, but feels a lot richer. On the inside.

The thing is that most of us just get stuck in a negative feeling not knowing how to get out. No one taught us to. We believe that if we allow ourselves to come closer to our pain, we are going to feel even more miserable. However, you will find that often enough we keep ourselves trapped within the boundaries of discomfort and the only way out is to experience the discomfort for a short while, go past the barriers in order to be free.

Have you ever been hurt by what someone said and just wanted at all cost to protect yourself and close down? This is our natural reaction to pain, but we have to understand that if we let it dominate us for too long – it cuts us off from the world, it cuts us off from life. In order to experience well-being, to be one through our mind, body and soul, we need to be able to go through the smooth and the tough parts of our journey. But what do we normally do? We want for the smooth ones to last longer; we fear to lose them and are afraid that the tough ones will come. That is living in fear. To be able to access true well-being we need to be connected, one with the forces of life instead of fighting against them.

It is like surfing. We get out there with our surf-board and see the waves rising in the ocean. We get up on our board and surf up a wave, down a wave and work with the forces of the ocean to stay on top of our game. Sometimes we are swept away by a wave and have our head under the water. No big deal. We get up again and use the experience we just had to be more efficient next time. Yet there are people who just remain swept away by their emotions, by their old thought patterns and struggle to keep their head above the water. They are not willing to surf with life's forces.

Our natural tendency is to protect ourselves from feelings and emotions that are uncomfortable or cause us suffering. We want to escape them as fast as it is possible and protect that little world that we have built with so much care inside our own minds.

The human condition is that we are on a daily basis confronted with pain and discomfort. The most common way to deal with it is to solve the outside problem, to find comfort again, to distract yourself, to eat something, drink something, smoke something to make ourselves feel better. And yes, seemingly those solutions give some short-term relief, however none of them provides us with a lasting feeling of peace and well-being.

By constantly being afraid and protecting yourself from the unwanted emotions and feelings you close yourself more and more in our own world. You feel that you are doing the right thing by avoiding situations that can potentially cause you suffering. You settle in your comfort zone, a place that feels so familiar and secure. You defend the boundaries of that comfort zone and inform people close to you what they can and cannot do, what is appropriate to say and what on the other hand absolutely cannot be mentioned. But notice that you are locking yourself away from the world. You are locking yourself away from life.

Michael Singer beautifully illustrates this in his book The Untethered Soul. Imagine a dog that used to be roaming around free and now has to live in the back yard of a house. The back yard does not have a fence as such, but the owners have buried some wiring and created a force field around it. They have also put a little collar on the dog's neck. Now the dog starts to happily run around and inevitably hits the barrier of the invisible force field. It gives the dog a little shock. It is uncomfortable enough to back off. Eventually it learns to move within the limits of the confined space in the back yard and stops trying to get out. But what if we are dealing with a very brave dog? What if it's willingness to be free was strong enough to try again? The force field cannot hurt it as such, it is just uncomfortable. Imagine it standing just at the border of the force field and not letting go. The dog makes two confident steps right in the discomfort and in a moment it is free. What seemed like a painful, insurmountable barrier was just a few moments of discomfort it had to withstand to find itself on the other side.

But how do we get through the barriers of our emotional discomfort? How do we get the courage to face our fears?

I would like to introduce you to an ancient practice in Tibetan Buddhism called Tonglen, which literally means "sending and receiving". The idea behind it is that the more you try to escape fear of painful situations –

the more you will actually get trapped in them. Tonglen gives guidelines on how to set yourself free from the fear of pain and learn to stay present with whatever arises in your life. You have seen that life is no string of joyful events – sometimes it's bright and colourful and other times dark and gloomy. Since we cannot influence all the situations and circumstances that arise – isn't it better to find a way to deal with them? Instead of clinging on to things that have hurt as and staying trapped with them, isn't it better to find a way to release and let go?

The first basic notion of Tonglen is the feeling of openness. See, when you feel pain you instinctually tend to close off. You create a sort of a protective shield that doesn't let anything to come through. Notice that nothing comes in, but nothing gets out either. You lock yourself in with your pain. The idea is that it essential to create a feeling of openness in your heart and mind for the negative emotion to pass though you.

The second notion is the hardest one to grasp for most people. Rather than escaping pain at all cost – the way out of it is actually through it. Remember the dog that had the courage to withstand discomfort and get through the force field of the back yard? Why did it do that? Because its longing for freedom was stronger than the fear of momentary discomfort. We are no different. Through Tonglen practice we learn to understand that locking away the pain is a sure way for it to stay with us for a long, long time. Instead we can have the courage to go through it. Feel whatever it is that makes us suffer – humiliation, loss, resentment and then make enough space for it to let it pass through our system.

Instead of avoiding pain at all cost we learn to navigate through it. I found this step in itself truly liberating. What we often experience is the fear of being in contact with pain. When we let go of that fear and step into the experience of pain – magic happens. The pain starts to dissolve. And by experiencing the pain completely on the in-breath and asking for relief on the out-breath we help the pain to pass through our system, instead of blocking it inside.

The third notion in Tonglen is the one of our shared humanity. If you look at literature throughout centuries you will find that human emotions of anger, joy, humiliation, pride have been around for as long as we can trace humanity. Meaning that situations change, history evolves, years pass, but the basic human emotions stay the same. The anger a person was feeling in the 18th century when being betrayed by a friend is the same anger we feel today. Through practicing Tonglen you acknowledge the fact that while you are sitting in your dark room feeling alone and isolated, there are thousands of people all over the planet – men, women and children who are feeling the same thing. You are not alone. Yes, their situation is different, but the feeling that permeates their being is essentially the same. Through Tonglen you awaken compassion towards all people that share your same suffering. And that compassion and openness can be a truly healing experience.

At a first glace it might seem counter intuitive – why should I step into the pain, that will just make my suffering worse! What you will find is that it brings a big sense of relief. You actually go past the fear of feeling uncomfortable to accepting whatever you are feeling at this moment. As Pema Chodron describes it in her book Living Beautifully with Uncertainty and Change, "Tonglen is a core practice of warriors in training, the most effective tool for developing our sense of oneness with others."

For some people the idea of Tonglen might seem like too much too soon, which is absolutely fine. Perhaps just the notion of our shared humanity can provide that glimpse of openness for you in situations of suffering. And maybe one day you will find that the Tonglen practice is just what you need to go through a challenge in your life.

Now let's see how to practice Tonglen. You can essentially practice it anywhere and anytime you feel emotional discomfort, pain or even when you witness the suffering of others and have a sincere wish for them to be better. When your child or your mother is ill for example. You can do Tonglen for them with the wish to send them relief.

The practice of Tonglen has four stages:

1. **Get in contact with a feeling of openness**. You can look outside and see the vast sky or simply think of the immensity of the ocean, a vast field, a view from the top of a mountain. Stay in

contact with this concept of openness and spend a few moments connecting to this feeling while having the image in your mind. Place your hands on your belly and feel it rise with every in breath and fall with every out breath.

2. **Work with textures**. Before getting in touch with the feeling that is causing you pain - get your system accustomed to breathe in the notion of discomfort and breathe out relief. On the inhale visualise breathing in a thick, hot texture and breathe out open, cool and light. When you breathe out feel this light radiating out from all the pores of your body.

3. **Breathe in pain – breathe out relief.** Gently shift from breathing in the hot and thick texture to breathing in your discomfort. On the in-breath have the courage to fully get in touch with the feeling of your discomfort, your pain and on the exhale breathe out relief. When breathing out have an image in your mind of what relief would look like. While breathing out relief feel your body start to relax. Feel relief radiating out through all the pores of your body, see it as that fresh, bright light. Repeat this at least 5 times and notice how you feel.

4. **Extend relief**. Take a step further and while breathing in your feeling of discomfort, anguish or pain become conscious of the fact that thousands of people on this planet are feeling exactly the same. You are not alone. On the breath out send relief to all the people out there who are feeling what you are feeling right now.

Notice that by doing Tonglen you are not working with the outside situation, but with the way you perceive it on the inside. You slowly learn how to go through both the bright and the rough parts of your life without locking yourself away for too long. It is a gradual process that does not happen overnight, but you will see that step by step you learn how to stay supple even in the moments of pain. There are various ways you can practice Tonglen for yourself and for others and you can find more interpretations in the books of Pema Chodron.

Let's look at an example of when you can use this practice. Say you got absolutely mad at someone, because what they said goes so much against your view of the world and you start to get trapped in your own feeling.

Now it might take you a few days to get over this feeling of rage and you will be playing dialogues on repeat in your head. Dialogues that prove that you are right and they are wrong. You will be selecting words you would say to this person if you happened to cross them on the street. Imagining how your conversation will take place. Notice how much precious vital energy you use to keep this all up! I am not saying you should forget about what they said or accept them being right, what I am saying is that it is just not worthwhile to sit there for too long.

Try Tonglen the next time you get mad at someone. Allow for the first instinctual reaction to take place and notice the place in your body that starts to tense up. Your shoulders might stiffen or your stomach starts to clench into a knot or your jaws tense up. Just notice where it is that you feel tension. Now with that awareness start the practice of Tonglen. Look up at the sky or bring to your mind an image of spaciousness. That space that you are inviting in your mind is vital for the emotion of anger to pass through. It needs enough room to be able to leave your system. It might seem counter intuitive at first, because you would naturally feed that feeling with inner dialogues and trap it within yourself even more. Just acknowledge and accept that it needs space to the able to work its way out.

Slowly start to breathe in and out into that place in your body where you feel tension. Maybe your fists are clenched. Feel that with every breath you take they start to relax just a little bit more. Notice that by keeping that image of openness and spaciousness in your mind, you start to create a space within yourself vast enough to release the anger. While you breathe in and out feel your clenched fists slowly starting to open up.

Now you can work with textures. Coming closer to acknowledge your feeling, instead of running away from it. On the inhale breathe in hot, dark and thick, which might be qualities of the anger you are feeling and, on the exhale, breathe out light, cool and bright. When you breathe out just feel how those fists open up even more and how your shoulders slowly start to relax. The whole idea about doing Tonglen in this way is that when you get really mad at someone your whole body starts to tense up. Your muscles just instinctually become stiff and your mind closes off. You become rigid. Now remember those tall palm trees by the beach? The only reason they survive the harsh winds is because while staying whole and one with themselves they have a quality of flexibility innate to their being. So, it is with us. We need to understand and accept that at times being rigid is a sure way to be hurt.

The next step is to move on and decide to get through that barrier of momentary discomfort and get to the other side. Decide not to poison yourself anymore with that feeling of rage and make two confident steps right through it. So on the inhale you breathe in your anger and on the exhale breathe out relief. While you are breathing out visualise a feeling of relief radiating out 360°. On the breath out see it radiating from all the pores of your body, just like cool steam evaporating from your skin. Repeat this at least 5-6 times and notice how your body feels. Notice that from being rigid and stiff your body slowly starts to give itself permission to relax into whatever it is you are going through. This step is truly liberating because you learn that no matter how rigid the outer circumstances might make you feel you have the ability within yourself to go beyond it.

You might decide to stop here, check in with your body and notice how much of the tension has been released. Or you can take it a step further and, on the inhale, breathe in the awareness that there are thousands of people on this planet who are feeling mad right now just like you. They also have clenched fists and tense jaws. You are not alone. You can breathe in this notion of your connectiveness to all of those people and breathe our relief. For yourself and for all those beings that experience just what you are going though. And that feeling of oneness with all of those people might be just what you need to start opening yourself up to the world.

It might take some time for you to get accustomed to this counter intuitive practice and you might initially be ready for just the first two steps, which is ok. It takes courage to step right into what is causing your suffering, but slowly you will see that it is the only sure way through it.

You gradually train your ability to stay with whatever emotion comes up within you and look it right in the eye. You might find that what took you days to overcome in the past you are now able to handle in a few hours. What left you lying awake at night and haunting you with incessant dialogues now might be over in an afternoon. Slowly you will see that you are able to walk around in the world much freer and not constantly afraid that someone might say or do something that will make you feel deeply uncomfortable. You can handle it.

You have the power within yourself to decide to be more open to life and the different colours and shapes that it takes. To be one with the forces of life through your mind, body and soul. You might feel overwhelmed and scared at times by a challenge that has come your way. Just remember that the more rigid you become the more likely a passing storm will hurt you. Find a way, the one that works for you, to cultivate the feeling of openness and flexibility so vital to withstand any passing hurdle.

And most of all be kind to yourself. Have the patience and courage to accept just being deeply human.

Love,
Elena

About Elena Berezina Velema

Elena Velema is a personal development coach, author and parenting expert. She shares with her readers insights on how to overcome the tendency to want to control events and circumstances and instead surrender to the flow of life. For over a decade Elena has been in the training business and worked with a variety of international organisations including the United Nations. Elena is an accredited Master Practitioner in NLP, certified coach and a professional trainer. She is a business owner and runs "Streamline"- a training and coaching company in Monaco. Elena works with clients from all over the world helping them to align with their goals and find ways to connect to their true authentic self.

 "Those who flow as life flows know they need no other force" - Lao Tzu

WORKERS HAVE FEELINGS

By Carina Bernardino

It took me 36 years to internalize the most valuable lesson we can learn: We are responsible for ourselves and for our life.

Of course, everyone's understanding of this phrase will be different.

I grew up in a small village where human values reigned, reality was not so important, what others thought more so, when I was 14 years old and sat sobbing in my room with pain in my soul, my mother came in and, scolding me crying, yelling if I wanted everyone in the village to know…. well, tears are not words…. how would people guess??

Being the youngest daughter, I grew up with the trauma of not being unconditionally loved all my life, I sought this love first with my parents and then all the people close to me, I thought that if they love me, then I am important.

This feeling of not being loved made me suffer but at the same time it created a resilience and independence in me that sometimes revealed rebellion and radicalism, it made me search within myself for what I really wanted. I was always criticized whether I chose left or right, so I started doing what I wanted, at the age of 13 I decided I wanted to be a hairdresser because I wanted to see people smile, happy and feeling good about themselves At 15 I started to work and study, I fell in love with the art of hairdressing and I always did my best to improve every day. At 16, my father loaned me 2 Dale Carnegie books that would change my life. I also fell in love with understanding how the human mind works, what's behind every gesture and behaviour.

And after 20 years my dream of writing a book is materializing, even better than I had anticipated, together with extraordinary people who are dedicated to improving the lives of other people too.... multiple blessings

What I want to share with you is how to awaken your inner self, so that you know and understand how it works, knowledge is power, but only when put into practice, I will show you how you can achieve different results in your life, become who you want to be and live life as you want to live it.

It all starts and ends within us.

1 Evolution and the human being

For the last few centuries the human being has been evolving, undergoing constant transformations:

At this moment we are entering the era of personal fulfilment, where the focus is on the emotional side, we've already realized that money is not synonymous with happiness and we all seek happiness.

We leave an industrial era where we went through a lot of physical effort, where people followed rules and did not question governments or religions, just followed the pattern.

In the era of freedom, of hippies all that mattered was peace and love, the heart was awakened, the home of our emotions, we could speak, express ourselves we moved on to the era of dreams where people began to question the truths they believed about their life.

Then came the technological age, new levels of evolution and production capacity, with women gaining more and more freedom of expression, entering the job market and being an integral part of communities, men and women wanting more, things, objects, conditions for the children, with the mind always in control, I have to do this, have to have that, achieve that goal.

Then came the era of having, appearance, it was more important who was famous, earned a lot of money, had a good house, car etc., There were those who did and those who didn't pretended they did. I always said, what we see is not reality.

Now we are entering the era of being, where more and more people are seeking answers they do not find on the internet, in books or magazines… they search within themselves based on what they feel and desire from the bottom of their hearts, looking for a purpose greater than themselves, because even reaching our goals is no longer enough, this need for personal fulfilment is part of human evolution according to Maslow's theory and thankfully, more and more people are becoming aware of their own power and role in this world, the fact that you are reading this book proves that you are part of that group of people, congratulations on that.

2 How it works

Those of you who have not found their greater purpose, should never stop seeking, it is there.

We are born with only two fears:

Fear of falling and loud noises, we are loved, nourished and cared for.

From 0 to 7 years old our brain is in theta mode, absorbing information and believing in it, as an absolute truth, coming from our parents, family, teachers and society, from there the conscious mind starts to act and we filter the information that comes in and we decide what our belief is in relation to something.

So we have two minds, the unconscious that has absorbed all the information so far, and the conscious mind, which begins to filter and place the info in another compartment, called the house of beliefs.

We go on with our lives, carrying out the most varied roles, parents, husbands, wives, children, friends, colleagues… and every day our thoughts and behaviours come from our unconscious and are responsible for our results, for example when we stop ourselves from doing or saying something out of worry what others will think, this stems from our childhood education where we are taught to behave in specific ways so others do not think badly of us, this conditions our thinking. In the first place we have the unconscious saying: I will not say it, I may be wrong, they will think I am stupid, then it determines behaviour, we remain silent, the result was not our true self. As a confident adult today and trusting what we know to be our truths, when the conscious questions the unconscious, and asks in what do I believe and what is the worst thing that can happen, it does not change who I am. The belief is theirs, the reality is mine, following the example ... then it leads to different behaviour, we gain clarity in what we believe and assume our real truth.

We have many unconscious behaviours, outbursts of anger, hurting others without wanting to, or episodes of desperate sadness, they are mostly in the unconscious as a result of traumatic moments we went through. If we analyse these behaviours and emotions, we can access the unconscious and go to the moment it happened, understand it, transmute it and release is in order to live today with conscious choices, behaviours and states aligned with what you really want and believe in.

Of course, for that we need to silence our mind that exists for our survival and not happiness. Our mind for survival is on continuous alert for information.

So we are constantly being bombarded inside our own heads, the conscious brings rational thoughts, of what we need to believe, and the unconscious opens doors to a world of emotions and memories to be processed.

Understanding our behaviours that are the result of past traumas and bring us unwanted states and knowing how we function as a human being brings us the power to consciously change these states, through tools and techniques that are already scientifically proven to result and transform.

3 Linked body and mind

Anger and sadness contaminate our body.

Cortisol and epinephrine are produced when we feel anger or sadness, it leads to increased blood pressure, increased glucose, which in turn can lead to diabetes, heart attack and can ultimately lead to death. We can and must encourage our body to produce dopamine and serotonin to balance this out, as those are responsible for well-being and pleasure, which is what we all seek.

It is proven that we can alter our state physiologically by adopting specific gestures or techniques, this leads to the brain producing ideal and wanted hormones. Imagine a person who looks down, his shoulders are slumped, speaking softly, is he a happy or sad person for you? Now imagine that same person with his head held up high, his back straight and speaking assertively. Happy or unhappy?

When we want to transform, change comes from putting it into practice in a conscious and consistent way, eventually the result will come.

What is your usual posture? Observe it throughout the day and adjust it according to how you want to feel.

I'm going to ask you to think about a person you admire, some characteristic that stands out that you would like to have, close your eyes and think about that person, observe the body posture that person has, the way he walks, the tone of voice ...

And you will put yourself in exactly the same position, walk in the same way, speak in the same way until you feel that characteristic you admire so much ...

If you did this exercise, you will have experienced how we can access resources that are within us, I usually say that we are all made of the same colours of the rainbow, simply in different condensations that make us all unique, but we have everything within us.

This is the part of evolution that is surfacing and starting to transform humanity towards its emotions and essence.

4 Heart

The house of emotions

When we feel good or bad, these are just emotions and sensations that are brought by the organ that emits the most energy from the human being, the heart.

We are emotional people, most of the time we act and react based on our unconscious mind without control over these behaviours until we put into practice the awareness that we can choose how to react simply by choosing how we want to feel in relation to whatever it is and then we gain the power to direct our life.

For example, when someone hurts you, you can react emotionally by being aggressive, react without thinking or you can keep silent and suffer inside and carry that event with you for years and be a victim to it or you can choose and be in control of your reaction.

Have you ever experienced this kind of situation with someone, where you could not let go of it? Let me share my technique with you, next time you find yourself in this kind of situation, stop and ask yourself the following:

- What is the result I want to achieve in this situation?
- And to have this result what behaviour should I choose to have?
- Have I ever experienced this chosen emotion/ behaviour? feel it
- What and how am I going to talk? What am I going to do?

Know that whenever there is a situation between 2 people the responsibility of each person is 50%.

Thinking consciously about the situation, rationally understanding the reality of that situation gives us the clarity to discover the best and most ecological way for us to react and take us into the direction we want.

Dr David Hawkins calibrated emotions with energy and concluded that there are 2 types of energy, expansion energies such as love, joy and peace, and contraction energies such as fear, anger and sadness just to name a few examples, we cannot be vibrating in two different energies at the same time, so if we can change what we feel through our mind, we can choose how we feel and change our vibratory pattern, if there are emotions of contraction, they are just invitations to healing, and when there are expanding emotions, notice what you are doing, thinking, listening, feeling and do more of it, consciously choose, set reminders, do something that reminds you and leads to this high and expansive energy state.

Reality is subjective and the other does not perceive the same as us, so there is no point in being stuck with the same feelings that contract the chest and cause us suffering, when there is an alternative:

Connection between mind and heart, understanding emotions and reframing each situation through the conscious thought of knowing ourselves and knowing where we want to be, how we feel and how we want to feel, using the body to change to ideal states of mind and heart towards our goals and becoming better parents, husbands, wives, brothers, children, colleagues our mission and greater purpose, towards our essence

5 Purpose

The call of our essence

As children we dream that we will be astronauts, scientists, writers, the most amazing things, but at the same time we are conditioned to believe: you will not earn enough money to do that, you are not clever enough, stop dreaming and study.... many limiting beliefs cloud our purpose, our true voice and freedom to be really who we are. Until one day we realise that we want that freedom we felt as a child, to believe in the things we want.

- What would you do if you could really do what you wanted and nothing would stop you? how would you spend your days?

- Imagine that you are on top of a mountain, with millions of people watching you, the world is ending and you have to tell the world one last message that will be recorded for generations, what would you say? What message do you have to give to the world? Think and write your answers, in it you will find your deepest desire for your purpose.

There is something in us stronger than our thoughts and emotions, something that animates the body and makes us vibrate and evolve every day, practicing meditation is a way to get in touch with that part of us that is our base.

We are an essence that has a body, a mind and a heart and these 3 parts must be aligned to access the purest essence and act on it, letting life flow and enjoy, life can be much simpler than it seems.

When we are aligned with our individual mission, we find the motivation and reason to do and act, there are no goals too small or big. What we have today are people disconnected from themselves who do not make the right conscious choices to achieve what is really important to them.

6 New concepts

And what does all this have to do with ONE?

Being a hairdresser and dealing with people who have different energies and are going through physical and psychological changes, I realised how much my study and transformation has helped me in overcoming personal and professional challenges. As a result, I was able to stand out, to evolve and I started attracting different customers, they weren't only looking for a haircut or make-over but they also had personal problems. Together we would explore these and by asking powerful questions, we would arrive at a solution. It was a concept that integrated beauty from the outside with beauty on the inside.

If we are all the same, work in the same way it is safe to say that if one succeeds, we all succeed, because we are one within the whole.

We deal with people on a daily basis, so emotional intelligence is necessary to create quality relationships and team cohesion. If we are efficient in technical work, we must also be excellent in human capacity.

Improving communication with ourselves, adopting habits that strengthen us, being aware and consistent, we achieve what we want.

Using techniques, tools and knowledge that allow us to know ourselves, to change our state, to change our behaviour, will change the results.

My mission is to use my resilience to inspire and help people to find themselves within themselves, to be their best version, to build a world where people are free and feel inner peace.

Combining personal and professional development in companies is a quick and highly transformational way to achieve a global awareness.

The more people are aligned and living according to their true purpose the more happy people we will have and the less suffering there will be in the world, instead there will be more kindness, help, generosity and peace of heart....

In order to achieve this, using the techniques and continuing our personal development is the key to success!

If we are all the same, we all work in the same way, it is safe to say that if one succeeds, we all succeed, because we are one within the whole.

Love
Carina

ABOUT CARINA BERNARDINO

Born in a small town, Carina was determined to become a hairdresser and started work at the age of 15, thriving and learning every day and seeing a rise in happy clients who don't just come and see her for an amazing hairstyle!

With a passion for understanding how the human mind works, Carina chose the path of personal development, through reading and personal development coaches.

Today she is a coach and master NLP, she helped hundreds of people. Today she focusses her coaching on hairdressers and teaches them how to overcome exhaustion and have a client return rate of 99% so they not only can have a fulfilling career but also as personal, emotional life with inner peace and purpose.

"The more people are aligned and living according to their true purpose the more happy people we will have and the less suffering there will be in the world, instead there will be more kindness, help, generosity and peace of heart...."

REINVENTING MIDLIFE FOR THE OVER 40S

By James and Claire Davis

Transform the quality of your life so you can be more, do more and have more over 40

Who We Are And Why We Focus On Midlife

We're Claire and James Davis, a husband and wife team specialising in midlife health and happiness. Not only are we mid-lifers ourselves but we're a multi-award winning duo and owners of world renowned fitness brand 38 Degrees North and creators of the phenomenally successful, five star rated 'The Midlife Mentors' podcast, which has hit the top ten charts in both the US and UK.

We're on a mission to help stressed, dissatisfied and unhealthy people over 40 transform into the best possible version of themselves so they feel alive, excited and in control of their lives again.

We've drawn on nine years of working with thousands of clients and almost 3 decades of professional experience in psychology, NLP, stress management, physical training and nutrition to develop a world leading, science based formula that is not just about dramatically improving your physical body and health, but one that fundamentally enables you to reclaim the power in your life, relationships, and mindset - so you're free to thrive.

As well as being regarded as authorities in the field of holistic wellbeing, we continue to be a force of truth, authenticity and integrity in the industry – demystifying the fads, fake promises and pseudo-science that plague our news feeds.

We're proud to have won Certificates of Excellence for our 5-star reviews, as well Top Influential People In Fitness, World's Top Health Retreat and Innovative Company of The Year.

Plus we're grateful for the wonderful press we've had - the likes of Tatler, Conde Nast Traveller and also The New York Times and Sunday Times.

But honestly - our validation doesn't come from pieces of paper. Our purpose and passion is what people say about us - the lives we touch - the impact we make. It gives all of this meaning. It gives us a huge kick to know we're making a difference in the world.

We focus on midlife because we're mid-lifers and recognise the stresses and strains that come with this time of life. Career, financial commitments, children, ageing parents, less time, an expanding waistline, and often a lack of intimacy and connection in relationships. We also understand the ageing process and hormonal changes occurring in the body that affect how and when we train.

Sadly, research of first world countries has found that 47.2 is statistically the unhappiest point in your life.

We don't want it to be and it doesn't have to be. We've seen too many friends, too many clients, hit midlife and think, "this is it, it's all downhill from here" and give up. No, no, no - this is just the start for you. It's the beginning of the next phase, where you get to decide what the quality of your life looks like, with the wisdom that comes with age.

Why Midlife Can Be Challenging

We're Generation X, aka Generation Squeezed, or often known as the forgotten generation. Everyone talks about the Boomers, the Millennials and Gen Z, but little is spoken of us. We're in the business of changing that, because as we see it, we've hit midlife and there's no one supporting and guiding us through the mental, physical and emotional challenges - with truth, authenticity and expert knowledge.

We're sure you're all familiar with the cliched concept of the midlife crisis? If you'd like to know more about it's fascinating origins, check out our podcast on the subject, but in brief, a psychoanalyst called Elliot Jacques coined the phrase in a 1957 presentation.

He framed a case study of a client and stated it thus: ""Up till now, life has seemed an endless upward slope, with nothing but the distant horizon in view. Now suddenly I seem to have reached the crest of the hill, and there stretching ahead is the downward slope with the end of the road in sight—far enough away, it's true—but there is death observably present at the end."

Later Jacques admitted that he had in fact been talking about himself. Although the phrase "Midlife crisis" didn't come into popular usage for some years after, it's by no means a modern invention.

Dante referenced it in his 14th century Divine Comedy. "Midway upon the journey of our life / I found myself within a forest dark / For the straightforward pathway had been lost."

Today aside from realising our own mortality, we can recognise a multitude of factors at play which often unsettle midlife.

Internal factors include perceptions of declining health and vitality, even libido. Questioning our beliefs, our looks. Then we have cultural and societal factors. Invariably we compare ourselves to others, question our progress and wonder if we should have achieved more.

These feelings are psychological but also physical. As we age our human growth hormone declines, our testosterone levels decline and of course for female's there's the peri menopause and menopause. The symptoms of these changes include decreased muscle mass, weaker bones, disturbed sleep, lower energy, a slowing metabolism and greater likelihood to store fat.

That's the bad news - and of course this can make some midlifers give up hope.

However, the good news is that we can absolutely do something about both the physical and psychological factors, and that's what our whole approach is based on: solid research that's created phenomenal results again and again for our clients. Practical solutions that take into consideration the midlife body, mind and lifestyle.

Our Approach

The Midlife Method has evolved from almost 3 decades of experience in psychology, NLP, coaching, stress management, personal training and nutrition. For the last 9 years we've run fitness retreats working with thousands of clients. We began to see similar themes and issues with our midlife clients, and as midlifers ourselves we wanted to find a holistic mind, body, soul solution that would dramatically improve their quality of life. So they could increase their chances of living longer, healthier and happier.

As personal trainers we realised working on just the physical aspects via diet and training wasn't solving the underlying causes, and didn't address happiness. That's why the first thing we work on with any client is mindset.

You can eat well, and train smartly, but if you haven't focused on strengthening your mindset and emotional wellbeing, you won't sustain success.

For this reason, The Midlife Method is deeply grounded in positive psychology research, utilising NLP to affect change, and syncing the body in line with the changes occurring in midlife, so everything's working in balance - from the inside out.

In the next section we'll look at our 6 pillars and how they optimise midlife health and happiness.

The 6 Pillars For A Great Midlife

We base our approach around 6 pillars. Many of them interact with each other, and by ensuring each is kept in balance, we can sustain success for the whole being.

In this chapter we'll also look at the role of self-identity which is the cornerstone to any goal you wish to reach. We guarantee if you're feeling stuck and frustrated about a lack of progress in any area of our life - this is where you need to start. Why? Because you cannot out achieve your own self-identity.

We'll finish off the chapter by giving you a free real time exercise video you can do anywhere, anytime, as well as advice on how to maximise fat loss and increase fitness.

And we couldn't leave you without giving you our great way to start the day centred and empowered.

To help it all make sense, we want to share the 6 pillars that make up The Midlife Method:

1. Exercise

Your body is designed to be moved, and as we age the adage "use it or lose it" is definitely true. Yes, we need to take more care of joints and muscles, but moving the body will actually prolong your quality of life, if not lengthen it as well.

As we age, hormonal changes in the body mean we lose muscle mass and strength. We begin to lose flexibility, and can start to put on weight as we begin to move less and our metabolism slows down.

Exercise provides multiple benefits, not just for our bodies, but our minds as well.

Firstly, blending cardio training (for overall fitness and heart health) with resistance training (weights), increases muscle mass, fires up the metabolism (both of which will burn more calories), builds stronger bones, strengthens the immune system, and by including stretches, we ensure greater mobility and flexibility.

If that's not enough reason to move, recent studies have also shown regular exercise actually slows brain ageing, and that's in addition to all the feel-good neurotransmitters, such as dopamine and endorphins that are produced when we move our fabulous backsides!

2. Nutrition

We love our food! So our approach is based on sensible sustainable nutrition.

Nutrition is just that - how we nourish our bodies, and as we age, why shouldn't we also enjoy things in life that make us happy. It's not about restriction. It's about finding a balance and knowing the right strategies to help keep your midlife body fat down and your energy up.

We're anti-diet and anti-fads. We advocate making informed food choices and not going hungry or obsessing over food and drink.

If we were to sum up our approach in a few words, we'd advise:

Choose whole foods where you can. Cut out hidden sugars from your diet by learning how to read food labels. Aim for a rainbow of natural colours on your plate. Watch your portion size! And finally, from field or sea to plate with as few steps in between as possible.

We also live by the 80/20 rule on nutrition. Aim to be mindful and make good choices 80% of the time, the other 20%, don't over indulge, but don't be too strict on yourself. Emotionally it's better for you to live this way. Plus, most neurotransmitters are formed in the gut (which is another reason not to live with the denial of dieting).

3. Understanding Hormones

In a nutshell there are a whole load of hormonal changes going on as we age. Two of the main hormones in decline are testosterone and human growth hormone (HGH).

Training in certain ways, orders and timings can actually help raise your testosterone (yes ladies this is good for you too) and HGH levels. In effect helping you stay younger.

We're going to share one hack here with you later in the learnings section of this chapter.

4. Mental Resilience

Stress is a major player in our life at midlife. It can feel overwhelming and alienating. Burn out is not uncommon and we strongly believe more should be done to help you cope with the day to day pressures you're under.

With backgrounds in stress management, positive psychology and coaching, we provide science-based strategies to help you reclaim your power, focus on life balance and build a more positive, confident outlook.

Mental resilience and wellbeing are also linked to exercise. The more exercise you do, the less likely you are to experience anxiety and stress.

5. Emotional Wellbeing

We could call this spirit, or soul work! It's the connected-ness to the truth of you. Your potential and creativity. Your need as a human to grow and expand in life. The need to move forward and not stay still.

You see - at midlife, a vast majority play not to lose, as opposed to the 'playing to win' mentality we had when we were younger.

We've accumulated more things: wealth, properties, social standing, reputation etc. The flip side is that we have more fear about potentially losing these things, which in turn makes us resistant to fully embracing change and living to our highest potential. We get stuck in a rut, feel bored and stagnated and it's these feelings that lead to unhappiness.

The work we do here is about giving yourself permission to 'follow your bliss'. To perhaps redefine what the next chapter of your life looks like and know that it's possible.

We give you tools to unlock a new self-identity, create deep and fulfilling relationships, become a better communicator and feel excited about the future.

In fact, later in this chapter we'll give you one of the most powerful, practical tools for creating a new self-identity - which is the key to living an extraordinary life you deserve.

6. Accountability

Being accountable means, you smash through your excuses for not doing the things you know will get you the life you dream of. It's a crucial aspect of our approach, because we know the power of feeling like someone's got your back. Research suggests that when you have a community, a mentor - you're more motivated to stay on track as you don't want to let them down.

It's why we have a thriving community that makes people feel connected, understood and supported. It's often this final piece of the puzzle that people overlook. It's also why we ourselves have mentors. We understand the value of an outside perspective to pick you up and keep you taking action.

As we always say - it's not impossible to do it on your own, but it's a lot harder.

Your Starting Point - Creating A New Identity And Living It

Your identity determines who you are. Which may sound obvious, but so many people overlook their existing self-identity when wanting to make changes in their external environment.

In fact, addressing this one thing is the linchpin to having what they want.

There's a psychological theory called congruence theory, and it's one of the main drivers of human behaviour.

In brief - we consistently act to keep our behaviour and our beliefs aligned, or congruent. When either our behaviour is out of line with our beliefs, or our beliefs are out of line with our behaviour, we'll adapt one or the other to move out of the state of dissonance this creates, and back into congruence.

So how can we use this to help us achieve our desires?

Put simply, when we want to become "new" in some way - lose weight, get fit, be more confident, we need to actually adopt the beliefs underlying this "new me" and start living them.

Say we want to be more confident, but our inner belief is that we lack self-confidence. Then all the work in the world on confidence without shifting this inner belief is not going to help.

This is why people yo-yo diet, why lottery winners spend all their winnings, why people succeed at a goal for a while, only to sabotage it further down the line. Because their new behaviour is incongruent with their inner beliefs about themselves.

Where we go wrong is working from the Have, Do, Be principle.

For example, how often do you all say things like - Once I have more time, I will do more things with the kids and my partner, then everyone will be happy? Once I have more confidence, I will do internet dating and I will have a loving relationship?

We're here to tell you this is totally wrong. The Have, Do, Be approach is what causes the greatest unhappiness in your life.

We're going to show you why, and how to change it for success. This chapter will give you an understanding of why you haven't got the results you want so far. Until now. Because you've been operating from the wrong perspective.

We're going to concentrate on the mindset and beliefs that will get you the life you dream of. Because no amount of DO-ing will help if you don't have this figured out.

Why?

Because what we think in our mind is what we become. This is based on science. Einstein. All the greatest thinkers, scientists and philosophers. They all knew this.

"We cannot solve our problems with the same thinking we used when we created them" Einstein

"We are what we think. All that we are arises with our thoughts. With our thoughts we make the world." Buddha

We've both experienced this in our own lives. Learning, but most importantly using this mindset and self-identity exercise has been a game changer. It lifted the veil on what was holding us back. It works for us, our clients and it'll work for you.

You see - until our early thirties we didn't realise just how much our mindset and thoughts held us back. We didn't know how to use our mind to cultivate true happiness or lasting, loving relationships. We spent thousands on mentors, coaches and courses to give us the answers.

Like most people we tried to find it in external things. Marriages, alcohol, experiences, new business ventures. It felt like we were on the hamster wheel, and exhausted. Disconnected from something.

The issue is that we were trying to change external stuff - outside of us.

But beyond all our qualifications, all our experience, all the striving, seeking answers and some meaning to it all, there was one component that never changed.

Us. Inside. Our thinking. Our beliefs. Our identity.

You see - like you probably are - we were hoping to change things, without looking at the story we were telling ourselves on the inside.

So hear this and let it sink in.

You cannot become the person you wish to become. Healthier, slimmer, an entrepreneur, wealthy, kind, giving, inspiring - unless your story internally is in line with it.

This is called our self-identity.

Self-identity is incredibly powerful. It dictates what you experience in your life. Period. What's more, you cannot out achieve your self-identity. We'll repeat that - you cannot out achieve your self-identity.

If you wish to be slimmer you must think like a slimmer person. You must identify with being slim. If you identify with being overweight and yo-yoing all the time - that is locked in to your self-identity. That is what you think you are.

If you wish to be a millionaire, you must identify with being one. If you think you're poor and always only have just enough in your bank account - you will never be wealthy because you identify with only having just enough.

You have to BE before you DO and then HAVE.

But 99% of people have got it all wrong.

You are what you think. You create your outside world. You must BE it in the mind, then DO with that state of mind, then you'll HAVE it in reality. That's why poor people stay poor and rich people get richer. It's why some people walk in a room and people flock to them and why others disappear into the background. It's why some attract opportunities left right and centre and others don't. It's the story of themselves internally reflected back at them externally.

So, let's dive into this a little deeper and look at your life. Let's look at where you're at and where you want to be.

Firstly - You might ask - how do I know what my self-identity is?

The easiest answer to that is look at your current life. Look at yourself in the mirror. Are you overweight? Look at your bank account. Is it always in the red? Look at your relationship. Do you always argue? Do you always push loved ones away? Look at your career. Do you like what you do? Or do you feel trapped because of money?

Right now, think about these areas. What is it telling you about your self-identity?

The main reason for this is the subconscious mind is designed to play the same loop over and over. It wishes to stay safe in its own self-image. Telling it to DO external things that aren't in line with its TRUTH about you is setting you up for failure.

So guess what? We MUST change our internal self-identity FIRST. We must BE first.

So here's the next part that we've used in our own lives to phenomenal results. And it's exactly what we help clients with in the very first instance. Having looked at your current situation like we've suggested above. Ask yourself…

What self-image would I need to have in order to achieve and have X?
What beliefs would I need to have to achieve X?
Write them down. Spend time really understanding this.
These are the things you need to start believing about yourself.
So how do we start to install these new beliefs?

Having done the above exercise, we want you to write out 5 affirmations that affirm the identity and beliefs you wish to adopt. So we start to literally reprogram the mind. We are internally becoming that person so we act in that way and in time the outside conditions of our life will reflect it…

It could go something like this….

- I am capable and smart enough to start my own business
- Every day I grow in confidence and self-worth

- I am easy to love
- I see myself getting slimmer and healthier every day
- I make good choices when it comes to food
- I do not look to food for comfort
- It is easy for me to stay calm in stressful situations
- It is possible for me to get out of debt and become financially free

These are rewiring your brain. The power of auto suggestion will literally create new neural pathways in the brain. These pathways become stronger the more they are fed positive thoughts, beliefs and emotions. Science has proven this time and again - showing that the human brain is highly dynamic and capable of being shaped and reshaped.

The more we feed it the same messages and experiences over and over in our imagination, the greater the ability to create new neurons and connections until it's rewired to that belief or thought.

We can literally reimagine our self-identity by rewiring the brain and then it becomes a belief. When we have a belief, we act in accordance to that belief....

We ourselves repeat affirmations every single day and every single night. Every opportunity we can. They have changed our life and they have changed the lives of our clients and millions of others around the world. We know that 90% of your success in anything is mental. Not doing. Not acting. But thinking, being - first.

Start telling a new story. Repetition is key to mastery. Build that belief and make those pathways work for you not against you.

So here's the challenge for you.

Go through the steps we've discussed above.
Then write out....
My old identity is: and write out your old identity

My new identity is: and write out your new identity

Then say this out loud….

"I release my old identity. I commit to saying my new identity affirmations out loud every morning and every night for 5 minutes."

Now, some of you are going to say:

Will this work for me?

Yes - because it works for everyone who is consistent with it. Athletes, millionaires, the world's most successful people. Us, our clients. This is what they understand and practice. You see until now you've been doing it back to front. Trying to change the outside without looking at what you already are now. You're trying to change external habits, whilst still believing you're something else. Fundamentally you've never acknowledged that your life now looks a certain way because of what you believe about yourself. Now you have a chance to rewire your brain.

You might also say…

I don't have time to myself to implement this? What about my children, my job, commitments? Well some tough love. That's just another form of avoidance.

Procrastination. Until some point in the future when you feel more ready. Truth is - you'll never feel ready and you'll never find more time. You have to make time and jump in with faith. And the affirmations take 5 minutes. Morning and evening.

When you prioritise and prime your mind for success and happiness, the rest of your life will positively shift. In every single area.

You might also say…

I don't believe in it - well - here's some research proving it

The development of self-affirmation theory has led to neuroscientific research aimed at investigating whether we can see any changes in the brain when we self-affirm in positive ways.

Research using MRI scanning has suggested that neural pathways are increased when people practice self-affirmation. Specifically, the area related to positive valuation and self-information becomes more active.

Let's look at some more research from a variety of psychologists:

- Self-affirmations have been shown to decrease health-deteriorating stress (Sherman et al., 2009; Critcher & Dunning, 2015);
- Self-affirmations have been used effectively in interventions that led people to increase their physical behavior (Cooke et al., 2014);
- They may help us to perceive otherwise "threatening" messages with less resistance (Logel & Cohen, 2012);
- Self-affirmation has been demonstrated to lower stress (Koole et al., 1999; Weisenfeld et al., 2001).

So, we have the research to back it up. This stuff is proven and it's being used by top achievers for success right now. You're no different and there's nothing special about us or them.

We believe in you. And you deserve this chance to live the rest of your life in flow. Not struggling. Excited about life. Alive and looking forward to every day.

Aligning The Body For Optimum Health

Because we want to give you more than one actionable takeaway, we're going to share our workout tip that more than any other, has positively changed our lives and the lives of our clients.

By adding this little trick to what we'll teach you about exercise, you'll see phenomenal results.

This one secret is the greatest take away from our 9 years of running retreats and coaching. Clients message and call us time and time again to say excitedly

"Claire and James - this is what changed it all for me."

We're talking about fasted HIIT (Hight Intensity Interval Training).

When you move your body at intensity for short periods of time, you get incredible results. A HIIT session should be 10 to 20 minutes long, and it should have short bursts of intense work, and short periods of rest.

We realise that might be a little confusing. So…we decided to give you access to an example HIIT session, filmed at our home in Ibiza. It's real time and no equipment is needed. It gives you a great little taster and is perfect for beginners. A warm up and cool down is included.

You can access it by going to this link….

https://youtu.be/AT8xSAkLu_U

Now listen - if you're not particularly fit, please don't worry. We all need to start somewhere and you can work up to the real time HIIT session mentioned above. Simply start with steady state cardio like walking, jogging, swimming or a bike ride and always check with a medical professional before beginning a new exercise programme.

Now, we'd also love you to do this session first thing in the morning. Here's why…

You'll get an energising boost of feel good neurotransmitters that will keep you on a natural high all day.

And, you will be able to make dramatic changes to your body composition by burning through body fat.

Here's the basic science. You've fasted overnight so your residual glucose and glycogen stores are low. These are what we use for energy. As they're low, when we train at intensity for short bursts, we'll burn through those stores and then tap into body fat for our energy needs.

Now, because we create an oxygen debt with the intensity, when we combine that with being fasted, we in effect turbo charge our metabolism and spike it for the rest of the day at least - meaning we burn more calories through the day.

Without going too much into the nutritional or science, because we don't want to overload you - doing your HIIT fasted first thing in the morning will super charge your fat loss results.

This amazing method when combined with resistance training, is super effective at "future proofing" your body into older age.

Now remember, these workouts are less than 20 minutes. We want you to commit to these. If not now - when? Put in the diary. We want you to quit making excuses. Regardless of how outside your comfort zone it feels. Two to four times a week maximum is enough.

As Einstein said - The definition of Insanity is doing the same thing over and over again. You gotta do something different if you want change. So put it in the calendar for tomorrow morning. Before you go to work. And remember, as Bruce Lee says - Long term consistency trumps short term intensity.

Set Your Intention: Start The Day Right

One last point we'd love you to take on board, is starting your day the right way. So many of us get up and let the outside world in before we have centred ourselves... the news, TV, radio, emails, social media...

Sadly - all you're doing is giving your power away. This will have you feeling ungrounded and frazzled all day. So instead, assign yourself a 10-minute block each morning when you first wake up as time for you.

Do this exercise each morning - it's what we do without fail and it's what we insist our clients do while we work together.

Write down 3 great things from yesterday

Write down 3 things you're grateful for in your life
Write down 3 things you'd love to get from the day
Write an affirmation

That's it! What you're doing in those ten minutes is being present. You're also reflecting on your existence, what you have now, rather than what you don't have and finally, you're taking time to connect and be grateful.

Trust us, this alone is a complete game changer for your mental and emotionally wellbeing. When we begin to focus on the good in our world, we allow more in. It might feel weird at first, but stick with it and you'll start to feel the difference.

That's it! We wanted to share so much more, but we're limited with our space here in this fabulous book with so many other great authors. We hope you've enjoyed the words here. We hope they've been enlightening, practical and inspiring. Thank you for reading. Now go and claim your best life. You deserve it and it's yours for the taking.

Love,
James and Claire

About James and Claire Davis

Claire & James Davis are a midlife, multi-award winning duo and owners of world renowned fitness brand <u>38 Degrees North</u> and creators of the phenomenally successful, five star rated 'The Midlife Mentors' podcast, which has hit the top ten charts in both the US and UK.

They are passionate about helping stressed, dissatisfied people over 40 transform into the best possible version of themselves physical, mentally, emotionally and spiritually. Working with thousands of clients they have seen how intrinsically linked the mind and body are. Training one or the other in isolation will only get you so far, which is how they have developed their mind, body and soul approach. To help you evolve to the highest version of yourself.

They have drawn on their qualifications spanning psychology, NLP, stress management, physical training and nutrition to develop a world leading formula that is not just about dramatically improving your physical body and health, but one that fundamentally enables you to reclaim the power in your life, relationships, and mindset - so you're free to thrive.

Claire & James are well regarded as authorities in the field of holistic wellbeing. They continue to be a force of truth, authenticity and integrity in the industry – demystifying the fads, fake promises and pseudo-science that plague our news feeds.

They have built their business on simple steps that provide huge change. The science-based method promises strength and resilience in body, mind and emotional wellbeing– giving clients the ultimate step by step toolkit they need to transform their quality of life - so they feel alive, connected and the best version of themselves.

"Now go and claim your best life.

You deserve it and it's yours for the taking.

ENERGY IS THE KEY TO YOUR HEALTH...

By Martine de Petter

←—∞—→

Before I reached forty, I was not a particularly healthy person! Neither physically, as I was born with a heart malformation and suffered from asthma when I was a child, nor emotionally and mentally, as I discovered rather soon in my life, that my mother did not desire my birth and never missed a chance to remind me! As a consequence, I was often ill and grew up quite insecure with little self-confidence! At forty my life changed. Fed up with my marketing and logistics consultant job, I started Martial Arts, i.e. Qi Gong and Karate, two disciplines, which subsequently opened for me the doors of Tao Philosophy and Chinese Medicine.

I enrolled in Shanghai (China) University and became a Doctor in TCM, Acupuncture and Moxibustion. Not only did I find mind fulfilment, I also managed to cure myself progressively of "most" of my health problems whether physical or emotional! I say "most" as it requires continuous effort and mind/body training to get results!

Thanks to the principles of Chinese Physiology I acquired, I was able to understand the reasons of my childhood illnesses and consequently treat them and cure them all except my heart malformation, which I have managed to keep under control without synthetic medication. A diet based on fruits, vegetables, some grains and fish, lots of water, daily exercises and meditation keep me fit and healthy!

The Universe came to my rescue at a desperate moment of my life when

I thought there was no solution for me and I was close to suicide! It showed me the Way, through the Principles of Tao, which I discovered in a book I bought in a bookshop where I had never set foot before and was on the other side of Brussels! When I first read the book, it did not interest me at all. I thought it was full of sh…! I indulged in self-pity and cried all day and night! Then quite bored and depressed, I decided to try the exercises explained at the end of the book. They were supposed to give you energy. I had nothing to lose! I did two exercises! I felt good! I did them all, all fifteen of them! I felt great!!! I re-read the book!

Its title?
"Harmonisation with the Invisible Forces of the Universe".

It was all about Yin and Yang, Chinese Medicine and how to heal oneself with Energy. I returned to the shop and bought more books. I was hooked!

As I found the answers to my health questions in this book, I decided to study these disciplines in order to help those who were suffering like I had been and were not as lucky as me to find solutions to their ailments whether emotional or physical!

My journey had started and never stopped! After my graduation as a Doctor in Chinese Medicine, I created ESTAR, a centre of Traditional and Classical Chinese Ancestral Techniques.

ESTAR means Energy, Strength, Therapy, Acupuncture, Revitalization.

CENTRE ESTAR

The Centre ESTAR was founded over twenty years ago in Ibiza, where I have lived ever since, with the sole aim to help those who visit to achieve wellbeing and improve their health. During my extensive experience in the sector, I have attended to more than 4.500 people, whom I have helped to improve their state of health and their quality of life.

My work is based on *Traditional and Classical Chinese Medicine* known for its benefits in dealing with all kinds of ailments and diseases, as its priority is to look for the source of the problem for further treatment.

Each session that I conduct in my centre begins with a comprehensive diagnosis to determine what kind of therapy or treatment is the most recommended for each case.

Some of the methods carried out and which are contained in this type of medicine are, for example, *Acupunture*, which consists of the stimulation of certain points of energy with fine needles, *Dietotherapy*, which focuses on treatment by food, *Moxibustion*, based on the application of heat using Moxa, and *Tuina*, Chinese Physiotherapy, which helps to treat all kinds of physical injuries and contractions.

Other techniques, I use, are Qi Gong (breathing with slow movements),

Qi Nei Zang (liberating energy stuck in the belly due to blocked negative emotions) and Wai Qi Liao Fa (Energy transfer).

I am also specialized in *Cellular Medicine*, specifically *Morphological Blood Analysis and Cellular Therapy,* which consists in analysing the morphological state of the cells in order to improve health and prevent diseases. In this way, I can discover what are the strengths and weaknesses of each organ thanks to a deep study of the body and come to a better understanding of how the organism of each individual functions. It enables me to diagnose deficiencies and excesses of nutrients, processes of oxidation, imbalances, etc.

This analysis enables me to detect diseases at an early stage, discover the cause of the disease, come across food intolerances and, based on this knowledge, design a personalized treatment.

In the Centre ESTAR, I have merged Chinese Medicine and Cellular Medicine in order to give myself a very powerful tool of Diagnosis and Treatment that has given significant results to my patients.

I want you to feel good, on the inside as well as on the outside and, for this reason I perform treatments of Chinese Cosmetology or Mei Rong. Mei Rong was originally created as an anti-age system for members of the Emperor's Court.

In Chinese Cosmetic Medicine, beauty is the expression of inner

health. Thus Chinese Cosmetology is a cosmetic therapy based on the principles and techniques of *Traditional and Classical Chinese Medicine* to rejuvenate and balance the body from the inside out.

In the Centre ESTAR, my cosmetic diagnosis seeks out energy imbalances that cause skin problems and premature aging, namely imbalances of Xue (blood), Qi (energy), Yin and Yang.

I offer an *Anti-Age Cosmetic Therapy* in 3 phases: firstly, re-balancing of the bodily energies responsible for the problem, secondly local treatment of the problem and thirdly a change of diet and lifestyle.

In addition to relying on the methods and the techniques of Chinese Medicine, I equally target my goals with the external use of natural plants and the therapeutic and vibratory properties of Essential Oils.

TRADITIONAL AND CLASSICAL CHINESE MEDICINE

If you peruse my website (www.estarmtc.com), you will see that I refer to Chinese Medicine as *Traditional and Classical Chinese Ancestral Techniques,* and Morphological Blood Analysis as *Nutritional and Micro Nutritional Evaluation*! Why? For the simple reason that the Balearic and Spanish Government do not allow Practitioners of "Alternative Medicine", even if they have done a Doctorate (like I did), first to bear the title of Doctor and secondly to refer to their techniques as treatments.

There are a few words I am not authorized to use. If I don't comply, I will be sanctioned! So I don't do a diagnosis, but an evaluation, I don't speak about illness, but an imbalance. I don't perform a treatment, but a re-balance! I don't have patients, but clients. I certainly cannot use the words Chinese Medicine. I can refer to it as Chinese Energetics, or as I do, Chinese Ancestral Techniques. This is ludicrous, as Chinese Medicine has been called like this for 6000 years!

Occidental Doctors have nothing to fear from Chinese Medicine, or Ayuvedic Medicine, or Tibetan Medicine. Whatever the technique used, as long as it gets results and helps the patient, that is what matters!

So how does Chinese Medicine work? How can it help you?

First of all, we have to make a difference between Western and Eastern Medicine. Doctors in the Occident will treat the symptoms of an illness whereas Chinese Doctors will, of course, treat the symptoms as well but they will look for the origin (cause) of the symptoms and treat the illness at its root. The purpose here is not to give you a lengthy and theoretical essay but rather to explain, in a simple way, what results and benefits Chinese Medicine will bring to your health when you apply certain basic rules.

Every living organism on Earth has energy, be it man, animal, plant, or mineral. In fact, the same Energy can be found in the Macrocosm, the Universe, as in the Microcosm, the Human Being. What affects one affects the other and vice versa. Energy vibrates at a certain frequency. If the frequency is too low or too high, there will be disharmony. Energy in excess or in deficiency will create unbalance.

Where does this Energy come from?

One part of the Energy comes from "Heaven". It feels aerated, warm and light. The Chinese call it "Yang". It is the dynamic part of the Universal Energy. It is the air we breathe. It is our breathing. We stop breathing, we die!

The other part comes from "Earth". It feels dense, cold and dark. The Chinese call it "Yin". It is the nutritional part of the Universal Energy. It is the food we eat. It is our nutrition. We stop eating, we die!

Man living between "Heaven" and "Earth" is influenced by the interaction of these two polarities Yin and Yang. To help my patients understand it better, I compare our body to a car. A car, in order to function properly, needs an engine and petrol. The engine, with no petrol, will overwork and burn. The car will not move. Too much petrol will flood the engine. The car will not move. Just petrol and no engine, the car will not move. In our body, we can compare the engine to the Yang Energy, the dynamic of our organism (the air we breathe) and the petrol to the Yin Energy, the nutrition of our organism (the food we eat). A harmonious balance between the two (breathing and eating) is necessary for the good functioning of our body. Excess or deficiency in one or the other will create a disruption in the circulation of the Energy (called Qi) and Blood (called Xue) and generate either pains in our muscles and/or articulations or an illness in one or several organs.

Let me give you an example to illustrate this. A lady patient comes in with severe constipation. In the West, she will be advised to eat more fruits and salads in order to have bowel movements. The more raw food she will eat, the worse her condition will get. She is stuck in a vicious circle. Why is this? Food has energy too. Food has a certain type of nature, either Yin or Yang, referring to the thermal impact it has on your organism. Food, due to its particular flavour, will affect the function of a specific organ. Constipation in Chinese Medicine is considered as Fire in the Stomach, which in turn will provoke dryness of the Large Intestine, due to a lack of organic liquids. Stomach and Spleen are working as a "couple". The Stomach, being more Yang, needs to cool itself down and prefers food with a cold/fresh thermal impact like fruits and salads, or even cooked food with cold nature. The Spleen, on the contrary, is more Yin and needs the warm nature of food to be able to function properly. So eating too much raw and cold nature food will disrupt the balance between the Stomach and the Spleen and create what the Chinese call Fire in the Stomach and Deficiency of the Spleen, which is the cause of what we know as Constipation. After making my diagnosis, I treated my patient with Acupuncture but also with Dietotherapy, which is the art of treating with food.

Hence, I advised her to eat more cooked and warm nature food to improve the function of her Spleen. A week later, she had daily bowel movements. She got rid of her constipation!

As you can see, we are affected by what we eat but also by what we think! Each organ, when it is unbalanced physiologically, develops a negative emotion. Let us go back to the Large Intestine. Its primary function is to eliminate food waste, under the supervision of the Stomach/Spleen "couple". I give you another example. A few years ago, another patient of mine was treated for severe pain in her arm with acupuncture by one of my students, but with no results. I examined the woman, pressed on a specific point of her forearm that provoked an immediate shooting pain in her arm. I knew then precisely what was the matter with her.

"What's troubling you?" I asked her.

"Nothing!!!" she answered aggressively.

As she refused categorically to tell me what was wrong, I then pressed on the point again but this time harder! The pain was so strong that she started to cry! I had the reaction that I wanted! In between two sobs, she explained to me that, in the last six months, she lost both her dad and her sister. As the father was ill, his death was expected. But it was not the case of her sister. Apparently, her sister went into hospital for something totally benign and never came out of it. She could not accept her death. She was furious against the doctors and could not get rid of her anger and frustration. She was obsessed with her sister's death and utterly blamed the hospital for it. The point I pressed was a point of the Large Intestine. **Mental Constipation**!!! As I said earlier on, the Large Intestine's function is to eliminate waste, but not just food waste, also emotional waste. I treated her with acupuncture. She cried the whole time and let out her pain, physical and emotional. One session was enough. I never saw her again until she came back 18 months later with the same pain!!!

"What's wrong now?" I asked her.

She replied in the same aggressive manner. She then told me that this time she was mad at her brother-in-law.

"Whatever for?" I asked again.

"He has another woman!!!" she continued. "He can't! I will not allow it!"

"Good on him!" I said. She looked at me angrily. Patiently, I then explained to her that if he wanted to rebuild his life with another woman, first of all, it was none of her business, and secondly, he had every right to do so! I applied the same treatment as before and her pain went away!

With these two examples, I wanted to show you how the mind affects the body and vice versa and how Chinese Medicine offers solutions, through its various treatment methods to align Mind and Body.

Qi Gong

There exists a lot of technical literature, either books or Internet, about Qi Gong. As there are many ways of spelling it: Chi Gong, Chi Kung, Ki Kong (Japanese version), I will in this Chapter, stick to the new nomenclature i.e. Qi Gong and concentrate in giving you the main principles and concepts of this Ancient Chinese Martial Art rather than write about techniques, which really have to be shown.

Two Chinese characters or ideograms compose the words Qi Gong:

Qi = Energy and **Gong** = Development or Workout

So Qi Gong is a Workout to develop our Vital Energy.

The Qi Gong is a method of control, regulation and regeneration of the vital energy. It is the base of all the Chinese therapies and all the Chinese Martial Arts.

Qi Gong has principally dedicated itself to health and longevity.

The Qi being the source of life, to understand the way it functions and how to regulate it, enables us to live a long healthy and strong life. Do not forget, as I explained earlier on, that man is conceived according to the same layout as the Universe, according to the principles of Tao, philosophy upon which Qi Gong, Chinese Medicine and all Chinese Martial Arts are based, and that if we go against the nature cycles, we expose ourselves to illness. It is hence in our interest to adapt our way of life to the way of nature. It is precisely what "Dao" (Tao) means which can also be translated by « Way of the Nature ».

I am a Grandmaster of Tao and Qi Gong. I was taught and trained by a Shaolin Monk over thirty years ago. I created a school called ESTAR DAO JIAO. Basically, DAO means "TAO", and JIAO means "SCHOOL". But Jiao is not a physical school, a geographical place. It has to be understood as "TEACHINGS". During my classes, I explain how to feel the Energy within you, to feel the difference in your body between the Yin Energy and the Yang Energy, how to move it through breathing and slow movements. Two key words are "intention" and "attention".

It is your intention that is going to move the Energy in the part of your body where your attention is focused.

The regular practice of Qi Gong combined with abdominal breathing enables you to reach a physical and mental balance as well as a larger and freer conscience opening more and more deeper psychical levels.

In fact, through a state of harmony and emptiness where perfectly harmonious breathing leads you, you will have access to your pure and original consciousness what Ancient Taoists and Buddhists were seeking during their whole life to attain "Illumination". According to Taoist Principles, we have three bodies that cannot be dissociated from one another i.e. the physical body, the energetic body and the mental body. The more aware you are of your breathing, the more energy you are going to accumulate and the more relaxed you are going to feel. So practising Qi Gong is another perfect way to align Mind, Body and Soul.

I have been practising it for years. It helps me to control my heart condition. I was born with this heart malformation that sometimes gives me hypertension attacks. When my blood pressure is too high, for instance 170/95, usually due to some emotional stress (yes! I am human too!!!), by breathing consciously during five minutes, I can reduce it to 127/78!

There exist various types of Qi Gong, such as Taoist, Buddhist, Martial, Medical and Mental. Qi Gong can also be divided in two distinct practices i.e. Nei Gong (internal development) and Wai Gong (external development). I practise and teach them all. Taoist and Mental Qi Gong to control my emotions, Medical Qi Gong that I prescribe to some of my cancer patients and Martial Qi Gong that I use in my Karate Training. It is not the purpose of this chapter to expand upon these various types and practices that could be the subject of future texts.

In conclusion on Qi Gong, I leave you with these wise words of Miyamoto Musashi:

"There is nothing outside of yourself

That can ever enable you to get

Better, stronger, richer, quicker, or smarter.

Everything is within.

Everything exists, seek nothing outside of yourself."

MORPHOLOGICAL BLOOD ANALYSIS

This type of analysis differs from regular analysis done in your local hospital. The latter one gives you a quantitative report of your blood count, whereas the morphological blood analysis, I perform with my patients, gives you a qualitative report of blood cells.

Let me explain. I pinch your finger and take ONE drop of your blood that I put on two glass samples. I cover one of them with a fine slide and let the other one oxidise. Then I examine the two samples in the microscope using the Dark Field Method. As my microscope is connected to my computer, and my computer to a TV screen, what I see in the microscope, you will see it on the TV screen at the same time as I do.

The first sample, the covered one, is the Live Blood. So, basically, together with the patient, we look at the morphology of your blood cells (red cells, white cells, plasma), how they behave, if the circulation is fast, slow, completely still, the size and shape of each cell. There are over 800 unbalanced morphologies. Each unbalanced morphology gives me an indication to what the cell lacks to function correctly. A cell is a living organism. So it is being born, lives, feeds and dies. It will need several nutrients in order to perform its metabolism like vitamins, minerals, amino acids and oxygen.

The metabolism generates waste (what we know as toxins) that is going to be disposed of by the white cells (our immune system).

I have fused my knowledge of Chinese Medicine with my knowledge of Morphological Blood Analysis into a very powerful tool that enables me quite instantly to diagnose the problem of my patient and treat him accordingly, without synthetic medication. I only prescribe natural products (vitamins, minerals, amino acids, enzymes), plants and herbs and aromatherapy.

ADVICE

In this whole chapter, I have tried to demonstrate to you the importance of balancing our Mind and Body. It is better to maintain this state of balance daily before pain and illness appear. For this, we dispose of an army of tools. My fellow colleagues, all experts in their fields, have done the same throughout the whole book by explaining to you via their techniques and knowledge how you can align Mind, Body and Soul!

The Tao teaches us to live according to the Principles of Nature. The Energy Laws that rule the Universe apply in the same manner to the Human Being. This is what Chinese Medicine and Qi Gong are all about. It teaches us to breathe consciously the Air and Energy surrounding us and eat consciously the food the Earth provides us i.e. fruits and vegetables.

Lao Tzu, the father of Taoism, explains in his famous Tao Te King in 81 chapters what the Tao is not!!! The first Principle of the Tao Philosophy is "Wu Wei" or "non action". This principle helped me to finally understand that I had to establish the connection between my mind and my heart.

Wu Wei turned my life around at an angle of 180 degrees. It taught me to deal with my emotions in another manner. An emotion is just a motion of energy, an e-motion. Before I was putting the blame on everybody else for what was wrong in my life. Through time and exercises, I learned to recognize my emotions, accept them, live through them by myself without it affecting anyone, let them pass and not accuse the others of being the triggers of my emotions. It took me a while but I succeeded. I also know exactly what to eat when I have an organic imbalance using the appropriate food to correct the problem. I am not perfect, far from it. We are human beings and we make mistakes. This is why we are on Earth to learn this experience. With time, I have learned to know what my strong and weak points were and deal with them accordingly, applying the healing methods that work for me.

For me, it's Chinese Medicine and Qi Gong! I practice Qi Gong every day rigorously and cure my ailments following the principles of Chinese Dietotherapy. If I slip one day, I get back to it the other day. I drink a lot of water daily, pray and meditate every day, focus on gratitude, try to stay away from negative energy and people, detox once a week physically and every morning emotionally and mentally, eat and breathe consciously, focus on remaining aware, connect with my Divine and Inner self as much as I can and above all focus on Love.

This book is all about healing and aligning your Mind, Body and Soul. Choose the methods that work for you. It might be Chinese Medicine or Qi Gong or any other technique proposed to you by my co-authors.

I care about you. Remember! I have been there! I have suffered! But I found the way to heal, to go from fear to faith, faith in my Divine Self, faith in my Power through daily and rigorous Mind and Body Balance! Get in touch with me or come and see me, I will be happy to assist you. I am looking forward to helping you!

Love,
Martine

ABOUT MARTINE de PETTER

Born in the University Town of Louvain in Belgium on 24th June 1953, Martine de Petter lived and studied in her birth country until she reached 40 when she made a 180-degree turn in her life.

After having spent many years in telemarketing, marketing and logistics consultancy and feeling unfulfilled, she decided to follow her heart. She quit her job, was called a fool by her friends and colleagues and started to study Martial Arts, the Philosophy of Tao and Traditional Chinese Medicine, sold everything in Belgium and moved to Ibiza! Her studies brought her great mind, heart and soul satisfaction. She became Master and then Grandmaster in Tao and Qi Gong, Doctor in Chinese Medicine (Graduated from Shanghai University, China) and Specialist in Morphological Blood Analysis, Black Belt 3rd Dan in Karate.

She is a member of SAC, Societat de Acupuntores de España y Cataluña, and Pefots (Pan European Federation of TCM Societies).

Now at the of 66, after 20 years, she has a well-established practice in Ibiza, helping people to find themselves and recuperate their health by means of Traditional and Classical Chinese Medicine, Qi Gong, Chinese Cosmetology, Morphological Blood Analysis and Coaching. Through the ups and down of life, she learned quite a few lifesaving lessons which she tries rigorously to put in practice daily: amongst them, self-love and self-forgiveness. Her patients are touched by her positivity and joie de vivre, her patience and dedication. They consider her a friend more than a doctor.

"Before you heal someone, ask him if he is willing to give up the things that made him sick." Hippocrates

Your Last Break-Up Holds The Key To Your Next Breakthrough

A journey of self-discovery, self-healing and transformation.

By Cristina Drannikow

If this chapter touches your curiosity it is no coincidence. In fact, consider it a sign. Maybe you have passed through a break up or you are playing with the thought "I love you but I love myself more".

Either way, breaking up is never easy. It is ugly, messy, painful, complex, stressful, multi-dimensional and at a certain moment, simply unavoidable. It brings to the surface sadness, anger, anxiety, regret, loneliness, certain loss of identity, deep wounds and traumas, all together, not necessarily in that order. If you have kids, well, all the above simply multiplies. Yet at the same time it creates a great opportunity for self-discovery, healing, awakening to a new version of yourself. All in all, you can face a breakup as your worst nightmare or make it a great opportunity to surrender, to find your own divinity and to embrace the power that makes you a Goddess on earth, an Empress.

Writing this chapter allowed me to revisit the last six years, to re-read the journals and to see how far I have come. Today, I thank the father of my son and myself, because if it wouldn't have been for that encounter, my life as it is today wouldn't have happened. Thanks to the depth in which I have fallen, I have discovered my purpose in life, helping other women to step into their power and make from this breakup the threshold of their breakthrough.

When I tell this story, I like to use the symbology of the Tarot simply, because I use it as a tool to converse with the unknown and I like the imagery it provides.

IT ALL STARTED WITH THE TOWER

In a tarot spread, the tower, comes like a divine intervention to break obsolete structures. To open our minds and our existence to something even bigger. It is the lightning that breaks the castle in two, throwing the guardians to the floor. In my case it couldn't have been more literal.

It was seven 'o clock on a cold winter morning in the middle of Uruguay, looking at the last fumes of a fire that destroyed one of the houses that I had just rebuilt and refurbished, six months ago.

The Tower. There it was, the beginning stepping over the threshold of a fiery end.

The Universe showing a big sign "That's all folks".

Months before that morning, the tower came several times, in hunches, feelings and internal pressure, aka a weakened health. Yet, I didn't want to listen. I was trying to feel different, remaining the same. I was trying to patch up the painting of my life, when in fact the structure of it, the core of my life was quietly rotten. "It was going to collapse anyway".

My marriage was on the brink of divorce many years before, yet I was failing to look at it that way. Somehow between becoming a mother, living in a foreign country for twelve years, closing my ten-year-old business and saying goodbye to my father, I lost myself. Maybe I just avoided myself altogether all those years…also possible.

But that day, that fire showed me that my life as it was, could not continue any longer. That fire was my full stop.

After living in the Netherlands for almost thirteen years, my father passing away in South America, my ex-husband facing bankruptcy we decided to move to Uruguay, to a farm in Punta del Este one of the most sought-after holiday destinations. Needless to say, the farm was in a catastrophic state. I even remember a wall in the main house downstairs that had like five different types of mold.

Like my life, that house needed a deep restoration.

The starting point was to take some time off. And before that was to give myself the permission to do that. See? In my head I was having the following dialog: "are you really going to go on holiday now? You just moved to a holiday place." And the truth was that I wasn't only in need of a holiday, I needed space to figure things out without being confronted with all the things that were broken and on the verge of collapsing, and that included my own dreams, fantasies and illusions.

The winter in that part of Uruguay at that particular moment of the year was cold, windy and damp as hell, somehow crawling into my soul. I started to play with the idea of closing everything, packing a backpack and taking a journey to India, searching for my own guru, my own guide, my own salvation.

Needless to say, that I couldn't. I was a mother of a five-year-old kid. This wasn't just me and my existence or just a backpack.

So, in the spur of the moment I decided to take him with me. No, not to India. I had found a retreat, in sunny Costa Rica, a Mindfulness and yoga retreat.

THE HANGED MAN

Do nothing and look at things from another perspective…

As an Aries, I have a pretty restless nature. I don't do "not doing anything" …well at least, I didn't at that time. I always had to be busy, I had to feel that I was hustling, not only doing things, but also planning or creating things. "Being busy with a project was my motto". Not doing was not an option. Till then. Because my whole existence was crying out loud not to do anything… for a while at least.

The hanged man, in the tarot is being represented as an upside-down person, hands tied at his back with a crown on his head. Basically, letting things be just as they are. Not doing anything. It is in the act of not doing that the light will come through. That is exactly what I needed at that moment, where my soul was as painful as my wrists stretching on the yoga mat.

That week in Costa Rica I learned the power of surrender. I cried, a lot. All the tears I hadn't allowed myself to cry over the last couple of years. I experienced deep energetic healing and the transformational power of collective Metta meditation. I met wonderful women, each with their own background and at that time I got a glimpse of what was to come, after having this beautiful awakening session with whom I like to call "my rock and roll monk".

Seeing things from a new perspective is key to the process of getting out of a breakup. Putting some distance is extremely important, as much as finding a calm centre within ourselves.

During a break up there are soooo many dimensions involved. There is the emotional one, the mental (and by this, I mean things can get pretty nasty here…from both sides), the relationship dimension, the family dimension, the financial part all of it condensed in one single act of BREAK UP. (or divorce or separation…)

Now, taking some time off of it all is a must. You do not need to go as far as a retreat to Costa Rica… but make sure you take time. You let the waters cool down, you put some distance between the other person and yourself. You can't drink from murky waters; you need to let them settle down for a while.

And then… you just start all over again.

Step by step…."despacito, pasito a past…" (the song of Fonzi calls)

The only thing that has no solution is death…For the rest, everything is ….FIGUROUTABLE.

And slowly (sometimes too slowly for my restless nature) the fog starts to clear from the pathway that was meant to be mine.

But first, I needed to surrender even more.

THE DEVIL

The unconscious chains that bond us. Our Ego. The automatism of our instinct. The devil shows us how to enter and remain chained to relationships.

Mostly we enter relationships not knowing. Not knowing the other for what he or she is, but most importantly, not knowing ourselves. We get "entangled" in an unconscious web of projections, power games, guilt tripping, overactive emotions. We get further and further away from our hearts, sometimes up to the point of ending like "The war of the Roses".

One of the points I want to draw special attention to here is that in a relationship power games appear, involving more than the couple at play. Collectively we women hold the anger and frustration of many women and the women before them that suffered at the hands of men, that were not free, were not respected and they couldn't find in their husbands a friend, even a partner. Mind you, historically women couldn't be alone, because of the patriarchal system, that didn't allow them to be financially free, that treated women as stupid, were put into a golden cage or made to be prostitutes, yet, how can you prove yourself in life if you cannot even grasp an opportunity? It has just been during the last century that women obtained the right of expression, to vote, to own property, could even have their own signature, could be treated independently from the man (mind you, my mother had to put "from" before her married surname…indicating that she was from the family of my father… that was the 70's, in Argentina). And as much as we want to look at ourselves as "modern women" inside of us there are generations and generations of women that couldn't be free, that couldn't be at the same "level" than men. So, for years and years in the collective unconscious we were not able to make decisions, to see ourselves as powerful beings.

And men collectively hold a deep unconscious guilt for not being able to trust women, to act authoritarian, with violence and pride. And they also couldn't have a strong bond with women. It is through honouring those old feelings, by giving them a place in our hearts they still find the strength to stay alive.

And then, when we feel untangled from one relationship, we hop into the next one, thinking that the last guy was the problem. Even if one part of us thinks: "If only I will find the right one this time|, another part knows that "being rescued by the next guy" was not the answer.

If I wanted my life to change, I knew that I needed to change.

I started a "Conscious Path of Transformation", to understand what was happening "on the back stage of my existence, AKA my unconsciousness".

THE JUDGEMENT

Something new is being created. A new version of myself is arising from me breaking down.

As I opened up to my own change, the universe that surrounded me started to change, including my relationship with my ex-partner.

In that path, I have learned that we are co-creators of our reality, which means that everything that is in my existence I have created it, either consciously or unconsciously. How? Our souls are having a human experience and from a higher perspective our souls have chosen this life to make an evolution, to grow. Unfortunately, we do not grow from pleasurable experiences, so we create painful ones to pass through the "college of life" and that includes our partners.

Getting my power back was getting in touch with my own unconsciousness, with my family programming, my fears, my wounds and my shadow. Getting my power back meant that I know that I always, always, always have a choice, even when I can't see it yet, even if my view is limited by my ego. Because my Soul, my true being always knows, and knows better.

The soul always knows the way, yet we fail to listen to the instructions. That's why, finding the calm centre is so important. In that way we can listen to the whispers of our soul.

Most of the time, we are too busy listening to our ego, who has a pretty loud voice. Our ego holds our fears and our belief system. When that is positive, it adds to our lives. Yet when it is negative, it needs to be addressed and healed. Our belief system is not only ours, is the belief system of the family we have been born into, the culture we have been born into, the time of human kind we have been born into. We carry in our unconscious field the knowledge, and the information of mankind.

How does this apply to the relationship with healing yourself and healing your partnership? Well simply because we are not an island. We are a system born inside a system (which is the union of two systems) and we live culturally in another system. Going into too much detail here is not the idea of this chapter, but let me explain the basics. Everything from the past influences you, mostly unconsciously, but you are the result of the complex dynamics of your family system, the way your parents got together, loyalty issues can pass from generation to generation, if there have been wars, children born dead or unborn through abortions or miscarriages, migrations... The way we relate works as follows: It is like going to a supermarket, and putting things in the basket, at a certain point you come to the counter and need to pay. If you do not pay, the next generation has to do it, and so on and so on, until someone (usually the seeker, the black sheep) starts a process of unravelling and healing (basically paying) everything that was left to be paid. (and that usually is through depression, illness, divorce, etc...). Once we see, integrate what was left, honour the destiny of those left behind us, life can flow with more freedom. The "density" of automatic responses diminishes.

We cannot change the past, yet, through knowing and accepting our past, we can heal our present. There is a lot of love in family systems, but beyond the love from the day by day actions, there is a "bigger love", a love experiencing itself through life. When we heal our part in the family system the family system can breathe alleviated, ushering us to a great life.

Another part in the healing process was understanding that I am light and shadow at the same time, and so is the other person. In a relationship there are "no good, neither bad" people. There are two people having an experience together. If I have an abusive partner, I do need to start asking myself first: where am I in my own existence being abused or repeating that pattern, and then asking where in my "family system" can I find that pattern. And forgiving and healing both. Also, which benefit do I get from "being the good one", usually it is a feeling of superiority that lies waaaaay deep down there.

Exploring our shadow is painful, complex and a bloody dirty job. It requires not only raw honesty with~ourselves, but also an immense amount of unconditional love, compassion and forgiveness. A very humbling process, let me tell you. Again, the "other" as such becomes less important. It is me hurting through the actions of the other person. If my partner is unfaithful, why did I loved myself so little as too allow all that? Where wasn't I committed that I have chosen someone that is non committing? Who else in my family system has been unfaithful and am I being loyal to? See what I mean? The other is there just to act as a reflection of those things that need to be looked up and healed within ourselves.

I AM is a great statement…I AM RESPONSIBLE FOR WHAT I AM, is even greater. What is to be responsible?

We usually understand responsibility to the degree of our duty. I am responsible because I go to work, earn my money, pay my taxes, etc, etc, etc. Yet to be responsible means, to be able to respond. Respond as an adult to what life is giving me.

In this case, I am not responsible for what my partner is or isn't, does or doesn't. I am responsible only for who I am and what I do (or bring to) the relationship. In a relationship there are two parties, each of them responsible for fifty percent of the equation.

By healing myself, I recover that fifty percent that was lost in that relationship.

THE EMPRESS

The Empress the Arcana III of the tarot. The union of the Divine Masculine of the Arcana I, the Magician and the Divine Feminine Arcana II, the High Priestess. The Empress sits comfortably in her throne, knowing that her power comes from her embodiment of a goddess on earth. In her power she IS abundance, fruition, love and pure creativity. The next Arcana is The Emperor, yet she is not waiting for him, since she doesn't really need him. If he arrives, it is to reign together, side by side. Yet for the moment, she sits there, enjoying her creations, and why not, the view as well.

The Empress is not a warrior anymore, she has already conquered her terrain. She doesn't hustle, she knows about divine inspiration for action and divine timing for fruition. She knows about receptivity. (which sometimes, when women need to be the feminine and the masculine in the upbringing of our kids we tend to forget).

She is this divine wise woman, knowing that inside of her, the Universe resides. She knows that her compass is her heart and she arrived home. She is not afraid to touch happiness and sorrow. Knowing that she is here to learn, experiment, transcend, be happy and enjoy this earthly and divine experience.

She has made her breakthrough.

I myself have made that breakthrough, and so can you.

Independently from getting into a relationship later on, you can feel fulfilled today from a place of utter freedom, deep love and compassion, understanding and nourishment for yourself and your loved ones. When you can pull yourself out, you know you can do anything. You can make the decisions that are important to your life and the life of your kids from a POINT OF POWER and a Center of alignment, a place of connection with source and the earth. When you heal yourself, when you put the pieces of the puzzle that is your life together, you become invincible and incredible magnetic.

I don't know if you are going to find a "good love in the next relationship" yet I do know that you will enter that relationship differently, and if it doesn't work, you know who you are, making your own choices and owing your life.

PRACTICAL TIPS ON HOW TO GO FROM A BREAKDOWN TO YOUR BREAKTHROUGH

1. KNOW THAT ALL IS WELL. EVERYTHING IS PERFECT AS IT IS. Yes. I know it is difficult, that you are on an emotional roller-coaster, that you feel you don't understand. But believe me, there is a bigger plan out there for you.

2. TRUST THE PROCESS. AND SURRENDER. The more you stop resisting, the smoother it goes. It is not a lineal Process, you will go up and down, relieved and overwhelmed, you will loose sanity and gain it again. You will loose friends, and gain new family members... THIS ALL SHALL PASS. The pain, the tears, the overwhelming sensation of loneliness. You have lost a partner (or husband or boyfriend) but you will gain yourself in the journey.

3. FIND A SUPPORT SYSTEM. It has to work for you. I did several transformational courses and support therapies. Finding other people than your friends will put some distance from it all, and you will be able to see the bigger picture.

4. UNDERSTAND THAT BREAKING DOWN IS THE MOMENT OUR LIGHT CAN COME THROUGH. It is the way Life or The Universe (or whatever you like to call it) is testing your strength, pushing you to another level. Always, remember the words of Franklin D. Roosevelt: "A smooth sea never made a skilled sailor."

5. CREATE A SACRED PLACE OF PEACE FOR YOURSELF. A calm Center. First internally, by concentrating on your breathing, on your alignment with source, and with connection to the earth. Remembering that YOU ARE LOVED, WELCOMED, VALUABLE, IMPORTANT, AND DESERVE TO BE HERE. CREATE AN EXTERNAL REFLECTION OF THAT INNER CENTER. It could even take the shape of a small altar or

sanctuary, where you put those things that make you happy, or give you peace or bring you nice memories. Connect with the joy of that creation. if you created that, you can create more and more nice things in this life.

6. START A JOURNAL. Pour it out there. During this period writing saved my life. Even if you feel it is non-sense. Where do you think this article came from? I went through the first stages of my transformation all again. And guess what? I am soooo loving who I have become! And furthermore...I am proud.

7. FIND YOUR CENTER OF POWER. If you like images or visioning, imagine sitting in the throne of The Empress and overlooking your surroundings (what is happening to you) from that POINT OF POWER. Breathe, they're...how does it feel? What do you feel when sitting there?

8. PRACTICE FORGIVENESS. Especially of yourself. The person that made the choices is not the person that is here right now reading this. So, forgive that person back there, because she made her choices from another level of consciousness. You have Monday's newspaper now, but you didn't have it back then.

9. CONNECT WITH THE NOURISHING PART OF THE EMPRESS: from this power point, from this sacred throne start loving yourself. Truly and fully loving yourself. Start by asking: what do I need right now? Remember, especially if you have kids that you cannot give from an empty cup. PUT YOUR MASK FIRST. (like they say in airplanes)

10. KNOW THAT YOU ALWAYS HAVE A CHOICE. EVEN IF YOU THINK YOU DON'T. You actually do. If this makes no sense to you, just explore the other choices, or ask for someone to help you make a list of those other choices. Here is a practical tip: write the choices down on a white paper, close them. Put them on the floor and then, without looking just stand on them. Feel your body and how it resonates with the choice.

11. KNOW THAT YOU ARE ON A HEALING AND EVOLUTIONARY JOURNEY. That everything you have learned and healed will heal generations behind you and generations to come. Understand that many women before you

didn't have the choice to separate, or didn't have the courage, and you are changing that.

12. THERE IS A REASON FOR EVERYTHING. And there is a lesson in everything. Your ex-partner happens to be your mirror and your teacher of all those things from yourself or your (family) system that you couldn't see, that you needed to heal, to transform.

13. CONNECT WITH THE CO-CREATOR THAT THE EMPRESS REPRESENTS. Imagine yourself sitting in this throne, in the forest, surrounded by abundance, by love, by prosperity, by health. Knowing deep within that you are infinite, that all is well, and start dreaming your new life. You deserve it. Give yourself the gift of dreaming, through this, A NEW VERSION OF YOURSELF.

14. HONOUR YOUR STORY BY SAYING YES TO IT AS IT WAS.

15. AND DONT FORGET YOU ARE AMAZING. AND MAYBE YOU JUST NEEDED TO LOOSE THE SECURITY OF THE FLOOR UNDERNEATH YOU TO UNDERSTAND HOW POWERFUL YOU ARE. TO TEST YOUR SELF CONFIDENCE. TO KNOW DEEP WITHIN YOURSELF THAT YOU ARE BIGGER AND BRIGHTER. TO TEACH YOURSELF THAT YOU ARE WONDERFUL AND THAT YOU CAN INSPIRE OTHER WOMEN ON YOUR PATH, BY BEING THE PERSON YOU NEEDED TO BE WHEN YOU WERE IN THEIR SHOES.

Love,
Cristina

ABOUT CRISTINA DRANNIKOW

I HELP WOMEN THRIVE & Unleash that Inner Empress they have....

By embracing change, I work with my clients on a self-discovery journey that transforms their current limitations, suffering and pain towards a place of power and possibility.

My zone of genius is helping women change their limiting beliefs by healing their conscious and unconscious patterns.

Through this inner alignment they can jump into "the quantum version of themselves": empowered, confident and creative. Living a fulfilled joyful life.

Thriving then becomes easy. It's easy to expand and inspire others…it's easy then to transcend.

My Yedi skill?
A deep sense of clarity combined with unique intuition and the wisdom that comes having lived several lives in one. (yes, a little bit like a cat...)

MY STYLE?
Earthly and Divine...my way is poetic yet direct, sometimes and when needed metaphorical, sometimes a little bit whimsical and other times is just "fuck the unicorns and the fairies!" It's damn practical.

I combine several techniques as a transformational coach, formed in Family Constellations, Therapeutic Narrative, NLP and Generative Transe.

"We shall not cease from exploration, and the end of all our exploring will be to arrive where we started and know the place for the first time."

T. S. Eliot

STRESS, ANXIETY, DISEASE AND HOW A FUNCTIONAL MEDICINE APPROACH CAN HELP.

By Udi Gon-Paz

←∞→

We all encounter physiological and emotional challenges that become a barrier keeping us from having the life we desire. Today I would like to talk about some of these challenges and how many of them can be overcome. My name is Udi and I'm a Functional Medicine Practitioner (I'll tell you more about functional medicine in a moment) who is based in Monaco but serves clients globally through Telemedicine sometimes also referred to as Telehealth (more about that later).

One of the most common questions that I get is what kind of medicine I practice. Am I an alternative medicine therapist, an integrative medicine therapist, a holistic medicine therapist, a natural medicine therapist? The answer? I'm none of the above! I prefer to classify myself a Wholistic Medical practitioner who employs principles of Functional Medicine.

In fact, I trained as a lawyer and businessman and when, at later years, I became unwell I couldn't see how the body could be separated into specialties. I just could not imagine that somehow all the symptoms I had were unrelated. So, I kept searching for a different approach and I became interested and later trained in clinical nutrition and stress management as a way of helping to improve my own health and later-on, once I became certified and licensed in these fields, that of my clients.

Through my learning, experimenting and experience I realised that although therapies such as alternative, integrative, holistic and natural therapies might be less toxic and even effective for some people, they don't always help us understand and treat the person, often they treat the symptoms of the disease. I also discovered that stress is almost always the fuel of almost every disease and very often it is not just a trigger or an aggravator, it is a disease by itself.

Finally, I discovered the type of therapy that I wanted to practice. It's called functional medicine, or systems medicine which I believe that it's the future of wellness and the medicine of tomorrow. It is an entirely new direction in the world of health and illness and every new client is an exciting new challenge for me.

So, first thing first: what is Functional Medicine?

First, it is profoundly science-based. It has emerged from new discoveries in what we call systems biology — the understanding of the deep interconnections of the basic systems of the body.

That's because, in systems biology, NAMING diseases becomes increasingly meaningless as we understand the inner workings and function of our cells and biological systems within the context of our entire organism.

You see, disease occurs because of the body's attempt to correct underlying imbalances. It is the body's best attempt to deal with a difficult set of circumstances.

Healthcare professionals who practice functional medicine believe that health depends on your constitution, which is partly genetic, and partly determined by your lifestyle and environment. Your constitution can also be called your "biological print." This determines your resilience and capacity for self-repair and healing.

Functional medicine is founded on a number of key principles.

1. We are all different and genetically and biochemically unique and have to be treated as such.

2. Everything that happens within us is connected in a complex network or web of relationships. Understanding those relationships allows us to see deep into the functioning of the body.

3. Our body has the capacity for self-regulation, which expresses itself through a dynamic balance of all our body's systems.

4. We have the capacity to enhance and optimize our organ reserve and prevent nearly all the diseases associated with aging.

5. Last but not least – health is not just the absence of disease, but a state of profound and resilient positive vitality.

This new type of medicine is personalised. It treats the individual, not the diseases. And it supports the normal healing mechanisms of the body, rather than attacking disease directly.

But what does this in practical terms means for you?

Well, here's some examples: It means that for an infection or cancer to take root, a weakened immune system is required. It means that imbalances in your intestinal tract's bacteria flora trigger inflammation throughout your body and can lead to autoimmune diseases and arthritis. And it also means that deficiencies in folate and vitamin B12 are likely to prevent your body from producing the neurotransmitters that help to balance your mood.

When you have health problems such as these, you have a choice. You can choose the drug-based treatments of conventional medicine, or you can help heal your body using principles of functional medicine. So, you can either take antibiotics or use toxic chemotherapy drugs to attack the infection or cancer, or you can discover how and why your immune system is not protecting you. You can take powerful anti-inflammatory medication for autoimmune diseases or you can change your diet and feed the healthy bacteria the fibre it loves, and even help to "re-plant" new healthy bacteria back in your gut.

You can take an antidepressant for depression or you can take folate and vitamins B12 and B6 to help your neurotransmitters, including serotonin, function in a better way.

Having mentioned antidepressants perhaps it's time to talk about stress in a little more detail.

Stress usually starts as pressure – from ourselves or others – and if we are unable to cope with this pressure, we start feeling stressed. The effects of stress will differ from one person to another, but if left untreated (as mentioned above) it can lead to illness.

There are many things that may cause stress, such as work, relationships, family issues and financial problems. For some, stress causes them to adopt unhealthy coping mechanisms such as smoking or drinking - and while this may feel like a quick fix, these habits are harmful to our health and in the long run the stress itself still isn't being addressed. Now, let's look at stress in some basic detail, including stress definition, symptoms and what you can do to manage it.

What is stress?

Stress is an inherent reaction embedded from our history as cavemen (and women). Back then people had to deal with threatening situations, which caused our brains to release a range of 'stress hormones such as cortisol and adrenaline to provoke what is known as the fight-or-flight response. The fight response would give us a burst of energy, readying us to fight for our lives, while the flight response would encourage us to flee from danger and get to safety. A third classification of response is 'freeze' (which is beyond the scope of today's chapter).

These days we rarely encounter such threatening situations (save such circumstances as when our mother-in-law is due for a visit), however our brains continue to react in this embedded manner when we are under pressure. When this happens, and there is no option to fight or flight - the stress hormones can build up and affect our immune system and blood pressure. Over time this build-up of stress can affect our mental health as well, leading to anxiety, depression and other mental health challenges.

Causes of stress

Causes of stress will depend on each individual - so what may cause stress for one person may not be stressful to another. Having said this, however, most stressful situations are associated with situational changes or a lack of control. Even if the change is a positive one, it can still cause stress.

Some common stressful triggers include:

- getting engaged or married
- moving house or relocating
- having a baby
- serious illness
- bereavement
- Divorce

As well as such triggers, stress can also be caused by enduring circumstances, such as:

- being unemployed
- having financial problems
- relationship difficulties
- caring for a disabled family member/friend
- Problems at work

Occasionally, the absence of change or activities in life may also be the source of stress.

Stress symptoms

As mentioned above, stress is experienced in different manners by different people and some personalities find themselves more susceptible to stress than others. However, there are certain symptoms that are frequently associated with stress. These can have an emotional as well as physiological affect.

Emotional stress symptoms

- feeling agitated, frustrated or quick to anger
- feeling overwhelmed and teary
- feeling anxious
- having a low sense of self-esteem
- Avoiding other people and social situations

Physiological stress symptoms

- using alcohol/drugs/food for comfort
- difficulty sleeping
- digestive problems and upset stomach
- feeling dizzy
- sweating excessively
- Experiencing chest pains or palpitations.
- Tremor or shaking

The physiological side effects of stress are caused by hormones which are released by our brain during the fight or flight response - these include adrenaline and cortisol.

Adrenaline

When adrenaline is released it causes rapid changes to our body, increasing blood flow and speeding up our breathing rate and heartbeat. You may become pale, sweat more and your mouth may feel dry. This hormone is designed to help us either fight or flight in response to the stressful state of affairs. When the threat is physical, this works well and once the danger has passed, the body recovers. When the threat is emotional however, the effects of adrenaline subside much more slowly - meaning you could feel tense and anxious for much longer. If the situation is enduring, you could feel the effects of adrenaline long-term and this is when your body and mental health begin to suffer.

Cortisol

Cortisol is present in our body constantly, but levels increase when you are faced with danger, or a stressful situation. In the short-term, much like a rush of adrenaline, the effects on your body are positive and help you deal with an immediate crisis. Long-term stress however can cause a constantly raised level of cortisol, which can have a number of harmful effects, including:

- blood sugar imbalances
- suppressed thyroid activity
- high blood pressure
- lowered immunity
- Increased abdominal fat storage.

Is there a difference between stress and Anxiety?

People often confuse the two or used the terms interchangeably. I think we can summarise the differences as follows:

- Stress is usually the result of external pressures – we can also say that stress is the reaction to a problem and anxiety is a reaction to the stress. This is not to say that anxiety cannot be a reaction to external stressors. But essentially, stress is "the feeling of being under too much mental or emotional pressure," while anxiety is "a feeling of unease, worry or fear." (definition from the UK NHS website). Why is the distinction important? Stress can often be dealt with in a much more practical manner; whereas anxiety may require counselling, medication, or other professional psychological treatment

- Anxiety tends to linger after the issue is resolved whereas stress doesn't - the National Institute of Health's U.S. National Library of Medicine says, "Stress is caused by an existing stress-causing factor...[while] anxiety is stress that continues after the stressor is gone." Basically, stress can set off a case of anxiety. Once again, the distinction is important because although anxiety can definitely be triggered by stress, sustained or chronic anxiety needs to be treated as its own issue, rather than as a by-product of stress. You can't alleviate an anxiety disorder with a holiday or a visit to the spa (no matter what some less enlightened people might tell you).

- Anxiety involves needles and often irrational worry – although symptoms of stress and anxiety can often overlap and be confusing, there is one tell-tale symptom that signals anxiety and only anxiety: a persistent feeling of apprehension or dread in situations that are not (rationally) threatening. The kind of counselling given to someone coping with a great deal of stress will be quite different than the course of treatment from a person suffering from generalised anxiety disorder.

- Panic attacks are triggered by anxiety and not stress - A panic attack is actually a very specific experience of heightened fear of discomfort that often involves sweating, trembling, pounding heartbeat, heart palpitations, nausea, chest pain, the sensation of choking, chills, and numbness in the hands or face. A panic attack begins suddenly, and most often peaks within 10 to 20 minutes. Some symptoms continue for an hour or more, and many people go to the emergency room during their first panic attack, because they are convinced that they are having a heart attack or some other terminal health problem — so, yes, it's a very different experience from just feeling a little panicked about having burnt your toast. If you've experienced a panic attack, that's a sign of anxiety — and a sign that you could benefit from professional help.

People's tolerance of stress and anxiety differs, meaning for some the effects will be severe but for others they will be manageable.

When should you seek help for stress?

The issue with stress is that it exists as a problem that feeds on itself, and over time lowers your ability to cope. Because of this - the sooner you seek help for stress, the better. Since stress is frequently viewed as simply a 'part of life' it can be difficult to know when outside support is required. As a rule, you should look to seek help if the following is happening:

- stress (and the effects of stress) dominates your life
- stress is affecting your physical health
- you are using unhealthy coping mechanisms and methods in dealing with your stress
- You are experiencing angry outbursts that are affecting those around you.

Treatment for stress

Recognising the negative effect stress is having on your life, and understanding that this is not OK is an important first step. Once you have admitted to yourself that you need support, you can look into the various treatments available.

One form of therapy that has been recommended for those struggling with stress, and certainly my favourite and the one I treat my clients with, is HeartMath. HeartMath is a new technology that has broad-based applications in stress reduction, rehabilitation, and performance enhancement. HeartMath techniques have been proven to facilitate rapid, profound, and enduring improvements in a wide variety of conditions. The HeartMath methodology is a scientifically validated way to reduce stress, and more importantly, to transform the negative emotional and physiological effects that occur when you experience feelings of stress or a stressful event. Heartmath is different from other stress relieving activities, such as listening to music or taking a warm bath because those activities take place after the event has passed. By the time you wind down, you've already experienced the harmful, often unpleasant effects of stress. The stress hormone cortisol, for example, stays in your system for hours once it is released in to your system. High levels of stress hormones can have a serious negative impact on your physical health. So, the key appears to be learning how to transform your reaction to stress, and therefore stop the emotional and hormonal fallout that follows.

What is the science behind HeartMath?

In studying the science of the heart, The Institute of HeartMath has discovered is that your heart rhythms have an impact on your thinking. When your heart rhythm is coherent (smooth and orderly), you are able to access higher-thinking centres in your brain, so can think more clearly and see more options or solutions to problems. When your heart becomes incoherent, this access becomes inhibited and you are likely to find your reactions are slower and you are not be able to think so clearly.

Studies have found that people in a coherent state are noticeably able to improve their thinking and performance, whether they are making decisions or playing sports.

Over time, coherence also helps to reduce the 'stress' hormone cortisol – which is produced whenever you experience feelings of frustration, anxiety, anger or despair – and increases the 'vitality' hormone DHEA. Ideally, these hormones should be in balance, but when you experience frequent stress, cortisol can become too high and DHEA depleted. This pattern is found in most major diseases and is associated with accelerated aging, brain cell death, impaired memory and learning, decreased bone density, impaired immune function, increased blood sugar and increased fat accumulation around the waist and hips.

How does HeartMath work?

HeartMath provides techniques that can be practiced daily to help you actively reduce stress in your life. With HeartMath, you learn a simple coherence technique that can help you 'reset' your physiological reaction to stress as the event occurs.

Just a couple of HeartMath breaths can help you stop the hormonal cascade that triggers the release of cortisol – and you stay coherent (i.e. calm and in balance). When practiced regularly, research has found that the exercise can help you to feel better emotionally and improve your intuition, creativity and cognitive performance.

Which conditions can be helped with HeartMath?

Heart Rhythm coherence feedback (HeartMath) can be very useful in the treatment of chronic anxiety, stress, depression, anger and other emotional issues. It is also an effective addition to treatment programs for chronic conditions that are associated with or exacerbated by emotional stress, including fibromyalgia, chronic fatigue, hypertension, asthma, environmental sensitivity, sleep disorders, diabetes, cardiac arrhythmias, hypertension, congestive heart failure, and many others. It has been proven particularly effective in cardiac rehabilitation programs to help patients reduce stress and increase cardiovascular efficiency. HeartMath can also be used for performance enhancement and for reducing test taking anxiety.

Everyday stress management

There are things you can do yourself at home to help manage your stress. There are several excellent HeartMath tools that were developed for this purpose. Mental health experts agree that the following tips can help with everyday stress management:

Know your stress triggers

If you're not sure what it is that's causing your stress, it might be a good idea to keep a journal and note down any stressful episodes over the course of a fortnight. Aim to include as much information about your experience as possible, including the time and place, what you were doing, what you were thinking about, how you felt physically and a rating out of 10 of how stressed or anxious you felt.

Using this journal, you should be able to figure out what your stress triggers are, how you cope with pressure and how you could potentially change your reactions.

Look after yourself

This means getting enough exercise, eating well and taking time to relax and mentally focus out from obsessing over the causes of your stress.

Health professionals agree that exercise is a useful tool when tackling stress as it releases 'feel-good' endorphins, helping you to physically and mentally de-stress. Eating well is another important factor. Eating an unhealthy diet puts your body under physical stress, which can aggravate any emotional stress you may be feeling.

Taking time to relax is another key part of self-care and is essential if you want to reduce your stress. Aim to dedicate a certain amount of time every day to relaxation, whether that be HeartMath meditation, practising yoga, reading, or simply clearing out your own thoughts.

Take control

One of the main reasons people feel stressed is because they feel as if they don't have control of a situation. While of course it is impossible, nor desirable, to always be in control, you can choose to control your approach to a state of affairs. If you remain passive in your thinking (i.e. "I can't do anything about my problem") then chances are your stress levels will continue to increase. Alternatively, if you choose to accept your problem and seek to find a solution to it (which may involve you reaching out for help), you will begin to feel more in control.

Connect with others

When we are stressed it can be easy for us to hide ourselves away from the outside world and avoid social encounters. This can lead to a feeling of isolation and even increased stress. Talking through your problems with friends, family and even co-workers can help you feel more connected and may even help you view your concerns in a different perspective. Sometimes talking to someone else about their worries puts our own in perspective. Some people find it therapeutic to get out of their own head for a while, so why not consider volunteering?

Avoid unhealthy habits

When we are stressed it is easy to rely on unhealthy habits for escape and comfort. Such habits may include smoking, drinking, taking drugs or even overeating. In the long-run, these habits will only create new problems and as they don't tackle the cause of your stress, you will continue to feel the effects and probably with a vengeance.

Accept what you cannot change

If a difficult situation arises and there is nothing you can do to change it, take a step back and accept this. Recognise that there are some things in life you cannot control. Instead try to focus on what you are able to control. For example, if you are being made redundant there is probably little you can do to turn the situation around. What you can do however is control your reaction and what you do next - you can choose to see it as an exciting opportunity and begin a new job search.

Relaxation techniques

Learning how to relax properly is an essential part of stress management. There are many different relaxation techniques that you can try, many of which focus on relaxing your body and breathing in a certain way.

In preparation, look to set aside a few minutes a couple of times each day to relax and keep to this schedule. If you can, choose a quiet place away from distractions - if you have young children, why not have them join in? This can be especially useful before their bedtime.

Stress, Anxiety and the gut connection

When our body experiences stress, it causes a cascade of events that are intended to help us evade imminent danger. It shuts down non-essential activities such as sexual desire, reproduction and digestion, and uses neurotransmitters to direct its resources and energy to the brain and muscles. This has repercussions for the gut too.

A lesser known fact is that an unbalanced gut has consequences for your mood because bacteria can also influence anxiety and stress by their activities in the gut. They can play a positive role by enhancing our resilience to stressful events, but when the ecosystem is not balanced (dysbiosis), their activities can have a negative impact on our mental health. Dysbiosis doesn't merely have a negative impact on physical health, it can also have a negative effect on our mood, anxiety levels, stress resilience, and depression. That's yet another excellent reason to incorporate healthier food choices.

Gastrointestinal health is a favourite area of medicine of mine and books can be written about the gut stress connection. But for the purpose of our little chat today, I feel that saying less is more.

How does it all tie up?

Stress and mental health in general are individual. It takes time for a medical practitioner to understand what is stressful for each patient and to find solutions that work for each person. Though the medical system is changing, conventional medicine still treats disease in isolation, rather than looking at a person's whole health picture. I've found in my own practice that once we begin to take a more wholistic approach to symptoms and disease, we find that so many of our health issues are rooted in stress.

We are all aware that things such as traffic jams, lack of sleep, too much sugar and processed food, long hours at work or unpredictable situations can burden our bodies, but there are other triggers that can increase the stress hormone cortisol that may surprise you. All of them can easily be tested with advanced home testing kits. Here's some with their corresponding symptoms:

- *Food intolerances:* Symptoms may include bloating, wind, brain fog, fatigue, joint pain, diarrhoea.
- *Nutrient deficiencies:* Symptoms may include leg muscle cramps, food cravings, hair loss, fatigue, brittle nails and hair.
- *Hormonal imbalances:* Symptoms may include irritability, carb cravings, fatigue, hot flashes and/or night sweats, irregular menstrual cycles.
- *Over training:* Symptoms may include feeling depleted after exercise, fatigue, skipping menstrual periods.
- *Infrequent meals and snacks:* Symptoms may include light-headedness, dizziness, irritability between meals.

Each time our body has to compensate for the losses associated with one of the above triggers (or stressors), we put more strain on our body. And in many cases, the adrenal glands (our stress responders) release cortisol to manage the stress. Yet increased cortisol is associated with many diseases including Alzheimer's disease, heart disease, insulin resistance, obesity and Type 2 diabetes. Consequently, if we could figure out what is stressing us, we could potentially help prevent some of the most common diseases.

Emotional stress is frequently the hardest to solve for both patients and practitioners. Whether it's a troubled relationship, the death of a loved one, an unfortunate job situation or past trauma that hasn't been entirely processed, there are many emotional stressors your body has to struggle with on a daily basis. And even if it seems like the stress is only occurring in our mind, the adrenals are still pumping out cortisol in an effort to keep the situation under control.

It's sometimes difficult to figure out everything that may be contributing to your stress. I always ask clients to take an inventory of their triggers. This requires sitting down and listing the things in their lives that cause stress. I also offer a questionnaire that helps rating your stress and see how you compare to others. In addition, I use the HeartMath Bio Feedback system and I also ask about some of the symptoms I mentioned above to see if any physical stressors are involved -- because often these aren't considered by clients as real "stress." When we combine all of the data, we get a much better idea of what the causes are. Once this has been established, we can commence on our joint journey toward eliminating the sources of your stress and getting you nearer to a balanced and healthy life.

Telemedicine/Telehealth is your solution

Can't travel to Monaco for Functional Medicine consult? Not to worry, I offer remote care via Telehealth / Telemedicine for many people around the world. Many patients fly in from different countries to my practice – with these in person visits, we are able to establish a practitioner / patient relationship. For this level of care, I require that patients maintain a Concierge Level membership, with interim visits conducted via Telehealth / Telemedicine.

These services will consist of providing you with information and suggestions that are intended to assist you and your health care provider/s in using natural means to support your health. Telehealth education services are not intended to serve as a medical diagnosis or treatment of any kind. We offer access to medical testing around the world. Our Fees for Telehealth are the same as the fees that we charge for our telephone consultations and visits to the practice. If you want more information of all the services that are offered at our practice or to book an appointment, please call our practice or visit our website www. wholeiswell.mc

Love,
Udi

ABOUT UDI GON-PAZ

I'm a Functional Medicine Therapist, qualified in Clinical Nutrition and Stress Management Therapy. I'm certified by the International Association of Health Coaches, and by the Heartmath Institute as a certified <u>Coach, Trainer and Mentor.</u> I am dedicated to helping others understand the physiological and emotional aspects of their lives and the connection and overlap between these aspects. This in-turn allows people to make changes which I believe helps people activate their innate ability to self-heal when given the proper tools, information and guidance. By following a wholistic life style not only can they achieve an optimal level of wellness, happiness and extended longevity, but also reverse and at times cure chronic conditions. My methodology is based on practical application of combining the sciences of nutrition, stress management and physical activity which is custom fitted to each individual client's goals. We have access to advanced home medical testing from advanced laboratories, including DNA testing, which helps us in determining the root causes of many problems.

We all encounter physiological and emotional barriers and I am passionate about helping my clients find out what can be done to overcome those barriers in order to experience their lives in a way that makes them happy and satisfied.

Whether you are looking to improve your diet, reduce stress, stop your emotional eating, improve everyday functions of living, improve physical health, find your optimal performance zone, or excel at your sport or at your work (or very likely, a combination of these things because they're always linked to one another), my unique and customised 1 on 1 coaching is the solution for you.

"You have to put on your own oxygen mask first before helping others."

EMOTIONS MATTER

By Amy Gyles

←—∞—→

From early childhood we are unconsciously and consciously taught that our emotions are a bad thing. When someone cries, you are taught to hand them a tissue, a seemingly kind gesture but it also implies that tears are not allowed in that space. You're told as a child not to express anger, "don't be mad." Even excitement can be seen as too much. This constant stifling of our emotions can lead to serious problems. But it's not just outside influences that affect how we process our emotions. Our bodies will suppress emotions in order to protect us. Dissociation is a process in which our bodies will create a disconnect between memories, actions and surrounding events. When we are exposed to a traumatic event, excess stress, overwhelming grief or other intense emotions our body will disconnect from the thoughts or memories in order to protect us from having to process them. This may show up as a lapse in memory or a blackout. This is a common component of PTSD. When thinking about a traumatic event the person may have little to no memory of what happened. This feeling can be quite unsettling to the person living it, they may feel as though they've lost their memory or even parts of themselves. People with PTSD often struggle with identity because of this, it can also show up as a feeling of being broken or not whole. PTSD is an extreme example of this process however emotion suppression doesn't need to be extreme to create a lasting effect on your physical and mental health.

Emotions can hide anywhere in our bodies but certain patterns tend to occur within our 7 main energy centres also called chakras. The trapping of emotions causes energy blocks, basically a block in the flow of energy that stops the chakra from performing as needed.

The first of these chakras is called The Root. The Root is located at the base of your spine and pelvic floor. This chakra is responsible for our connection to earth, our ability to stay grounded is in this chakra. The Root chakra glows with a red colour of energy with an opening in the back of the body where energy enters and an opening on the front where energy exits. Because this chakra is where our connection to earth and safety is, it's common for fear to be stuck here as well. Fear is a normal emotion that we encounter in our daily lives and through traumatic events. When fear is stuck in our root it can manifest in many ways. Fear in your root can lead to an exaggerated fight or flight response, it may feel as though you're constantly on edge or on guard. This can lead to physical problems such as elevated stress hormones, adrenal fatigue, problems with the kidneys and muscles in the lower limbs. Psychological problems that stem from an energy block in your root could be memory problems (from chronic dissociating) and social anxiety.

The second Chakra is called The Sacral Chakra. It lies just below your belly button with an opening in the back of the body for energy to flow in and an opening on the front of the body for energy to move out. The sacral chakra glows with a soft orange colour. The sacral chakra Is about sexuality and creativity. Sexual trauma tends to be stored here, along with guilt, shame and feelings of not being good enough. The sacral chakra helps regulate the reproductive organs, bowels, bladder and lower intestines. Physical problems that can arise from energy blocks in your second chakra include but not limited to, ovarian cysts, bladder infections, constipation, irritable bowels, painful periods and irregular cycles.

The third chakra is called The Solar plexus. The solar plexus is located above your belly button and below your ribs, again with an opening in the back and front of the body allowing energy to flow through the chakra. The solar plexus glows with a soft yellow energy. Your third chakra is your power house, it's where your confidence lies, your personal power and professional success. The organs involved with this chakra are the stomach, liver, gallbladder, pancreas and large intestine. This tends to be where anxiety, self-sabotage and negative self-talk will hide. Physical problems that can arise from an energy block in your solar plexus include but are not limited to, reflux, diabetes, gall stones, problems with the liver and food allergies. Psychological problems can also stem from blocks in your solar plexus such as, anxiety, depression and low self-esteem.

The fourth chakra is known as The Heart chakra. It is located in the centre of your chest and glows with a soft green light. The chakra opens on the back to allow energy in and on the front of the chest allowing energy out. The Heart chakra relates to the heart, lungs and diaphragm. Feelings of not being loved, abandonment, rejection, fear, anger and sadness can be stuck here. Physical problems that can occur from energy blocks in the heart chakra include but are not limited to, heart disease, chest pain, palpitations, asthma, COPD and frequent colds. Psychological problems arising from a blockage in the heart chakra can be depression, low self-esteem and a tendency to push people away in order to protect yourself from heartache.

The fifth chakra is called the Throat chakra. The throat chakra is located at the base of the neck with an opening in the back of the neck allowing energy into the chakra and opening on the front allowing energy out of the chakra. The throat chakra glows with a soft blue colour. It relates to the thyroid, trachea and oesophagus. Emotions that tend to be stuck here include, anger, sadness and a feeling of not being heard. The physical problems arising from a block in the throat chakra can include, hyper or hypo-thyroidism, problems with swallowing and jaw problems. Psychological problems that can come from a blockage in the throat chakra can include, social anxiety, fear of public speaking or a loss of words.

The sixth chakra is called the Third eye. It is located on the forehead with an opening in the back of the head to allow energy in and on the front of the face to allow energy out. The third eye glows with a purple energy. The energy from the third eye chakra regulates the brain, pituitary gland and eyes. Emotions that tend to be stuck here include fear and sadness. Your third eye also controls psychic ability and intuition. Physical problems from a blockage in you third eye can cause migraines and hormone imbalance. Psychological problems can include hallucinations, or a feeling of disconnection.

The seventh chakra is called The Crown chakra it is located at the top of your head. The crown is our connection to God/source/the universe. The crown glows with a purple or white energy. Physical problems associated with a blocked crown include neurologic disorders and nerve pain. Psychological problems include a feeling of being disconnected.

Common physical ailments and their emotional cause:

Auto-immune disease - With auto-immune disease your immune system attacks your body in various ways depending on what type of auto-immune disease you have. In my opinion the auto-immune portion stems from-feeling that you are not good enough. some see it as a self-hatred or self- sabotage and yes those both play into the development of the disease but both of those boil down to-feeling like you're not good enough. This feeling of not being good enough or not worthy tends to settle into our bodies in early childhood. It becomes a core belief that we hold that literally makes our-body eat away at itself. Pinpointing the exact trigger for auto-immune illness gets more specific, you need to look at what body systems are involved and their corresponding energy centres.

Let's look at Hashimotos specifically. Hashimotos thyroiditis is an auto-immune condition where your body attacks your thyroid gland. If we look at the associated chakra, we can see the thyroid sits in the throat chakra. Since we know the throat chakra is about speaking your truth and the auto-immune component boils down to "not enough" then Hashimotos can be simplified to the emotion of not feeling like you're good enough to be heard. A lot of times this comes from something that happened as a child. it may have been a single traumatic event or repeatedly being silenced as a child.

Insulin resistance - Insulin resistance is a disorder where the cells in the body become resistant to insulin allowing excess glucose to circulate in the body, this can lead to type 2 diabetes. Insulin resistance relates to the Pancreas, which is governed by the Solar plexus. This is where your personal power and self-confidence can be found. because Insulin resistance is thought to be a problem with glucose or blood sugar a good emotional cause would be that you are simply denying yourself the sweetness of life. This rejection of the sweetness of life or joy can also cause depression and the two often go hand in hand. Because without joy, you would be left awfully sad. So, what makes people reject joy? I think it comes down to believing that you don't deserve to be happy. Something happened early on in childhood that let you believe you weren't worthy of being happy, who stole your joy?

Heart disease - Heart disease can include anything from clogged arteries, heart failure, arrythmia and structural abnormalities. Your heart lies in the area of the heart chakra, which is all about being loved and loving others. Heart disease can manifest from not feeling loved or constantly pushing people away to avoid being hurt (also a lack of love). Obviously if you're born with a structural abnormality a lack of love couldn't be at play, right? Energy doesn't die, it simply moves. So a mother who had a significant lack of love as an adult or child can pass on the imprint of that broken heart to her child. This is partly why healing yourself can literally change the health of future generations.

Stroke - A stroke is caused by a blood clot or a haemorrhage in the brain, these can be life threatening and cause lifelong damage. Strokes are related to the third eye and crown chakra; they tend to happen to people who are the back bone of their family. They constantly do for others without caring for themselves first.

Chronic pain - Chronic pain is usually caused by something that emotionally hurts you, it's important to note where the pain is to pinpoint the cause.

Back pain - Low back pain tends to relate to a feeling of lack. This tends to relate to money concerns and financial stress. Mid back tends to hold guilt, something you feel guilty about that is causing literal pain. upper back tends to be a feeling of being unsupported in life or carrying a burden (shoulder pain as well).

Knee pain- knee pain relates to your root chakra and tends to be something you "can't stand" or an unbending attitude. In this case side matters, left tends to be female or maternal and right male or paternal. For example, you might have right knee pain if you can't stand the way your father treated you.

Painful periods- Painful periods relate to your sacral chakra. There are many possible causes here as the organs involved give life and many emotions are tied into that. One example would be someone who suffers from infertility (emotional cause here too), every month when her cycle comes it is seen as a failure of her or her body. She begins to resent her body for not being able to do what comes naturally to others, this manifests pain around her cycle.

Hopefully you can now see how emotions play a role in the physical manifestation of illness or pain and how important it is to recognize and release trapped emotions.

Just as important as knowing what those emotions cause is knowing how to release them. Making sure your 7 major chakras are open and clear is a great start. Let's start at the bottom and work our way up.

Opening and clearing the chakra system:

A great way to start the process of healing your chakra system is to get outside and practice grounding. This simple meditation will ground you and help to clear energy blocks. Start by closing your eyes and visualize roots coming from the bottom of your feet, send those roots deep into the earth. You'll know you're there when you feel the pure loving energy at the core of the earth. Allow that energy to travel up your roots and into your feet, visualize it traveling up your legs, core, chest, neck and head. Send the light out into the universe with your intention to send it to source. Then visualize light from source going into the top of your head, let it fill you as it travels down through your body and out your roots back into the earth. This connects you above and below. Set your intention to allow your emotions to surface, whatever comes up is okay. When an emotion surfaces, thank it for releasing and breathe it out. To do this breathe in divine white light and when you breathe out see it as negative energy, the emotion itself or just dark energy, whatever feels right in the moment.

When visualizing the energy of your root itself you want to see the energy as a red circle that is every so softly swirling with its own force. Move your focus up to your sacral chakra again with the intention to release any stored emotions, your sacral should be a soft swirling orange colour. Continue this through each chakra, solar being yellow, heart is green, throat is blue, third eye purple and crown dark purple or white.

When you've looked at each chakra a good practice is to fill your whole being and aura with solid gold energy. Gold is protective and will keep out unwanted energy but still allows guidance from the angelic realm to come through.

You are not a victim of your past; you have the ability to heal yourself. Just because an emotion is stuck and causing a physical problem doesn't mean you're destined to have that illness for the rest of your life. You can look inside you, find these emotions and release them.

My goal in writing all this wasn't to point out that you're broken or flawed, in fact I want to point out the opposite! You are more capable than you know, shifting your mindset and releasing trapped emotions can heal you on a very profound level. How do I know? Because I've done it, not just for myself but for my clients as well. When I was thirty my life turned upside down.

Overnight I went from running often and working full time as a Respiratory Therapist to not being able to stand without losing consciousness. I went to countless doctors and specialists and my list of diagnoses just kept growing. At just thirty I was diagnosed with Lupus, Hashimotos, Poly Cystic Ovarian Syndrome, Ehlers-Danlos syndrome, Postural orthostatic tachycardic syndrome, gastroparesis, insulin resistance, eczema, chronic pain and dysautonomia (dysfunction of my autonomic nervous system). At one point I had a port placed in my chest for IV fluids just so I could stand without passing out. I had lesions in my brain, a mass in my liver and a mass in my left lung. Just a year after getting sick I was told I would probably be wheelchair bound and disabled for life but I refused to give up. I knew there had to be something they overlooked. How could I go from seemingly great health to being disabled literally overnight?

I started looking for more, there had to be! One by one I pinpointed the emotions attached to my physical illness. My hashimotos went back to feeling rejected by my father, he left when I was a teen and moved across the country, until recently I never told him how much that hurt. I wasn't speaking my truth. My Ehlers-Danlos syndrome, at its core was triggered by an unstable childhood.

My PCOS was my rejection of life. Being raped at four years old and again in college contributed to a constant fear of attack, I lived in fight or flight mode. This caused elevated stress hormones, metabolic syndrome, and chronic pain. I worked on myself for years and I'm still healing. But today I walked two and a half miles. The port was removed from my chest years ago and it's been 4 years since I needed IV fluids. No wheelchair, I cut up my handicap card and my leg braces are gone. I didn't heal overnight and more was at play other than solely energy work.

But my true healing began when I could see that my emotions played a massive role in my physical wellbeing.

Getting into alignment with your true self. We are what we tell ourselves, which is why the way you speak to yourself is a big aspect of healing.

Once you've identified and began working on releasing trapped emotions, you can start to bring yourself back in alignment with your true self. Shifting your mindset is a game changer for healing.

A good place to start is to come up with some personal mantras or affirmations to tell yourself daily.

A good mantra should be positive and in the present tense. Here are some I recommend for shifting your mindset:

I AM ENOUGH	I AM HEALING
I AM LOVED	I AM DIVINE
I LOVE MYSELF	I SPEAK MY TRUTH
I AM ME (good for PTSD and chronic dissociative states)	
I AM SAFE	I AM STRONG
I AM CREATIVE	I RESPECT MYSELF
I DESERVE TO BE HAPPY	I AM WORTH IT

Mantras will help shift the way you see yourself and your circumstances, you are not a victim. Something I've found that helped me with seeing my strength was to cut toxic people out of my life.

I don't allow people to treat me badly, I deserve better and so do you. Cutting people out of your life, especially family can be difficult. Once you've identified a toxic person in your life and stopped communication with them, take time to grieve the loss of the relationship you thought you would have with that person. When cutting out family this can hit pretty hard, take the grief in waves and be sure to offer yourself forgiveness along the way. You are allowed to be sad; you're allowed to be angry; you're allowed to grieve. An exercise that helps you let go is to write a letter to the person you cut out (YOU WILL NOT BE GIVING THIS TO THEM). The point here is to help you heal from them. Write a letter to them and write everything you ever wanted to say to them, really let it out. They won't be seeing this so don't hold back. Let the emotions surface and let them out!! it's time to heal.

Once you've had time to let that out, you're going to write another letter, this time to you from that person. Write everything you ever wanted to hear from them, be the apology they never gave. Let the emotions flow and take time to release.

When anger comes up, scream into a pillow, get a punching bag, or simply breathe it out (breathe in light, breathe out anger). When sadness or grief comes up, cry.

Once you've written both letters and had time to breathe take both and destroy them, you just put a lot of energy in those letters and it's time to transmute it.

Tear them up, burn them in a well-ventilated area then return the ashes to the earth when safe to do so. Set your intention that when the letters are returned to earth that the emotions attached leave you fully. This is as simple as stating your intention out loud.

It is important to rebuild ourselves and the most important part of this is Self-Care

Self-care is not just bubble baths and manicures.

Real self-care is about loving yourself so much that you won't want to repeat patterns that don't serve your highest good anymore. You've released a lot and it's time to focus on rebuilding.

I want you to love yourself, not just have chocolate when you want it but real unconditional love, shifting your vibration is a great way to start.

When we sleep our body tends to stay in the vibration we hold as we fall asleep, this is why what you do in the hour before bed is so important.

An hour before bed think of at least three things or people you are grateful for; I don't mean list them like it's Thanksgiving dinner. I mean think of each and really feel the vibration of gratitude.

Once you've listed and felt gratitude for at least three things or people focus on you.

Tell yourself what you love about yourself, list them. Once you've listed everything you love about yourself find one thing you don't love about yourself, but tell yourself "I love...". Add one thing every night until eventually you are loving every cell in your body. When you make these statements, you are literally sending the energy of unconditional love to yourself.

Part of self-care is knowing when to ask for help. Trapped emotions and energy absolutely contribute to the development of physical illness.

However, you may need more than just energy work to heal the physical.

It's important to know when you need help and ask for it. There are lots of healing modalities that work alongside or in place of western medicine. Some examples; homeopathy, acupuncture, massage, yoga, meditation, QiGong, Tai Chi, Sound therapy, Crystal therapy, Reiki, Energy healing and more.

Find what resonates with you and trust yourself in your healing. You deserve to heal, you deserve to be happy and you deserve to know that right now, in this moment, YOU ARE ENOUGH!

Love,
Amy

ABOUT AMY GYLES

I am a Reiki Master/Teacher, Intuitive energy healer, medium, meditation coach and mindset shifter.

I offer intuitive energy healings, Reiki, sound therapy, crystal healing, meditation coaching, Reiki certification and one on one support to make sure you are releasing the emotions and coming back into alignment with your true self. I specialize in PTSD, anxiety, depression and chronic illness.

When I work with a client I can see where emotions are trapped in them, what caused them and the potential or current physical problems that arise from those emotions. I can pull those emotions to the surface and work with the client to consciously release them. By doing so their body, mind and soul can heal as one.

On a personal note, I am a 35-year-old with and amazingly supportive husband and two magical and loving children. I developed my practice after learning how to heal myself from decades of trauma and physical illness that was seemingly "incurable." After finding the root emotional cause of my ailments I was able to release them and put the pieces back together. I understand pain, I understand the words "there's nothing we can do." More importantly I understand hope and that shifting your mindset and releasing stored trauma or emotions can help you see the light inside you that wants nothing more than for you to feel whole, happy, loved and to know beyond a doubt that you are enough.

 "You are not a victim of your past, you have the ability to heal yourself. YOU ARE ENOUGH."

THE MIND-BODY-CREATIVITY CONNECTION

By Nikki H.

Let's get right to it, shall we? Mind, body and creativity are connected. Creative activities and creative pursuits improve your physical health, mental health and brain function - woo hoo! - and here's how:

Multiple studies have shown that doing something creative or being creative

- reduces stress
- focuses the mind
- strengthens the immune system
- increases cognitive function and
- increases connectivity between left and right brain hemispheres

(Want to read more about the studies and the research? Check out the reference list at the end of the chapter)

Yep, creativity does all of this and more. Simply put, if you boost your creativity, you will also boost your mind and body, together ☺ Together - isn't that fantastic?!

How do you boost creativity, you ask? It's not a complex, complicated or overwhelming thing. It's as easy as pie actually.

At the core of it all is this: creativity is not limited to an activity, skill or project. Creativity can infuse all aspects of life. Let it. Live in a way that encourages and embraces creativity so you can always access it and it is always available to you. Think of creativity as a well - you want it to be full when you want to draw from it, at any time. Keep filling your well. Keep feeding it. It will never run dry if you do. (Oh and by the by, doing this is also a good way to thwart creative block)

This is the foundation in my creativity consultation work. There is endless creativity, available and accessible to you at the drop of a hat, and I'm going to share how you can tap into, harness and fuel yours.

Just remember to PLAY!

P - Practice
L - Look around
A - Adventure
Y - Yes, you
! - Play!

PRACTICE

Practice.
Do something.

The more you practice creativity, the more creative you become. That's how it works! It's like anything else you may practice: the more you do it, the better you are it.

It doesn't actually matter <u>what</u> you do. What matters is that you <u>do</u> it.

Don't just think about it. Do it.

Develop a practice for creativity. To develop any skill, you would make time to practice it. Let's take playing a musical instrument as an example - if you want to develop your musical skills, you set aside time to play that instrument. Creativity is something that you can learn (as research and studies have shown)-and the same principle applies: if you want to develop your creative skill, you set aside time to be creative. So put your creativity practice on your calendar. Schedule it as an appointment with yourself and don't cancel it for anything.

If you want to commit to your creativity, commit to it. I've seen it many times - we put everything else (and maybe everyone else) before our creativity time (and ourselves). It's usually: "I just want to finish what I'm doing and then I'll get to it" and "I just need to do one more thing" or this one's quite popular too: "It's ok that I missed my creativity appointment - I'll just get to it later" and then later never comes.

Does any of that sound familiar? If it does, resolve to look out for those kinds of claims and justifications and also be on alert for when you're putting other things before your creativity. And then choose it. Choose your creativity. Choose yourself. You have committed to your creativity. You have permission to put it (and yourself) before other things.

Remember in your practicing and doing creative things, set an intention for a supportive environment full of positivity and encouragement. And, if you do fall off the wagon, I'm here to tell you that it's totally ok. Don't give yourself a hard time about it. Just get right back on. Just like that. Don't stress about it.

Be encouraging and gentle with yourself. You're just trying it. You're learning. It may be frustrating; it may not go so well and it may not turn out the way you imagined it in your mind. You most likely will not create a masterpiece the very first time you try anything. Be ok with that. Maybe even expect it to be an epic fail and fail spectacularly - just have fun and relax about it.

Whatever you create, make, design, craft, write, and so on, suspend criticism - rather revel in the fact that you actually did it, that you harnessed that energy of yours into something creative. The act of doing it is what's important, not how perfect or imperfect you think it may be. There's no right or wrong here. It's all gravy.

Start. Give it a try. Write something, draw something, sing something, cook something, do something. Dance around in your kitchen. Journal about your day. What you choose to do is entirely up to you. Choose whatever speaks to your heart. Do what moves you. No censorship or judgment. Just go for it. The "doing" - and more than once since it's a practice after all - will flex your creativity muscle and it will get stronger.

TAKING ACTION...

Here's an exercise to get your creativity cooking. **You'll need to grab a pen and paper if you're reading this on your e-reader!**

Take out your calendar and schedule an appointment with yourself for your creativity practice. Treat it like any other important appointment - don't break it or push it back. If it helps, and you want to make it a little more official, write in "meeting with Nikki" (as in "Oh, I'm busy at that time I have a meeting with Nikki"). Write in the date and time in the space below. And if you know what you'd like to do for your creative activity, write that in too. There's space to write other notes too - perhaps on what you'd like to commit to, ahem. It's blank intentionally so you can doodle your notes thoughts rather than write them if you are moved to do so. Whatever floats your boat.

My creativity practice date: _____

My creativity practice time: _____

My creative activity: _____

Write down any notes/thoughts/commitments/reflections:

LOOK AROUND

Look around.
Pay attention.
Observe.

Creativity is everywhere. It is not just in the arts - in paintings, drawings, dance and music. It is in everything. In architecture, design, food, engineering, nature, even in how people live their lives. Notice inspiration and pick up on ideas all around you. Appreciate what you see. Be curious. Investigate. Wander. Wonder. Wander and wonder. Tuck all those ideas and inspirations into your back pocket. Let everything inspire you. Let that be fuel for your own creativity.

I had the honour of training and designing a breath-taking wedding with premier event designer and artist Preston Bailey. Preston is world renowned for his ability to transform spaces into magical, theatrical environments and for his art installations across the globe. His medium is flowers. He is also the author of 7 books and one of my favourite human beings on the planet. I sat with him on the day of the wedding and chatted about inspiration. I asked him the questions I love to ask creatives: "Where do you find your inspiration?" And his answer was "Everywhere." In art galleries, on his travels, in the apartment he loves living in, everywhere in life. He shared that he loves to look around, to see, to notice and to pick up ideas that are not related that can be translated into his work. Like many artists, designers, performers, writers, painters and other creators, what Preston sees around him inspires him and moves him and goes into his creative work. The same can be true for you.

TAKING ACTION...

Look up, right now, and look around. Write down 10 things that you see around you right now that you enjoy, that inspire you or that are fun ideas. It could be something like "the sky" or "the light bouncing off the window" or it could even be "the way the cappuccino foam twirls around in my coffee cup like a cloudy Flamenco dancer". Write down 10 - ready, set, go!

ADVENTURE

Adventure.
Have adventures.
Be adventurous.

Do something different. Mix it up. Try new things. Things you have never done before. Go into uncharted territory. Cultivate wild ideas. Be an explorer and a treasure hunter.

Being an adventurer doesn't have to be intimidating.

Read books and magazines that you haven't read before. Treat your taste buds to new food. Listen to other genres of music. Explore new places. Attend events you wouldn't normally - in your own neck of the woods or beyond. Ever been to a Shakespeare Festival, tattoo expo, tribal belly dance show, tiki festival, Renaissance Faire or rockabilly weekender like Viva Las Vegas? No? What are you waiting for?

Immerse yourself in new environments. Follow your curiosity and facilitate novel experiences for yourself. Take a class. Learn a new skill, a new activity or about how something is made.

While grand experiences are wonderful and encouraged, you really don't have to go far and wide to have an adventure. In your own city, there are all kinds of classes, activities, events and restaurants to try. But, on an even smaller scale than that, switch things up in your regular routines and ways. Take a different path to a regular destination. Change the order of your sandwich ingredients. Do one of your afternoon activities in the morning instead. Do you work in an office? Make a new spot your #officefortheday - it could be a garden, hotel lobby, coffee shop, museum, the beach, or perhaps an art gallery.

I love what speaker and author Matthew Hussey says: "Be a tourist in your own life." Embrace that idea, go forth and make every day an adventure, you explorer, you!

Adventure comes in all forms and your spirit of adventure is yours to cultivate. It's all yours for the taking. If you're a bit afraid or hesitant to try something, ponder on this for some encouragement:

Ten seconds of courage.

That's all you need to start and to pick an adventure of your very own. And think about what you have to gain from those ten seconds of courage - what do you get to explore, experience or enjoy for yourself if you have just those ten seconds of courage?

TAKING ACTION...

How about we put you on the fast track to adventure, shall we?

Find a fun or silly activity or class, sign up, register or pay for it, and write in your appointment on your calendar. try it solo or invite your friends along on your field trip.

Some ideas to get the fire burning: cooking, dancing, crafting, singing, fencing, circus arts, sandcastle building, improv comedy, underwater basket weaving, axe-throwing. Think of "on-a-whim" kind of activities that maybe you'd never do or something you've always wanted to do. You have permission to go for it right now. (If you need resources or more ideas, let me know. I've got plenty.)

And, just for fun, and to further encourage your creativity, do a doodle of your chosen activity or class on a sheet of paper. Remember, it's not about drawing a perfect drawing. Just have fun with it. You can even write it out in BIG CAPITAL LETTERS ACROSS THE PAGE if that resonates with you more. Yeah, baby!

YES, YOU

Say yes.
Say yes to the possibilities.
Cultivate an attitude of yes.

Say yes to the process - Go with the flow. Choose ease. There is no need to resist or battle.

Say yes to you - Be yourself. Honour yourself. Nourish yourself. Be kind to yourself. Give yourself space to explore your creativity. Let yourself breathe into it. Give yourself permission to be inspired, to explore, to just be.

Say yes to your own journey - You get to choose. You choose to be creative or not, to take action, to commit. Or not. You choose. You decide. One decision can change your life, right? When it comes to your creativity, what decision(s) do you want to make? What do you want to say yes to?

And I'm here to remind you that:

Yes, you can do it.

Yes, it is possible for you.

TAKING ACTION...

Take a few minutes to reflect, right here and right now. What do you want to say yes to? What decisions do you want to make when it comes to your creativity? Write it down in your journal or on a piece of paper and stick it on your fridge, notice board or any other area where you can see it.

I am saying yes to:

I am deciding that:

PLAY!

The exclamation mark in PLAY! is for "play". (Big surprise, I know ;))

Play.
Laugh.
Enjoy yourself.

Whatever creative project or activity you choose to do, have fun with it. Approach it with excitement (like a kid-in-a-candy-store kind of excitement) versus drudgery or dread. Do it with curiosity and a sense of wonder and adventure. Leave the heaviness or negativity behind. Don't take yourself too seriously. (Also, did you know laughter in and of itself supports creativity?)

Embrace the fun of it all, from the get go, and let go of any worry or stress you may have about it. Remember there is no right or wrong here. Just play and laugh and see what happens.

After looking around and adventuring, notice what lights you up. Notice what you gravitate towards. Do more of that. Be around more of that. Play in that. The possibilities are infinite.

TAKING ACTION...

Let's be encouraging of fun, laughter, excitement and lightness. Write a sentence or two here and answer this question: **What are you most excited about when it comes to creativity?** It could be related to what you have learned about creativity or about the mind-body-creativity connection, it could be related to your creativity practice or your adventure...what lights you up about it, right now?

I am over-the-moon excited about ...

RECAP

Let's recap what we've learned:

Mind, body and creativity are connected. Creative activities improve physical health, mental health and brain function.

Doing something creative or the act of being creative:

- reduces stress
- focuses the mind
- strengthens the immune system
- increases cognitive function and connectivity between left and right brain hemispheres

Being creative does all of this. And, very simply, if you boost your creativity, you will boost your mind and body, together.

Big picture: Live in a way that encourages and embraces creativity. Let creativity infuse all aspects of your life. Feed and fuel your creative fire.

How to-s: Boost your creativity with PLAY!

P – Practice
L - Look around
A – Adventure
Y - Yes, you
! - Play!

And now what?

Well...

I am committed to your creativity and I am here for you. If you have any questions about what I've covered, get in touch.

Now, go on, don't be shy. Go PLAY! Like I said, the possibilities are infinite. The whole world is your playground.

Love,
Nikki

References:

"Here's How Creativity Actually Improves Your Health" by Ashley Stahl

https://www.forbes.com/sites/ashleystahl/2018/07/25/heres-how-creativity-actually-improves-your-health/#3c0704f513a6

"How Being More Creative Improves Your Mental and Physical Health" by Colette DeDonato

https://www.lifehack.org/articles/lifestyle/how-being-more-creative-improves-your-mental-and-physical-health.html

"7 Mind-Body Creativity Hacks" by Rachel Shanken, LMHC

https://mindbodywise.com/blog/7-mind-body-creativity-hacks

"Why Weird Experiences Boost Creativity" by Scott Barry Kaufman

https://www.psychologytoday.com/us/blog/beautiful-minds/201206/why-weird-experiences-boost-creativity

"The Power of Humor in Ideation and Creativity" by Moses Ma

https://www.psychologytoday.com/us/blog/the-tao-innovation/201406/the-power-humor-in-ideation-and-creativity

About Nikki H.

Nikki has thrilled audience members and event guests for over 20 years as a dancer, performer, choreographer, instructor and producer. With her signature encouraging and playful attitude, Nikki has a knack for breaking down concepts, step by step, in a way that's both easy to follow and highly entertaining. Not afraid to be bold and daring or embrace the unusual, Nikki is known for her uncanny ability to dream up endless supplies of out-of-the-box ideas and to find delight and inspiration at every turn. She applies her experience and these traits to her work as a creativity consultant and muse, helping people unleash their creativity in projects, events, businesses and everyday life.

"The whole world is your playground."

How To Live Your Life Orgasmically

Sex is a skill and can be learned

By Klana

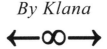

"I am convinced that, if everybody gets what they need, especially in the realm of sexuality, there would be no war on earth." - Klana

What do you struggle with most around sexuality, intimacy and relationship?

Are you not feeling yourself anymore? Do you feel lonely and empty and miss deep intimacy? Do you love yourself? Are you longing for a harmonious relationship and want a fulfilled sex life?

You might not be the only one.

This chapter will help you to take the first steps to self-love and more satisfaction in your life.

Imagine how it would be to feel comfortable in your own skin, be attractive and confident, free yourself from shame and guilt, experience more intimacy and enjoy amazing sex!

Being invited to be part of this book is a great honour and pleasure for me. Since I turned my life around 180°, I am realizing more and more who I could really be, the person who was hiding behind all the social masks that I had put on through decades of my life.

Bringing body, mind, soul and spirit together is the first step to move into living authentically and in the present moment. That means automatically you stop worrying, and enjoy more and more what IS.

After living a "normal" life in corporate Germany for many decades, the way to my real self, went from becoming a professional life coach to learning massages and different kinds of bodywork, getting a certificate in Sexological Bodywork and developing my spiritual gifts. Once I stepped on this path of change and transformation there is a constant moving forward to discovering new facets of myself and teaching the things I've learned to others.

Every human being should live their life in the way they want, and have a fulfilling sex life too.

I am convinced that, if everybody gets what they need, especially in the realm of sexuality, there would be no war on earth.

My story

I was 35 when friends asked me to go into the sauna with them. One part of me was interested, the other one was reflecting the fears of my mother: claustrophobia in the hot air. That's what I put in the forefront as an excuse for not joining them, but the real reason was that I was ashamed to show myself naked in public. Sure, we weren't prudish within the family, my parents didn't hide themselves in front of us, their children. Being naked was normal. At home.

I had this distorted image of myself. I was already very tall as a teenager, taller than the boys. Our dancing school offered events on Sunday afternoons. I loved ballroom dancing so I went there. But it was also frustrating because it didn't happen very often that a boy asked me to dance. Of course, thinking being too fat, too tall, not feminine, not to mention sexy, of course exuded through my energy field...

In retrospect it was no wonder that nobody wanted to dance with me, especially not the handsome guys.

On the rare occasion one of the not so cool guys came to ask this wallflower that was me for a dance: These shocked faces when I got up from my chair! Their eyes wandered up a long way to my face. That was quite traumatic and shaped the way I viewed myself.

So the first decades of my life, I mostly felt uncomfortable in my own skin and unattractive to the other gender. I was feeling lonely and unloved.

By the way, I overcame my resistance and went to the sauna with my friends. That opened a door: I met a guy there, who became my boyfriend.

You always have a choice.

If YOU don't take a conscious decision, someone else will.

Fast forward. After a career in corporate and several unsuccessful attempts to find the "right" man to be in relationship with, another door opened when I turned 50. I got a coach and took a very bold decision. I left my home and job in Germany to start a new life on Ibiza/Spain. That was something, I jumped into the unknown!

This mind guided woman, I used to be, always playing safe, found herself alone on an island without speaking the language, hating the heat, but being very curious what the coaching program she was about to take would bring her.

A lot of change and transformation!

Phoenix rising from the ashes. It was as if I had lived the wrong life all those years before. The woman that I am now has little to do with the mind driven, rigid person I used to be.

Now I feel much more like myself!

This is what I'd love you to take away from my story and this chapter:

- Learn to love yourself exactly as you are!
- Sex is a skill and can be learned

- It's never too late for change
- Be bold
- Trust in the universe/spirit/God/yourself, however you name it
- Drop your resistance and surrender to life

Way too often we are raised in families and environments that don't let us unfold the way we really are and then we forget who we really are.

Fairy tales, movies, magazines and advertisement show us how life and relationships "should be". What our body should look like. Which clothes we have to wear and which colours are on trend. No wonder that we easily feel inadequate. Nobody can fulfil these ideals.

Sexuality is a big topic for humans. Most of us think that sex is given by nature and everybody can do it. Of course, you can do it.

My opinion is, if you learn sex as you learn other things, you can have a much more fulfilled life. Few of us got helpful sex education when we were young and we needed to figure it out by ourselves. As a result of this, many of us fumbled around and had awkward experiences with a partner.

Isn't it time to bring your sexuality to a new level?

How about learning the skills and enhancing the quality of your sexual life?

I promise you; this will spill over into all other areas of your life in a very positive way.

Sexual Energy is Life-Energy.

We are quickly blaming our partners if we are not satisfied: "He doesn't care about me…, it's boring to only do it one way…, he only wants to fuck…, he is not doing what I really need…"

Often we think our partner will know what they have to do to satisfy us. How should they, if we don't know ourselves, if we don't know what's great for us?

You are responsible for your own orgasm, not your partner. That also means that you can have a great sex life even without having a partner.

So, I want you to learn how to love yourself first. Mentally and physically. Both go-together. I learned to love myself through the physical. In the training to become a Sexological Bodyworker I learned to discover my own body through a regular self-love practice. Getting creative, not just following the pattern that I used to practice since childhood.

When you start to discover your sexuality as a child you mostly develop shame around it. You didn't want to be caught by your parents, so you figured out how to get a quick release. You carry that behaviour into your adult life.

With my clients and lovers, I often see that they have that goal to get an orgasm and to give an orgasm. There is so much more to just achieving this orgasm!

If this is your only aim, you are not really present in the moment. Your mind is busy reaching the goal and you are missing out the beauty on the way. While both of you are being busy giving the other person what you think they want and need to orgasm, you are forgetting about your own pleasure, and will be frustrated if you cannot reach the summit.

Do you know what your partner wants? Or do you guess what they want because you learned it in a book, watching porn, or with other partners? You cannot be sure that it works with this partner too. Even though I am painting a black and white picture here to get across an easier understanding, people are very different. Especially women are complex when it comes to what they like in sex. Most likely you will have experienced this already.

Here we come to the next issue: The differences between men and women. A man usually loves to be touched directly at the genitals. A woman needs a lot of attention on other body parts first until you can even think to touch her vulva or her breasts. If you now come from your own feeling and want to apply it with your partner from the other gender, it won't work so well.

Men, if you really want to have her open up and enjoy what you are doing, please slow down, warm her up first and don't feel bad if she tells or shows you what she wants. Communicate your needs, ladies and gentlemen. You cannot always feel what the other person needs in this very moment. Even though you can feel it way easier if your whole being is in the present moment and not busy with reaching the goal of orgasm. Thank your partner if they tell you what they want from you. Sometimes you might not want to "deliver" that, and that should be ok too. I always want you to act consensual. This is very important for trust.

What I want to make clear is, that a fulfilling sex life is nothing "God given" but something you need to work on. Start with yourself. Explore yourself.

Find out what you like and what turns you on, try things out for yourself. Then share it with your partner. See if they want to explore it together with you. Sometimes it might be something that's not suitable for them or even scares them. Please respect this. Maybe at one point they are open to go a step further.

I once had a boyfriend who loved going to swinger clubs. This was a no go for me. He accepted this. I asked myself what the reason was that I didn't want to go there not even knowing what was going to happen there. I came up with a number of arguments why I was afraid. Being really honest with myself I detected that it was the fear that I might like it. This interfered with my upbringing, there was shame.

A lot of time passed and the topic occurred again and I noticed that I couldn't judge if I didn't try it out. What I needed was to feel safe. I talked to my boyfriend and he assured me that we could leave any time. I didn't have to interact with anybody I didn't want and he wouldn't do anything with anybody else but me in the club. With this agreement, I felt secure enough to try it out. It was interesting and not at all bad for me. So, I went with him a few times to different locations.

It's all about communicating your needs and find a way how you both can find an arrangement. I cannot say that going to swinger clubs became my favourite, however I had a good time whenever we were there, I overcame another bunch of inhibitions and made him happy.

I am an advocate of being in the present moment while having sex. No matter if it's solo sex or with partner(s). Many people "check out" into fantasies and loose the precious moments to feel those grand sensations to the fullest. If you like watching porn do it consciously.

A few exercises that helped me

- overcome sexual shame
- learn to love myself
- have a more fulfilled sex life with myself and with a partner

Here are a few exercises that I teach my clients to do themselves at home or in my women's retreats so that they learn to be more present and overcome shame.

My suggestion is to practice the following first on your own before you integrate it in partner sex.

Set the timer and do each of them 5-10 minutes.

Breathing

How to stay present? - Conscious breathing keeps you in the here and now. It also helps you to regulate your arousal. You might have noticed that when your arousal raises your breathing rate gets higher. That also works the other way around: breathe faster and you can raise your arousal, whereas slow, deep breaths calm you down.

You can do the breathing exercises first sitting in a chair or laying down and later add them to your solo sex practice.

1. Hold one hand on your genitals and the other one on your heart. That connects the two parts of your body that are so often disconnected. Inhale slowly and deeply through the nose, pull your breath from the earth, through your genitals up to the heart and release slowly through your slightly opened mouth. Continue doing this a few times and observe what's happening

in your body. The sensations and feelings will vary at different times you are doing this.

2. Circuit Breathing

    The important thing here is, to continuously breathe without stopping or pausing between in-breath and out-breath. Effortlessly let the in-breath flow into the out-breath which flows into the next in-breath... You can sit, stand or lay down.

    Breathe gently through your mouth. Relax your jaws and open your lips a bit.

    Feel how your throat opens and relaxes. Do not force your breath. You'll need a bit more effort for the in-breath than for the out-breath, in which the air gently falls out.

    This breath is particularly good to let the erotic energy flow in your own body and to let it circulate between you and your partner if you do this practice together. Feel how it builds the energy up, moves it and intensifies feelings and sensations.

    You can breathe through your mouth or breathe in through the nose and out through the mouth. Experiment!

3. Fire Breath

    Don't practice this one longer than one to two minutes.

    Coming from the Kundalini Yoga this is a powerful, arousing breath. For this one you only breathe through the nose. Emphasize on your out-breath.

    Breathe out and while doing that, press the air out pulling your navel quickly back towards the spine.

    To breathe in you just let you navel snap back forward again. The breath will fill your lungs automatically.

    If you take one hand to your diaphragm you can feel the power of this breath.

Start breathing every two seconds and move up to one or two breaths per second.

You can use the Fire Breath when you want to build up energy, any time before or during a sexual encounter, or if you want to be concentrated on some task during the day.

Try these breathing techniques first by themselves, then integrate them into your solo sex practices. Observe the different effects that they have on the flow of your erotic energy. You might notice that you take longer to reach orgasm if you use this or that breath consciously. That's great! That means that the breath moves your sexual energy through you whole body.

When we masturbate or have sex we usually hold our breath. That limits our sexual energy to the genital area. Whereas when we breathe fully and consciously, we fill our whole body with it. It takes longer but you'll have a bigger, deeper and longer orgasm.

We can only think one thought at a time. If you keep your mind busy with conscious breathing, there is no space for thoughts like "I will never cum", "Does he really love me", "Have I paid that bill?"

Movement

Another thing you can do is to move your body. If you are an agile person you already might be doing this. For me this was a great practice and I still love it.

Put some music on and let your body move. You can start on the floor or standing. Just move or dance. Be aware of when you start "performing", wanting to make it look nice. The point is to let your body do its thing. You will see how this frees you up. You can add physical touch to it. Maybe you even want to do a strip tease just for your own pleasure.

For some of you it might be even more challenging to do this in front of a mirror. For me it definitely was the case at the beginning. I was even ashamed in front of myself!

We all have challenges in different areas.

Then you can take movement into your bed or wherever you do your solo sex practices. By the way, I also recommend to experiment with different locations (shower, bathtub, whatever comes to mind). Always observe what difference it makes to your usual style of (solo) sex.

Let's break the patterns so that some extraordinary things can unfold!

Sound

Are you loud or quiet during sex? If you are like me, and rather quiet, I'd like to encourage you to introduce sound into your sexual practice. One of the things I took away from my swinger club experience was that it turned me on when people made sounds while having fun. So I experimented at home with myself. It worked, and the more I practiced the easier it was for me to also moan when I enjoyed myself with a partner. Yeah, I overcame another bit of shame!

Expressing yourself shows your partner that you like what they are doing. I do love to get feedback from my partners in some form. Do you, too?

Touch

Keeping the best for the end. Touch is my personal favourite. There are so many different qualities of touch I let my clients discover when they are working closer with me.

There are many variations between very gentle to very rough and even painful. For some people pain is very pleasurable. Usually it takes a certain amount of arousal for that.

When it comes to touch, I also want to motivate you to test what YOU like and in which intensity. You will discover that you prefer different ways of touch in different qualities depending on the situation and your level of arousal. This is important to know so that you can communicate with your partner while playing.

Try out how it feels to use a feather, hot wax or an ice cube on your skin. It will create different sensations on different body parts.

Imagine you find out that the gentle touch of a feather on your nipples drives you crazy? Or you realize that a clothespin at that particular spot and moment does it?

The possibilities are endless.

Being open to trying things out and explore on your own and with a partner will keep your sex life fresh and it will never get boring.

Important is to stay true to yourself and respect your boundaries and the boundaries of your partner(s). Even though expansion can happen if you stretch your own boundaries from time to time.

Everything, however strange it may appear at first, can happen as long as it is consensual.

I wish you an amazing and fulfilling sex life without shame or other things stopping you from your own pleasure!

Klana
The Pleasure Alchemist

To learn more about me and what I am doing go to www.klana.us or follow Klana.TV on Facebook

ABOUT KLANA

Klana worked in the corporate world for 30 years before she followed her curiosity to explore and discover her true purpose. Being devoted to her self-development and spiritual path, Klana has now been in the field of coaching, bodywork and (sexual) healing for more than 10 years.

She is passionate about this field because of her own struggles. Feeling like a misfit for many decades, not feeling sensual, sexy or feminine she finally realized that she didn't love herself.

Klana began her studies to learn more about how to overcome her sexual shame and how to have better sex and real intimacy. Over time she discovered her spiritual connections and is developing her clairsentient, clairvoyant and claircognizant gifts. She is a multidimensional healer, a professionally trained Life and Leadership Coach and a certified

Sexological Bodyworker.

Klana works with both women, men and couples. Her main focus is on emotional malnourished women who need help learning to love themselves so that they can have the intimacy and joy in their life that they desire.

She loves to help them bring mind, body, heart and soul into alignment and feel confident in their own skin.

"I am convinced that, if everybody gets what they need, especially in the realm of sexuality, there would be no war on earth."

ENERGY IS EVERYTHING.

By Sarah Lines

Albert Einstein said "**everything** is **energy** and that's all there is to it. Match the frequency of the reality you want, and you cannot help but get that reality. It can be no other way."

Alignment. So many seek alignment in life. Wondering how to achieve this lovely state of being.

In this chapter, I will address this important aspect in our lives.

A part of us is always seeking, searching, longing; longing to feel whole, complete and fulfilled. But many of us search for this fulfilment through external forces; love, money, success.

The truth is, when we fill up our cup from within, everything else falls by the wayside. When we transform our inner energy, our outer world will follow accordingly.

Yes, it can feel amazing to have 'stuff', but we can feel whole, complete, happy and fulfilled without these external forces. I have done this myself.

I was a chronic addict, homeless and totally lost, with no hope for my future. I had lost my home, my car, my belongings and the most heart-breaking – my children. I had become what I thought I never would. I was a destitute junkie.

I thought sex, money & having a partner in my life would fix me, fulfil me, nurture me. I was so wrong.

I floated through life, existing, feeling unsafe, scared, unsupported, unloved. I desperately needed validation. I needed to feel loved. And so, I drank, I drugged, I slept with whoever showed me attention. I so desperately wanted to be saved. I thought my knight in shining armour would come swoop me up one day and make all the pain go away, but he never came.

All of my relationships were toxic, unfulfilling, volatile. I didn't know about life and how to live. I didn't know I was attracting these relationships and situations into my life. I didn't know I was creating my reality; and that I could change this. I was enduring the dark night of the soul. I spent many years feeling distraught, deeply depressed, alone and just so sad.

But I found a way out, I found a way to be happy, without feeling like I had to please others so they would like me, without having to have sex with someone to feel love, without alcohol or drugs in my life to fill the emptiness, the unfillable void.

> *"Everything is energy and that's all there is to it. Match the frequency of the reality you want, and you cannot help but get that reality. It can be no other way."*

Albert Einstein

Healing within to heal without

When I finally had the courage to take a good, hard look within, miracles began to happen. I went where many do not like to go, the road less travelled. I looked over my whole life with a mentor and started at the beginning. I looked back at the conditioning I had been raised with and the beliefs I had taken on as a consequence. I looked deeply at the reasons behind my fears, my resentments, my harms. I opened my eyes to the part I had played in all areas of my life, releasing my victim mentality. And I forgave unconditionally.

The Universal Law of correspondence, states that our current reality is a mirror of what is going on inside of us, it is a direct result of our most dominant thoughts. If our life is filled with chaos and drama, as was mine, this is a direct reflection of what is going on inside of us. This is the danger in holding on to our negative thoughts, it becomes a self-perpetuating situation, a vicious cycle of self-sabotage.

If you resonate with this story, or parts of it, I want you to know there does not have to be this sense of "being stuck" or hopelessness. You have the amazing ability to Shift paradigms and transform your reality now.

Looking in the mirror, inside of yourself, not outward at others, can be hard if you have never done this before. You do not have the power to change people, places or things, but you can change you. This will literally shift your reality.

Three words: Thoughts, beliefs, attitudes. I believe this is why we are seeing such a boom in the coaching industry right now; we are ready as a collective to change and take our lives to the next level. We are ready to let go of these old paradigms holding us back from living our best life, moving onwards and upwards. This is why I believe having a coach or mentor is so pivotal to our human experiences at this time, having the guidance and support necessary to make these important life changes.

This is so doable. It can feel like the hardest thing to do but I promise, it is definitely the most rewarding.

The doors that will open for you when you decide to ascend are beyond your perceived limitations. You are an infinite being of love and the possibilities for you are endless.

"Be brave enough to heal yourself, even when it hurts."

Bianca Sparacino

We are all connected

The Universal Law of oneness states that we are all connected, as one, to one source. Absolutely everything we do, think and believe affects the collective conscious of the entire universe. This is a huge concept that gets missed by so many, and that's ok, this is all a part of the human experience, the journey, our path. We are each on our own unique paths, waking up one by one to new truths. All connected by the energetic matrix.

We can help people, heal people, situations and the planet without even being present in the same space-time. We can contribute to the health and happiness on the whole as one person just by sending love, being love and choosing love. Love-light always wins over the darkness.

If I feel affected in a negative way by someone or something I firstly come back to the realisation that I cannot control people, places or things; I do the inner work, whether it be letting go of expectations of others, forgiveness, acceptance etc and then I send them so much light. This affects myself in a more positive way, and the other person. Our thoughts are just so powerful. Look at the fires in Brazil and Australia, world-wide prayer affected change, we received rain.

You can consciously affect planetary change by sending light from above/source, down through your body, creating a white pillar of light; sending this light out through your feet, into mother earth, down to her very core. Mother earth gratefully and lovingly receives this beautiful energy and sends it where it needs to go most to humanity and the planet.

This in turn has a collective healing effect on every little thing, helping mother earth ascend in to her new 5D light energies, helping us all ascend into higher light frequencies on our collective journey of ascension, to new earth.

> *"We are all connected; To each other, biologically. To the earth, chemically. To the rest of the universe atomically. "We are all connected, to each other biologically. To the Earth, chemically. To the Universe, atomically."*
>
> *Neil deGrasse Tyson*

Energy Alchemy – Transform your reality

I came to understand this in my awakening journey. Somehow, Reiki found me in 2016 and I was off on a healing tangent. I had to know more, learn more, I was mesmerised. I wanted to heal the world! It was absolute magic to me. Energy alchemy is the process of transmutation and transformation. And we all have this capability. We are born with natural psychic-healing abilities, but we are born into this lifetime with amnesia, forgetting why we are here. The process of awakening helps reminds us of who we are and the reason we are here, the bigger purpose in life. And this is when we find our gifts are re-activated.

You know how when a child falls over and the mother will innately know what to do? She gives it her magic kiss and puts her loving, maternal hands over it. This is healing at its core. When I was a little girl, my dad would get migraines and he swore by having me kiss his head to make it feel better.

You can literally transform your reality through transforming your inner world. Our body is made up of over 70% water. Water has consciousness. We can make this water happy, healthy and supportive of our human vessel, or sad and destructive. Talk to the water in your body, fill your cells with light just by intending that it is so, tell yourself how much you love yourself every day in the mirror, affecting deep change. Sending yourself love, being kind to yourself, compassionate and forgiving.

If you feel you are a sensitive or empath, you may find yourself extremely affected by electronics, people and places. You may find yourself feeling sad without knowing why. Many empaths go through life believing they are just too emotional or suffer depression & anxiety, but the truth is, it is unlikely that these feelings are even yours. I highly recommend regular, daily energy protection to protect your own energy from that of others. Which have a negative impact on you. Each morning when you wake up, envision a golden light around your body with the intention that this will not allow anyone or any energies that do not serve your highest good to enter your space for the day. The more you do this, the easier and more effective it will be.

You may also like to call upon Archangel Michael to assist you. Ask Archangel Michael to be with you, removing all negative energies, thought forms, feelings and energies that do not serve your highest good; then ask him to surround you with his purple shield of protection and know that this is done.

Energy clearing and protection is so important in keeping your own energies clear and of a higher vibration. You can cleanse your energies before any protection technique with sage, incense, crystals, asking your angels & guides, a nice salt bath, or any method that suits you.

"The more you see yourself as what you'd like to become, and act as if what you want is already there, the more you'll activate those dormant forces that will collaborate to transform your dream into a reality" Dr Wayne Dyer

Simple daily techniques to align your energy

When you align your energies, things just seem to fall into place. Energy alignment can take on many forms. Energy is everything, so affecting change in your thinking will help with energy alignment, being more active will affect change throughout your being, eating healthier, loving deeply and so on. It is all connected, the mind-body-spirit, so what is one positive step you can take today that will infiltrate all areas of your life? Our energy body holds on to information, repressed emotions and trauma, as they get literally stuck in our body. All illness and disease have a spiritual cause and you can find much information about this, that all dysfunction in the body is caused by un-released emotions from this lifetime or past lifetimes. I have found this working with women, many fears and blockages that have been from a past life, so we clear this at the root, from that lifetime, from that memory or trauma. I had repressed emotions for so many years I didn't know how to allow myself to feel anymore. I learnt just how beneficial it is for me to sit with my feelings and allow them to flow through my body, instead of getting stuck causing me gall bladder problems, digestive issues, constant urinary infections, severe anxiety & depression, skin problems and the rest. As uncomfortable as this can be, we are allowing our shadow self to rise and more light to enter our body. Merging with our shadow through inner or shadow work is actually so powerful in rising into our authentic, beautiful, ascended state.

This does not have to be complicated, everything is connected, so you will find that by treating one part of your body, it will have a positive impact on your mind, emotions and physical being. For example, guilt and shame were a large part of my life. And I mean large, these feelings consumed me every day all day. I held this deeply in my sacral chakra, in my womb space. This physically affected my reproductive organs and I had 2 miscarriages. I also was having a lot of urinary issues and felt sluggish all the time, extremely fatigued, unsexy and just yuck. I started eating berries every single day, practising forgiveness of myself, and would place my hands in this area, imagining white light entering this area, allowing the warm, loving feeling to enter and clear this area. When the Chakras are open and clear, they allow a beautiful universal life-force energy to flow through our entire being, we feel well, happy, resilient and we live longer.

Just one closed chakra can affect the whole body. It is like blocked plumbing; the energy flow cannot pass through a closed chakra to the rest of the body and therefore negatively impacts other areas of the body-mind-spiritual wellbeing. To truly live in an optimal space of happiness and wellness, I recommend focusing on all major Chakras in the body, these are as follows: The Crown Chakra, Third eye, Throat, Heart, Solar Plexus, Sacral and the Root Chakra. All of these major Chakras are connected from the physical body to the spiritual. They energetically connect to organs, nerves and glands in surrounding areas. Easy ways to keep these Chakras clear are regular physical activity, eating plenty of fresh foods, meditating often, being out in nature, keeping crystals in your space and using essential oils or incense.

> *"What the universe will manifest when you are in alignment with it is a lot more interesting than what you try to manifest."*
> *Adyashant*

Living from your Heart space

We in society, have moved so far away from our inner being. No longer do we connect in, follow our intuition and take regular quiet time out to just be. We are a technological world, making decisions with our logical minds instead of our hearts and what we truly desire. When consciously connecting in with our beautiful hearts, our inner being, our soul; we can find major shift happen in our lives. Imagine a world full of people who are so deeply connected with their selves, their hearts. I believe we would see more people living their purpose and following their bliss, holding compassion and unconditional love for all kind. We would collectively raise our vibration, open space for others to heal in this lifetime, and ascend.

Purposefully connecting with our hearts, bridges the gap between the physical and the spiritual. It helps us realise the truth of who we are, who we all are on a soul level, infinite light beings of love. We can forgive easily and quickly, feeling love of self and others, opening up space for others to do the same, because when we heal ourselves, we heal others. This can change the world.

To connect with your heart space, you can create a few minutes each day, twice a day, three times a day, however often you can, to quiet your mind, tune in to you. You can begin by breathing slowly and deeply, focusing on the centre of your heart, imagine a green, pink or golden light, you are breathing in and out of your heart, and every time you exhale, your heart light expands and expands, filling up your entire body with love-heart light. You can take this a step further and breath this light beyond your physical body, creating a beautiful circle of light around you. You can send this light to family, friends, plants, animals, the whole entire world. This is a beautiful exercise you can do as one person to facilitate change beyond your perceived human thinking. Let's be the change we wish to see in the world. It starts with us, one heart light at a time.

"You cannot find your soul with your mind; you must use your heart."
Gary Zukav

The bigger picture

We are ascending. All of us. The plants, animals, humans, the planet. And we are not alone in this. Our galactic helpers have been watching, waiting and assisting with this process for a very long time.

Ascension is the process of moving our consciousness from one reality to another and becoming aware of the possibility that multiple realities exist simultaneously. Since a reality is a dimension, what we are undertaking is a dimensional shift. Embodying more and more light frequencies, ascending higher and higher into light, love and dimensions.

Why do we need help? For a long time, anti-awakening forces have tried to stand in the way of our divinity, of our ascension into our new earth of love.

Our collective Ego will attempt to sabotage our efforts to step into the light... the truth. This is the Collective Unconscious at play. This plays out as self-sabotage, gaslighting and control, betrayal, temptations, feeling unsupported on your path and so on. But light always wins, and we are well on our way during this time of ascension, into a new way of being. A lighter, brighter, loving way of being.

There has never been a better time on this planet than now, to focus on your Spiritual Journey of Awakening.

Our light Frequencies are raising higher & higher... and so is mother Earth's. You are responsible for your happiness & your growth in your journey and now is the time. Do what makes you happy and lights you up. Follow your passion and your purpose. When you say yes to you, you are saying yes to the Universe and divine support will carry and support you through.

Each time one soul wakes up, this allows space for another. and another. You are so much more thank you think, you are so much more than your human body, your perceived limitations. You are a divine spark of creator, powerful and infinite. Shine your beautiful light so that others may follow.

Now is the time to make magic happen.

Love,
Sarah

ABOUT SARAH LINES

Sarah Lines, from Australia, is a mother of 3 and a crystal and cat lover.

She graduated with a Bachelor's degree of Midwifery in 2013 but felt she had a deeper calling.

She has broken free from chronic addition, homelessness and helplessness into a life of peace, fulfilment and true alignment.

Sarah is a Quantum Reiki Grandmaster, a certified happiness life coach, a mediation teacher and a multidimensional channel and soul coach. She is the author of "The Roots of your Chakras", her mission is to serve humanity on a vast interplanetary scale through coaching and educating the mind, body and spirit connection as well as owning your power to co-create the reality you desire in this lifetime.

"Now is the time to make magic happen."
Sarah Lines

EMBRACING DIVINE FEMININE & MASCULINE

By Rene' Murata

←—∞—→

"When the Sacred Masculine is combined with the Sacred Feminine inside each of us, we create the 'sacred marriage' of compassion and passion in ourselves." – Matthew Fox

Compassionate leadership.

For some, this is an oxymoron saying that leadership is for the strong and compassion is for the weak. For those, however, that live, practice and embrace a more caring approach to leadership, they know that providing direction from a feeling place requires diligent effort. It entails consciously choosing our actions and words to be empowering, accepting and unbiased. Make no mistake, compassionate leadership necessitates that quiet strength that comes from being connected to our divine feminine and masculine energies.

So, where does one begin once they decide they want to lead from a place of compassion? How do you start to build and create a compassionate leadership style? You start with listening.

When I say listening, I am referring to something deeper than hearing another person's words or watching their body language. I am referring to that place, that feeling, that involves being in touch with your Inner Being, where you feel the energy of your responses and reactions within your body.

To understand what I am talking about, start with this. You receive a phone call from your best friend, and they are excited about something. How do you feel? More importantly, where do you feel it? Do you feel it in your heart space? I do. Identify WHERE you feel this feeling.

Next, think about a decision that was somewhat challenging. Recall how it felt while you were going back and forth with the pros and cons. Where did you feel the emotions? In your heart space? In your gut? In your chest? Once you made the decision, where did you feel that? Many people that I have worked with say that they feel the final decision in their heart space when it feels "right". That while going back and forth, struggling with the decision, they felt it alternately between their heart space, their chest and their gut, finally settling in their heart space. Pay attention to what you feel and where you feel it.

Now think about the energy you feel when someone approaches you and is upset with you. Again, WHERE do you feel this energy? How does it feel? Is it a knot in your gut? Is it a pain at the base of your spine? Wherever you feel these different energies is YOUR experience. It is important, though, to really pay attention, to KNOW where you feel them and what actions, words and behaviours drive the feeling.

Take some time to journal about the different situations and where you feel the energy of the situation in your body. For the next couple of days, when you are in conversation with someone, regularly check in to see where you feel the energy of the conversation. When you are reading or writing emails, posts, or blogs, check in to see where you feel the energy of what you are reading and writing. Get used to sensing the energy. Notice what thoughts, words, feelings come up in these conversations. Are there any patterns? Are there particular words that trigger you, particular behaviours? Write these in your journal.

Once you become aware, you can start to shift it. First, though, you must be aware.

Now that you have identified where you feel these feelings, let's look at what words and behaviours are triggering for you? What thoughts and feelings do you have? Are the feelings a learned reaction? Are the thoughts based on reality, or are they based on that small voice inside your head that wants to keep you "safe"? Ask yourself, why do they trigger you? What is the energy behind the trigger?

One of my biggest triggers was to be called controlling. When my son was 18 years old, he got up in my face and told me I was a control freak. I was triggered but managed to keep calm and asked him to elaborate. As he spoke, I kept an open mind and open heart. It was difficult to hear some of the things that he said. Yet, I just listened, the only interruptions were to ask for clarification. I listened viscerally. I paid attention to the energy of his words and realized that there was a lot of pain in his words. I felt guilty about the pain. I wanted to counter, to defend…to control.

When I couldn't handle anymore, I asked him to stop so that I could process what he had told me. I thanked him for his honesty, thus empowering him to continue to be honest with me. I spent the next couple of weeks really tuning into what I had heard and what I had felt. We had a couple of more very open, candid, difficult conversations about his feelings. Through this process we were able to heal a lot of hurt for both of us.

I also realized, during this period, that when I referred to someone as controlling, it was always in a negative context. I had made "controlling" a bad thing. Once I identified this, I was able to shift it. I was able to remove the negative energy of the word recognizing that there are times that "controlling" is a good thing. I also recognized that there are times when really, I am managing something, not controlling it. And when I am managing, I can allow more flow to occur. This further shifted the negative energy away from the word "controlling". Now, being called controlling holds no trigger.

After this experience, I really started to look at the language I and those around me were using. I started to see how much the language that we use defines us, and how much it divides us. It is used to create division in politics, religion, education, and between the sexes. Our vernacular is so divisive that people are often not even aware of it.

Take this example: a friend commented to me one day that she is bossy. I stopped her. "Bossy? How do you figure?" "Well", she said, "Since I am a mother to 3 teenagers. I have to be bossy." Bossy, for many, has a negative connotation and is almost always used when referring to a woman.

We would never refer to a man a "bossy", why do we for a woman? There are many examples of this kind of use of language. I once had a man refer to me as "Little Lady". I am 6'0", without heels. He was 5'6" with his cowboy boots, and he felt it okay to refer to me in diminutive terms.

Our language keeps us hostage to the distorted, wounded energies. If we want to live within our divine masculine and feminine energies, a good place to start is with our language.

Did you know it is your birth right to be full of joy, successful, happy, and abundant? So, why aren't we?

We live in this distorted masculine and wounded feminine energies where it is easy to point fingers, to blame, criticize and remain fearful and in shame. Shifting out of that requires work. It requires awareness, it requires vulnerability and strength.

Today, many people live wrapped up in the negative side of either their masculine or feminine self. We see it played out every day through racism, violence, pollution, and greed, to name a few. Yet, it is possible to bring the positive energy forward for both masculine and feminine and it is natural. And we need both. Both the masculine and the feminine.

Why? In nature we find many examples of the balance of two opposites: yin/yang, hot/cold, light/dark, joy/sadness. Without one, you would not have or even be able to recognize and therefore reference the other. Think about it a moment. How can you recognize and identify joy, if you don't know what sadness is? What about light, if you don't know what dark is?

We know what the negative energy is, we can use this information to choose our positive energy. Understanding this contrast actually makes it easier to shift, when we decide to do so.

Where to start… Think about people that you know that are good examples of "being in balance". They may be sensitive to other people's feeling yet remain firm in their convictions. They may have a strong drive to achieve something yet also know how to relax and enjoy life. These are people that have accepted both the masculine and feminine aspects of themselves.

Take a minute and list all of the positive traits that you admire about these people. Just like the things that trigger you, things that you admire are those characteristics that you already have inside you. You just might have to dig a little.

So, what did you find? Are you living in your Divine Masculine and Feminine, or in your Distorted Masculine and Feminine? Be honest. Here's an exercise to help you with that.

Create a table with four columns.

1. Write Distorted (Negative) Masculine in the far-left hand column and Distorted (Negative) Feminine in the far-right hand column.

2. Write Divine (Positive) Masculine in the centre-left hand column and Divine (Positive) Feminine in the centre-right hand column.

3. List as many qualities as you can think of for both the outside columns. These are the negative aspects. Don't get hung up on whether something should be in the Feminine or Masculine column. You'll find that several will fit in either.

Below is a sample/starter for you.

Distorted Masculine	Divine Masculine	Divine Feminine	Distorted Feminine
Aggressive			Manipulative
Judgmental			Jealous
Confrontational			Passive

Controlling			Mousy
Arrogant			Gossipy

Now here comes the difficult part. Circle the qualities from these columns that you embody. Be honest. These can show up temporarily, or routinely. For example, if you get upset when someone cuts you off, circle angry or aggressive. If you tend to gossip when you are with that ONE girlfriend, circle gossipy.

Now, go back and look at the ones you circled. Can you think of a more positive attribute that you could put next to it in the Divine column? Fill in the Divine column. This is not an exact science. The point is to find as many traits in the Divine column as you can think of that are a shift from the distorted.

When you add a positive attribute, cross out the negative one that you want to release.

For example:

Distorted Masculine	Divine Masculine	Divine Feminine	Distorted Feminine
~~Aggressive~~	Assertive	Negotiable	~~Manipulative~~
~~Judgmental~~	Discerning	Protective	~~Jealous~~

Now, go back and circle the positive traits that you ALREADY embody.

Once you have completed this, you can start to understand what energies you are embodying, and which ones you might want to shift toward and those that you would like to release. Think back on those words and behaviours that triggered you before. Also, think about the attributes that other people embody that you want to embrace. Are these listed?

I know that in the past I have been aggressive. Now, when I find that behaviour pops up, I can ask myself what it would take to shift to assertive. I know where that feeling lives in my body, I know what things trigger it, and I know where I want to shift it to. So, often, just the thought of the more divine energy is enough to make that shift.

A funny thing happens when you start to put all of this together. You start to live, think and be more compassionate. You start to look at other people and see them as human too. You stop seeing colour, religion, gender or sexual orientation as a divider and start to see these as flavours. Doing so changes your interactions with people for the positive.

This then empowers people to be fully themselves, to shine. When you allow people around you to shine, life becomes more brilliant. When you are in leadership and you empower the people around to shine, the job becomes easier…easier for you and easier for them.

Ultimately, that is the job of a leader. To inspire. To bring out the best in the people that work for them. Otherwise, you aren't leading, you are managing. So, when you bring all of this together, you have the essence of a leader. When you listen viscerally, you stop noticing things like skin tone, education, religion etc, and you start noticing feelings. Everyone has them. Everyone has hopes, dreams and desires for themselves and their families. A leader takes the time to listen.

When someone feels heard, they feel like they matter, thus they feel empowered. Empowered employees, clients and colleagues work harder, are more creative and are more collaborative. This has a definite impact on the bottom dollar making it a win-win situation.

Also, when you listen viscerally, there is a level of vulnerability that comes through, a rawness that tells the other person, "I am putting aside my agenda and making this all about you." This has so much power. I won't lie and say that being vulnerable is easy, but it makes a leader more approachable.

I have chosen to lead with compassion. It is not always easy. It is not always fun. Sometimes, it is plain difficult. However, it is always honest, always caring, and always improving. It also impacts every area of life, not just work.

There is a transformation that happens when you choose to step into your divine masculine and feminine energies…a transformation that reaches into every aspect of your life. It also becomes a mission to spread the feeling to other people, to help them attain transformation in their lives. This can be done in a variety of ways, through actions, through words, and through education. Below are some real-life examples of compassion in action. These are presented as examples that you can use and modify for your own use.

Practical applications for work and home

A long-time friend and I were talking. During our conversation, she said that I always held her at arm's length. In the past, I would have blown her off. However, I chose to listen viscerally, to really hear her and pay attention to what I felt and where. In doing so, I realized that I had always judged her openness. Upon further scrutiny, though, I realized that I was jealous of her ability to be so open. With this realization, I was able to shift my energy to one of appreciation for the gift that her openness brings, for the example that she provided. Once I stopped to listen to her, and really heard her, I was able to be honest with myself, and then shared this with her. My sharing was a vulnerable, scary thing to do. In the end, though, she felt more valued, I felt more in alignment with my divine self and we both felt more empowered to be fully and authentically ourselves.

My business was not doing well, so I sat down and had a difficult conversation with my employees about the financial hardships of the company. This level of vulnerability wasn't easy, but it was honest. I sat and heard each employee voice their fears and concerns. I listened beyond just the words, thus removing the defensiveness that I might otherwise have felt. By paying attention like this, I was able to "hear" and therefore address fears that weren't even expressed. This built a different level of trust and loyalty within our organization.

My marketing director and I are constantly talking about our word choices and our actions. Are they compassionate? Does this message portray what I want it too? If there is any doubt, we give it some time. For example, both of us will set up an email WITHOUT a name to send it to in order to play with the words to make sure that the message portrays the energy that we want it to represent. This is especially important when it is so easy in today's world to quickly write something and send it without any real thought about how someone on the other end will receive it.

If you are truly wanting, choosing, intending to shift from the distorted to the divine, you can use meditation to assist. I have a beautiful meditation that I love to use. It is simple and powerful, helping to release negative thoughts, beliefs and images that may attach themselves to you throughout the day.

Grounding Meditation:

Sit comfortably with your back straight, legs uncrossed, feet on the floor. Close your eyes and take three beautiful, deep breaths.

Imagine that at the base of your spine, there is a chord. Release it to Mother Earth, pull it off, cut it, let it fall away, whatever you feel is required to release it.

Then, imagine a new chord coming from the base of your spine, hip width. This chord is ruby red, thick, strong and supple. It goes from the base of your spine deep into Mother Earth, all the way to her core.

Now, envision a spinning disk at the top of your head, about 2 inches above your head, at your crown chakra. Allow it to open like a set of French doors.

Next, imagine a ball of white, gossamer light about 2 feet above your head. Envision that light coming down through your open chakra into your brain. As it enters your body, watch as it transforms all dark, dense energy to light and carries away anything it can't easily transform down through your body to Mother Earth. As this ball continues flowing through your body, it removes any and all structures and grids, releasing them into Mother Earth.

Feel the light flowing down, surrounding all the tissue in your brain, getting into all the nooks and crannies, clearing your pituitary and pineal glands, opening your Third Eye, relaxing the muscles of your face and continuing down and relaxing your jaw.

As this beautiful light continues into your neck, allow it to open your Throat Chakra, clearing the chakra; relaxing your neck and shoulder muscles, some of it continuing down your arms and out your fingers.

Allow the rest of the light to continue flowing down into your chest, opening your Heart Chakra, removing any walls or barriers around your heart, the light wrapping around the bones, ligaments, tendons and organs in your body, getting into your blood and clearing your blood.

Feel the light go into your lungs, liver, kidneys and gall bladder; flowing into your Adrenal glands to clear and regenerate your Adrenals. See the light open your Solar Plexus and Sacral Chakras.

Follow this beautiful, soft white light down into your pelvic area, allowing it to relax your hips, releasing any trauma and either transmuting it or carrying it on out through your legs, knees, calves, ankles and feet into Mother Earth.

Once the light has released all it has carried your body into Mother Earth, she can take it and regenerate or recycle the energy, using it for something else. Thank Her for Her assistance.

Now, allow this beautiful, soft, white gossamer light to come back up through your feet and back up through your body, clearing any residual energy that you are ready and intend to release. Feel the light carrying it up and out through the top of your head. There, it can be transmuted into Light.

Next, imagine this gossamer light expanding and raining light down around you. Allow it to clear any chords that are attached and removing any energy that is stuck to you. Allow it to also clear any structures or grids that are in your Aura.

Then, invite the Light to seal off any areas where you might be leaking energy.

Sit with this feeling a moment and allow a breath.

When you are complete, wiggle your fingers and toes to help bring you back before you open your eyes.

Allow a breath!

When you choose to embrace the Divine Being that you are, when you consciously choose your thoughts, words and actions to be of the divine, then you are living and leading compassionately.

Conversely, when you choose to live compassionately, you are choosing to embrace the divine masculine and feminine energies within you and thus embracing the essence of who you truly are and who you are meant to be.

EnJoy, Love and Light,
Rene'

ABOUT RENE' MURATA

Being a woman in a male dominated industry, Rene' spent many years trying to "fit the mould". However, after starting her own consulting business in the world of hazardous chemicals, she soon realized that it was a poor fit and decided to try something different. She started playing with her management style, and after a couple of shifts found her way to a compassionate, collaborative style. She began to see that leadership, true leadership, is about embracing both our masculine and feminine qualities. But it is more than just that. It is about embracing the DIVINE masculine and feminine that is within all of us.

After really developing a consistent and conscious methodology, she began working with other women who wanted to step into their power and express themselves more fully in the working environment. Realizing that compassionate leadership is something truly powerful, but not taught, she started CEO Essence to assist others who want to create more connection in their leadership. Rene' now works with individuals, organizations and leadership teams that want to bring more consciousness and balance to the workplace through understanding our masculine and feminine traits and how acknowledging both traits within each of us brings out our best self.

 "When the Sacred Masculine is combined with the Sacred Feminine inside each of us, we create the 'sacred marriage' of compassion and passion in ourselves." – *Matthew Fox*

WOMEN, SELF-CARE AND WELLBEING – A STORY OF 3 POWERFUL CHANGES

By Tatjana Obradovic-Tosic

I do not enjoy "GU-GU-GA-GA"

I still remember 2009 when my daughter was born. It was tough. In a foreign country, even though we speak a similar language, I felt very, very alone. No friends, our closest relatives stayed with us for a couple of months and that was it. My husband went back to work soon after she came to this beautiful world. I was an entrepreneur on a one-year parental leave. Lucky me, you would think.

In the late fall of 2009, after a particularly bad week with my 5-month-old daughter, I was exhausted. Days went by without sleep and with almost constant crying. And, as if that was not enough, my husband was late from work. You have to understand that usually, the moment he came home, I was out, I could rest, do nothing, stare at the wall, I could finally breathe. But not that day. He called me to tell me that he will not be home by midnight. I still remember, like yesterday, my reaction and his look when he eventually did come home. I started to cry as soon as he opened the door:
"I am so fucking lonely. I am tired. I did not have time to go to the toilet alone. Do you really think I enjoy talking GU-GU-GA-GA whole day? I do not! She hardly ate. I do not want to try anymore. I want to read a book, I want to go out, I want to have a coffee in silence. I want to dress like a normal human being, not with these breast pads full of milk,

sticking everywhere. I cannot stand this anymore."
I was at the point of having a nervous breakdown.
And he saw it.
Without a word he hugged me and kissed me.
He took my hand and took me to bed, gently pushing me to lay down.
As I had a caesarean, which wasn't performed that well, I still was not sleeping normally, he helped me with a half siting position, so that my wound wouldn't hurt.
He kissed me again and said, "Try to sleep".

You see, I was not feeling lucky at all. I have an amazing husband, still to this day, that breaks all patriarchal rules and codes when it comes to being a father because he is different. But, for me, that was not enough. I hated being on parental leave because I felt that I was missing out on the world outside. My daughter was born when I was 31, I was not young, we wanted the child, everything was as we had planned. But, no one prepares you for accepting yourself as a mother. They all prepare you to take care of the child.
I can say now – fuck that!
I needed someone to prepare me for myself.
I needed someone to tell both of us how to adjust to parenthood, with growing careers, and lots of interest around it.
In the patriarchal cultures we lived in, no one cared about that.
It wasn't even up for discussion.
"You are a mother, is it not enough that we gave you one year to be with your child (at that time, fathers were not allowed, now they are). Look at other states, women cannot take more than 6 weeks. How ungrateful can you be." That is what you got as a response.

And because I was not feeling lucky at all, I hated myself, my body, being alone. I hated having to wait for my husband to come home to have some ME time, and I am aware that some women do not have that at all.

I felt like I lost myself, as I knew that I am more than just a mom.

There I said it.

My mind was a complete mess, my body was distorted, and my soul was in some faraway place.

And my family's wellbeing was impacted by that.

I still feel that some part of my relationship with my daughter is affected by the lack of care for myself during the first years of her life.

The change did not come that easily. It took me almost 4 years to recognize that lack of self-care influences my wellbeing and my relationship with the world. It also made me understand why self-care is key to developing your soul, mind, and body for the purpose of wellbeing.

I felt such excitement and joy going back to work in 2010, but it was just an escape from being home. I somehow justified my long hours at work, with my business taking off the ground. But in reality, I was trying to be the old me, having lost all sense of identity, my mind body and soul were completely disconnected.

Fast forward to 2020, I have 2 children, I left my first company and started a new one, I changed 3 cities, 2 states and I still have my amazing husband by my side. I also have the business coach who stuck with me while I am achieving my big bold vision of changing the world by changing the lives of women. So many mentors that generously supported me along the way and 1000 successful stories of women because of what I am going to share with you today. Not to mention, that I am a TEDx speaker, and co-author of this amazing book.

You know, what I learned since 2009, is that going to the spa and taking care of your hair and your nails are not the answer to self-care. Even though it can help, and I fully understand that for some women it is the only ME time they have. Been there, done that. What I analyzed, studied, practiced and taught in the last 10 years is much more than that. **Self-care is a misunderstood concept, that took away so much power from women, instead of returning that power to them.** My mission is to give back the 2 million hours to women around the globe. You know why? So that they can use it for themselves. Why? Because, I saw how women change themselves, their home, their environment, and their community for the better, JUST because they changed the patriarchal norm of TAKING CARE OF SOMEONE ELSE. The wellbeing is connected to the individual as much as it is to the collective level. And for me, changing the notion of self-care for women on an individual level is a place of change for the world itself. Each of us counts.

3 powerful changes = 3 must haves for a self-care

I want to share with you 3 important, powerful changes I created in my life, that helped me and women I worked with to reconnect their body, mind, and soul, so that wellbeing is part of everyday life, not some isolated event in the spa once a year. Those are 3 must haves for self-care needs to be full and vibrant, so that all women experience life to its fullest, no matter where and how she lives and what is her lifestyle. These 3 powerful changes are explained in a way that is best to implement because it ensures that root causes are dealt with. This is a system I developed and tested, which gives long term results.

Change number 1 – Allow yourself ME time

This is the first change I created, and the first thing I teach women. When my daughter was 3, I started an online program that was focused on time management and productivity (how funny is that). Somehow, I thought that I am not organized and productive enough, so I do not have time for myself. My salary was quite low, but I knew that I had to change something, so I paid, thinking I will get the magic pill for an organization. What I got was a lot more than a pill, but there is one thing that I started to implement then, adjusted, twisted and tweaked to suit myself and my clients, and I am still implementing it. I want you to start this now before you do anything else. This is the best thing you can do for yourself, as nothing will work if you do not implement it.

I started journaling daily only on the following questions, and I want you to do the same:

1. Who am I when I have time for myself?

2. What do I need to allow myself in order to have time for myself?

3. Why am I a good mother if I have time for myself?

4. I am grateful for waking up and being, healthy, strong and confident. What do I need to do today, tomorrow this week, so that I wake up each day with this feeling?

Journaling changed everything. It brought me clarity, but also self-confidence. Women that I work with usually cry after answering these questions, as they discover something in themselves that is much higher, and much more connected to their inner being. If they do not care about themselves, they will not be able to care about others. It is common sense and a proven relationship. Without a ME time, we are stressed out, angry, with low self-esteem. None of this contributes to a good relationship with others.

As you will see by the end of this chapter, these questions are golden nuggets that can be used for any individual self-care practice:

- Who am I as a person that goes to gym 3 x a week?
- Who am I as a person who finished that course?
- Who am I as a person who sees her friends once per month?

Use it and adjust it to your needs. If you cannot journal every day, try a minimum once a week.

Change number 2 – Do serious talks

Some people call these "setting boundaries". I do not like that term (although sometimes I use it), as setting boundaries for me sounds like building walls. I did not want to build walls between me and my husband, my children, my father, mother and father-in-law or friends. I want them to understand what I want, do not want, who I want to be, what I would love to share, or don't want to share with them. And for that to happen, I needed to deliver some very serious talks. No one talks about this, because this is the hardest part of self-care. But trust me, if you do not do serious, open and structured talks with significant others in your life, none of your self-care practices will stay longer, and you will always have the struggle to implement it. I do not want you to get up earlier to meditate. You are already not sleeping enough. I do not want you to fit in self-care in your already busy schedule. I want you to clear that schedule now because you are having on your plate more than it is needed. So, what I will share with you now is a critical step you do not want to miss.

I still remember my colleagues and friends from work being quite sad and disappointed that I rarely had the time to see them after work and during the weekends. But I really did not have that need. It is maybe sad and perhaps even a little selfish, but we spent 12 hours a day at the office and there were only three of us. It was quite hard explaining that, as they really cared about me. I needed time to be alone, with myself, or with other significant people in my life. I needed to embrace myself as that person, to stop criticizing myself for doing that and accepting that I was more, and I want more

A client of mine a couple of years ago, received very little understanding from her husband whenever she wanted something for herself – having a massage, reading a book, going shopping, or coffee with friends. She wanted to set boundaries and told him, that from now on this and this time is for her. Of course, it did not work out. We created a plan on how she is going to have a serious adult talk with him (yes, you need a plan for it, because fight mode is never my approach). After implementing it, they have "the best marriage ever" (according to their words). He understood her needs and her feelings, but more than that he changed his role from "I am the man in this house" to "I am a partner in this house". I still keep in my journal her note she sent me one year after finishing the work – "my daughter told me today, that she never saw me and my husband happier".

So, I am sharing with you here, how to do it.

In order to have a serious talk with your partner, family, children, co-workers my trusted, proven process is this one:

1. Do Change number 1 – allow yourself ME time

2. Understand why you need time for yourself – write how you feel

3. Understand what you want to do in that time and when it needs to be done – write what do you want to do – sleep longer, read, walk or learn …

4. List what needs to be taken off your to-do list in order to clear your schedule

5. Schedule the talk and share the above 4 steps with significant others – include all family members. If you do not have family members talk to friends and colleagues.

6. Create a joint plan on how you are going to manage it.

7. Ask for a hug and give a hug to them.

It may take you a couple of weeks to do this, but trust me, it is worth it. This process bonds and connects people.

I implemented it with single moms. I implemented it with corporate directors. I implemented it with small business owners. They all tried setting boundaries, but it did not work. Creating a plan and delivering hard talks changed their lives.

Change number 3 – Build planning and productivity skills

In 2018, one year after I left my first company, I opened a second one. I gave myself time to adjust, study my target group and develop my business for one year, but then things were growing. And, once again I fell into a trap of never-ending work. Just, now I really did not have any excuse. I really loved, and still do, what I was doing, and I was losing sense of time when I was at work. I gained weight and was rarely active at all. I knew I needed to start with exercise, along with diet, but I just could not find the time for it.

As my husband started running, he challenged me to do the same. But I was coming up with every possible excuse. From children to a work schedule. I am a productivity strategist, and I was using my knowledge in order to master my calendar, appointments, clients, reports, consultancy work, everything but an exercise. It did not fit anywhere, as I needed to much time in traffic, or new clothes, or a change in a schedule which was not possible, or work on weekends which I did not want (Relate?). I knew from previous activities that when we allowed ME time for ourselves and we delivered a serious talk and got support and/ or understanding in our environment, the job is not done. I knew that productivity and efficiency are non-negotiables if we want to build a strong habit of care for our mind, body and soul.

I needed to find a way to stick to ME time activities.

I needed to make them priorities on my endless to-do-list.

So, how did I do that?

In this last chapter, I want to share with you the final step in my proven system. Building productivity and planning habits is the last thing you need to master, so that you have long lasting self-care practice.

But, before that let me share with you one excuse, most of my clients use to explain why they can not plan and schedule ME time. It is called "What if?". For example:

- What if my child has a birthday?
- What if I have to work?
- What if I get sick?
- What if I need to go somewhere?
- Add your own "what if" here _____

What I learned from them, is that if you do not have blocked time for yourself, the "What if" is much stronger than any reason, explanation or need for self-care. We, as women, are brought up to be caregivers, not caretakers. So, any time when a situation is not clear, we will not give ourselves a priority.

In order to make ourselves priority, it is not enough to put ourselves in the calendar once.

Remember this – you need to build a habit of making yourself a priority.

What I did with my clients is making them stick to a habit of blocking ME time in calendar, clearly and visibly (marked in a color they love), until it becomes natural like any other habit (usually after 66 days, but for some, it took less and for some, it took more). I want women to have a feeling of wellbeing that is coming from a strong connection between their soul, body, and mind. If their mind is finding excuses and "What ifs", we need to overcome it.

In my system I treat it like a habit building, that requires time and practice. This is exact process I use with my clients:

- Once every three months, you block all the ME time dates and time
- Once a week, when you do your planning system (I do it on Sunday), plan and schedule your ME time first. Mark those dates and time in the week ahead with a strong RED. Protect it.
- And then plan other obligations around it.
- Repeat, until it becomes a habit.

Yes, there are going to be times when life will happen, and a week will be without ME time. Trust me I know, and not only from my story. But, being strict and consistent with your planning routine will put you backtrack every week. So, do not be harsh on yourself if you miss a day or two, or a week or two. Start at the point where you left off and go on.

Life will happen

In January 2019, after 3 races of 10k, I started to prepare for a half marathon. But, by the end of February, I got a knee injury, which was not a disaster, but I missed several runs. That was not the end of the story. Immediately after the injury, I developed a very strange and strong allergy which stopped me from doing any activity as my oxygen intake was affected. I was put on medicine for the next 8 months. I was disappointed, and you can guess, due to the medicines, I gained weight again.

In September 2019 my doctor finally allowed me to start running again. I was really, really happy. My husband challenged me to run 100 days straight. He made me a program, starting with short and easily achievable distances. I was all in. And, again life happened. I missed a couple of days but succeeded to accomplish 95 days of those 100 days, with 2 breaks (3 days, plus 2 days). You know, old Tatjana would have beaten herself up over this. But not this time. I used the process explained in this chapter on repeat:

1. Change number 1 - I allowed myself ME time and journaled on who I am as a runner

2. Change number 2 - I did a serious talk about what needs to be taken off my to-do-list

3. Change number 3 - I blocked time for my run.

And I do not apply it only for running. It is February 2020 now, and I am preparing for my first half marathon in my hometown in June. I run almost every day, and if the weather is bad or I do not have time for a run, I take stairs up to the 12th floor 3 times.

I am not trying to show off, I am trying to show you that everyone who says that it is easy for women to take care of themselves is a liar. And very likely a male. And if it is a woman, she learned trough media and her upbringing that it is better to envy you, than to support you.

I wanted to show you with this chapter, that achieving a state of wellbeing requires taking care of your mind, body, and soul, and in order to do that we need a strong self-care practice. But, building that practice takes time, self-love, overcoming mindset blocks and allowing time for ourselves, some shitty serious talk and planning habits that stick. So, do not judge any women that has ME time. Support her and learn from her. I strongly believe that self-care is a rebellious act against patriarchy, and I also believe in what I said at the beginning of this chapter. A woman who practices self-care changes herself, her family, her environment and her community for the better. And by doing that we create a better world to live in, where wellbeing is a state of the individual as well as of the community.

So, do not be afraid to implement the 3 steps presented in this chapter, as well as to ask for support in doing that.

Being a part of this book, with amazing authors, we created a circle, that is ONE. Symbolically we create support for the collective mind, body and soul transformation. The circle is closed, but it does not have an end or beginning, so it is inclusive for anyone who wants to step in and create a new chapter in their life.

I can't wait to see and hear your story when you implement what I and all the other authors inspired you to do. Share your story with us, and welcome to the One.

With love,
Tatjana

About Tatjana Obradovic Tosic

Tatjana Obradovic-Tosic is a productivity strategist, a Facilitator, the TEDx speaker with 15 years of entrepreneurship experience. She is on the mission to regain back 2 million hours to women around the globe, so that they can use it for what matters to them. Tatjana works with women on allowing and creating the time for themselves by improving their planning skills, setting strong boundaries and changing mindset around ME time. She also has a podcast "Self-care Rebel", where she delivers some serious and hard conversations around women self-care as a rebellious act against patriarchy.

From her experience in working with more than 1000 women and 100 teams, she realised their major obstacle was having time for connecting the mind, body and soul. They learned from the early childhood that the wellbeing of others is their responsibility. They do not allow themselves to think and plan ME time. Once they do, their environment is not always supportive, on contrary, often they are isolated, scrutinised and rejected. Tatjana advocates changes in roles and behaviours within woman and around her, for her to be truly ONE and commit herself to the life she wants. Tatjana knows from her own experience of motherhood that it is not easy. But she also knows from experience that when you are the ONE, and your mind, body and soul is aligned, your family and community thrive. So, she is on the mission to make that happened. With a planner, markers and sticky notes, she makes the lives of women more colourful, with changes in roles and behaviours she creates the world as a better place to live in.

Tatjana has the most amazing partner in the world, who is really a model of what a committed man, husband and father should look like. You can always find Tatjana with a coffee mug in her hands, a planner in her bag and her 2 lovely kids in her smile.

"A woman who practices self-care changes herself, her family, her environment and community for the better. And by doing that we create a better world to live in, where wellbeing is a state of the individual as well as the community."

MY JOURNEY INTO COACHING.

By Jola Pypno-Crapanzano

←—∞—→

"The rhythm of the body, the melody of the mind & the harmony of the soul create the symphony of life"- B.K.S. Iyengar

When I look back trying to pinpoint one particular moment in my life that literally changed everything about who I am and what I stand for, it was my trip to Dubai and Abu Dhabi a few years ago. I believe that everything in our lives happens for a reason and that even coincidences and synchronicities occur to teach us specific lessons.

But before I tell you what happened while I was visiting UAE, let me rewind the tape even more and give you a better perspective. Let's go back to my childhood.

When I was a kid growing up in socialist Poland, I didn't have many of the advantages that kids had in the West. My biggest passion, and dream was to travel around the world and yet I didn't leave Poland till I was in College, using the money I made working at night assembling light bulbs in the local factory. Chocolate was a luxury, as was tropical fruit, I ate oranges and bananas once a year for Christmas, I'd never heard of McDonald's or any other fast food restaurant. And even though at that time it felt like a terrible in-justice, today I know it was in fact a blessing in disguise. I ate mostly organic food from my grandparents' farm, I actively spent time outside, I enjoyed sport and dance, I was a ballerina, ran 100 meters sprint, jumped long jump, played volleyball and even practiced aerobics. Needless to say, I was in top physical shape without ever having to worry about my weight, diet or any food restrictions.

Time went by, I moved to the United States and lived a very comfortable and abundant life. I never deprived myself of any types of foods, I continued being active even though I no longer practiced sports I still enjoyed the benefits of a fast metabolism, eating whatever and whenever I wanted: to consume a whole bag of chips or bar of chocolate even late at night was no problem at all for me. I never had to sweat in the gym, the word diet didn't exist in my vocabulary and yet I still looked and felt amazing. Since colourful and brightly packaged food was a novelty for me, I often indulged in processed meals never paying any attention to ingredients nor looking at the labels.

Then all of a sudden one day I noticed that my pants were a little tight, then I realised that on occasion I was sucking in my stomach, and I became that person who asks others taking pictures of me to crop them right above my waist line. "What happened?" I asked myself looking in the mirror astonished.

I was still in denial eating like food was going out of style Wow!!!

Finally, in a moment of awakening I realized that I no longer burned calories like I used to and that for the first time in my life I was gaining weight. I started to feel foreign in my own skin, disliking my own image and more importantly how I felt. I had no energy, I was feeling sluggish, I had headaches every day, I couldn't focus well, I was not happy.

"So what happened in Dubai Jola?" You may ask... Well...

I went on my first trip to UAE five years ago. I was always a "travelholic" and I especially loved to visit places I didn't know; Dubai was such a place for me. I also loved taking tons of pictures on my trips and that dream trip to Dubai and Abu Dhabi was no different, except for the fact that when I returned home I literally hated most of the pictures capturing my precious memories, I hated to share them with others because I didn't even recognize myself in them. I started frantically cropping them ... I was terribly upset. And then came the breakthrough

- I hit rock bottom – I realised that I needed to change the way I live, the way I eat, the way I move my body, because if I didn't change, my health was at risk. I made the decision to take care of myself and of the only body I was given. I started working out regularly, eating a balanced diet based on small portions, taking supplements, sleeping a minimum 7 hours, drinking a lot of water, walking outside daily and ... the magic started to happen. I began shedding the pounds like crazy. In five short months I lost 38 pounds and on my 20th wedding anniversary I was able to fit in my wedding gown and wore it to celebrate with my husband.

I not only looked amazing but more importantly 1 felt like a million bucks. My energy was through the roof, I was sleeping like a baby, my headaches were gone, mental fog disappeared. I became a brand-new person, people started to notice and ask the popular questions: "how did you do that?" "How did you lose all that weight so fast?"

At first, I answered everyone individually and gave advice but quickly I realized that I could become a fitness and wellness coach and help so many people to find their happy self, lose weight and feel strong and healthy again.

So I did that and for about two years, I ran small accountability groups and I coached women how to take care of their bodies by introducing them to a brand new lifestyle that had a combination of healthy habits, exercise, proper nutrition and supplements. My clients were getting great results and I immersed myself even more in studies related to the connections between the human body and the mind. I quickly realized that optimum health requires the mind, physical body and spirit to be in balance and that the mind and body are not separate, what affects one, affects the other. Everything starts from your thought and your mindset determines if you're going to succeed or not.

While I studied everything and anything on how to become a better version of myself, I came across New York Times bestselling author Brendon Burchard's teachings. I was attracted to the concept of high performance, which in essence is performing above standard norms consistently over a long term while maintaining positive relationships and wellbeing. When opportunity presented itself, I promptly signed up for high performance coaching, which helped me reach heightened and sustained levels of clarity, energy, courage productivity and influence. I loved the process because it was challenge based and future oriented and every session delivered a clear outcome. To say that the coaching had a huge impact on my life would be an understatement I really started firing on all cylinders. The idea of improving my performance in every area of my life to the highest levels possible was beyond attractive to me. I became obsessed with studying different methods and techniques on how to optimize human performance, and not just from a strictly physical point of view, but literally in all other aspects. I learned quickly that I am doing people a disservice by teaching them only how to improve their health without tapping into their mindsets.

So I decided that I wanted to start helping people in a more holistic way. I was hyper aware that the saying "the body achieves what the mind believes" is 100% spot on, after all I was the living proof of that. Without the powerful decision that I made and discovering the even more powerful "WHY", my transformation wouldn't have been possible. I did my research and I learned that if I got certified as a high-performance coach, I could immediately start changing peoples' lives in every possible way.

Once again, I made a powerful decision and with confidence, believing in my ability to figure things out I completed the demanding requirements of the High-Performance Institute and received my High-Performance Coach certification.

So now, two years after my infamous trip to Dubai I was not only enjoying the benefits of being healthy, strong and fit but also being one of only a few hundred elite certified high performance coaches on the planet, helping people with a world class coaching curriculum and equipped with the most powerful coaching tools I have ever experienced before. What I loved the most was that in High Performance everything was science based and measured, because like in the saying: "What you don't measure you can't manage and what you don't manage you can't improve". Based on their results, the clients report the highest satisfaction ratings in the industry: 9.6 out of 10.

So that's how it all started, like I said earlier I truly believe that we meet certain people for a reason, opportunities are presented to us for a reason, we may not understand certain coincidences at the time when they occur, but they all happen because the Universe/God/Higher Power whatever it is for you, has a bigger plan for your life. For me it was putting on extra pounds, traveling to an exotic place, hitting rock bottom and feeling unhealthy and miserable, which led to my dream work as a High-Performance Coach. Hashtag #ilovemyjob no longer sounds abstract to me. I am fulfilled and happy seeing a bigger mission and purpose in my life in helping other people transition from where they're at to where they want to be in life and in business. I also understand without a shadow of a doubt, that it's not enough to like something, the way I liked to be a fitness and lifestyle coach. Instead you have to truly love it the way I love what I do now. Digging deep into human psychology and physiology truly fascinates me. I love the quote by Harbhajan Singh Yogi;" Your mind, emotions and body are instruments and the way you align and tune them determines how well you play life".

The most remarkable transformations and breakthroughs my clients experience come from the profound realization of why they want to change in the first place. Let me share with you a technique you can use to discover your true reason why would you want to change anything in life. It is called "7 levels deep" and it helps you get to your true WHY. That's the "why" you'll always want to come back to when things get tough, when you suddenly lose motivation. So for example it is not enough to ask yourself just "why do you want to lose weight," because the answer will probably give you a very shallow reason like "I want to look good in my new dress at the birthday party", you must keep digging deeper: "why do you want to look good at the birthday party", and find the answer, and then ask again why, and again… 7 levels deep. Most likely when we get to level 7 you will get the real WHY you want to lose weight. It is a very powerful exercise and I encourage everyone to try it, by asking one's own questions. The clarity that comes out of it is unreal.

Our mind needs clarity so that the body will know which direction to move just as Tony Robbins says: "Where focus goes energy flows".

Clarity is power. When you have clarity on who you are and who you want to become, what you want to achieve, where are you headed, the path becomes easier. Distractions are easier to ignore and the likelihood of achieving the outcome you desire increases as well.

Another powerful exercise that helps tremendously with clarity, is to find three words that describe the best version of who you want to be in life and have them constantly in front of you, maybe even set these words as alarms on your phone a few times a day so that you get constantly reminded about them throughout the day. For example, my very first words were present, inspiring, persistent.

Once we have the mindset primed, it's time to take massive action. There are very few things as powerful as a good and personalized morning routine. Starting your day with gratitude, intentionally focusing on your own priorities and needle moving activities, is not an act of selfishness but the best thing you can possibly do. So plan your day carefully, avoid reacting and getting distracted.

Another very important thing is visualizing your future ideal life and reminding yourself about your big dreams and goals every single day. All high performers visualize the desired outcomes in vivid details, most notably Olympic Athletes. For example, finishing a race in a certain time, or scoring certain amount of points.

The next very powerful exercise is to write 10 biggest most audacious and crazy dreams you have, but like they already happened. Do it every single day and watch the magic happen. For example: "I travel around the world first class only", "I am an international best-selling author" etc.

Everything in this world is interconnected, so when we do something that affects our mind, it will ultimately have an impact on our body as well. Every thought, every emotion we experience will cause a reaction in our body.

Mind-body balance can be achieved when we establish a dialogue between our mind and our body. In order for them to function correctly, they need to be able to connect one to the other.

Here are my 7 favourite tips that help to restore that balance between mind and body so that they'll communicate more efficiently and in effect you'll become a healthier, happier more accomplished person.

1. Sleep

There is deep science about sleep, but regardless if you are an early riser or a night owl, you need to get enough sleep to recharge and rejuvenate your body and mind. Quality sleep affects every area of our life, it is one of the best ways to ensure energy the next day, and enough hours will boost it quicker than you think. Sleep can also help you improve your overall vitality, your sex life, help you lose weight and keep it off. Sleep helps in the process of making decisions and finally sleep offers real healing on a physical, mental and spiritual level. For the absolute optimal performance, the amount of sleep required should be minimum 7 hours per night, ideally 8-9. You should aim at going to sleep and getting up at the same time every day, you should eliminate any electronic screen time at least an hour before going to bed. If you are having hard time falling asleep try to go for a walk outside, do a short meditation, take a warm relaxing bath, drink a glass of water or herbal tea, read a book, listen to your favourite calming music, drop the temperature in the room and keep it dark. Do not press the snooze button in the morning instead when the alarm goes off immediately get up. Everything you do, you do better with a good night sleep.

2. Meditation

According to hundreds of scientific studies, meditation is literally a life changer. Take time each day to quiet your mind and meditate, because meditation is one of the most powerful tools for restoring balance to your mind and body. In meditation you experience a state of restful awareness in which your body is resting deeply while your mind is awake but quiet. Meditation improves your wellbeing both psychologically and physically so every day you should set aside some quiet time. A key to restoring and maintaining vitality is becoming conscious of your present thinking patterns, choices you make and how they may be affecting your health. Clear your mind of all the accumulated debris and clutter from technology and media, to-do lists and negative thoughts. Concentrate on positive aspects of life and repeat positive self-talk mantras. There are many types of meditations but regardless of which one you use, it will create a sense of calm and inner harmony and it will alter consciousness, help find awareness and achieve peace. According to Emily Fletcher, mantra meditation creates the key type of meditation to increase productivity and creativity by approximately 30%. Scientific research also proves that there are numerous health benefits from meditation: decrease of hypertension, heart disease, anxiety, insomnia and addictive behaviours.

3. Exercise

Moving your physical body is one of the most important factors in finding the mind body alignment. First thing in the morning, as soon as you wake up stretch out your whole body to shake off morning laziness, get your blood flowing, release the stiffness and you will be invigorated to tackle your day. All wellness experts agree that exercise triggers physiological changes in your body, your strength and mobility, your energy levels, your longevity. Science is also finding more and more proof that exercise is a key factor in optimizing mental performance. Exercising regularly will increase the size of your hippocampus, the part of the brain involved in memory and learning.

Research also has shown improvement in the function of the prefrontal cortex and medial temporal cortex of people who work out frequently. So you should exercise regularly, every day or at least 3-4 times per week. You need to work both on your strength and endurance. A morning workout triggers feel-good endorphins and lowers elevated stress hormones.

The key to good performance is using your whole body and mind in an intelligent way. You want your thoughts to improve, not impede your physical performance. If you understand the relationship between the mind and body, in which physical move is always accompanied by mental move, it will lead to improved performance. And finally there is the low impact but incredibly powerful kind of movement called yoga, which helps not only train your body from the neck down, but also the muscle between your ears.

4. Nutrition

What you eat will not only have a direct impact on your body and health but on your mind as well. When these two are not receiving enough nutrients, they can't function properly.

Eat high-fibre, low glycaemic foods. Vegetables are the number one energy-boosting food and they should make up a third of your diet. They prevent you from feeling hungry too soon and prevent highs and lows in blood sugar. Fruits are great too, but try not to eat too many high-sugar varieties. There are some very effective supplements that can increase your energy and mind body balance: Ginseng- strengthens the body, helps overcome stress, increases mental alertness and energy, enhances one's sense of wellbeing and boosts sex drive. Rhodiola- boosts physical endurance, energy and moods and heightens mental clarity, sexuality and post exercise recovery. Reishi – stimulates the sexual energy and overall vitality. Vitamin C– helps to produce the adrenal hormones and reduce stress, gives strength to bones, muscles and blood vessels. Vitamin B5- reduces adrenal fatigue due to stress.

5. Hydration

Water is essential to your health and weight management. Drinking water helps maintain the balance of body fluids. General recommendations are 1/2 ounce of water for every pound of your body weight, in other words you should drink minimum half of your body weight in ounces of fresh water. For example, a person who weighs 130 pounds needs to drink 65 ounces (8 glasses) of water per day. Drinking water helps your body perform at its top potential all day long. A glass of warm lemon water first thing in the morning gives your digestive system a kick and starts energizing your whole body. It helps purify your liver and boosts your metabolism, improves your immune and cardiovascular system, helps with heartburn and constipation, freshens up your breath and increases your energy.

6. Fresh air

There are many important benefits of getting fresh air: it is good for your digestive system, helps improve blood pressure and heart rate, it makes you happier, strengthens your immune system, cleans your lungs and finally gives you more energy and a sharper mind.

You can improve all these things and better align your mind and body by simply going for a half hour walk outside. If you can't do 30 minutes do at least a 15 minutes' walk, rain or shine every day no exceptions, especially if you work all day behind the desk. The fresh air and brisk walk will energize you and sharpen your overall focus.

7. Travel

Travel is a part of my life I am most passionate about besides personal development. And even in travel I can clearly see the connection between body, mind and soul. In all the years of travelling the world, I can pinpoint the times in the past when I would go places almost to check them of my list. I was in different places on the globe, different countries, but often I was present there only with my body. My mind was scattered all over the place, I was thinking more about snapping perfect photographs rather than actually experiencing where I was.

So often I would watch my videos or pictures from trips and realize I don't fully remember experiencing it. Nowadays I travel much more consciously, I pick destinations that are meaningful to me, do the work to prepare even better than before so that I can immerse myself and truly experience with my mind being engaged and my spirit connected. Now every single trip brings me ten times the joy.

When you think of things in life that are important to you and you are passionate about, ask yourself "Am I fully engaged in them with my whole-body mind and soul?" Think and journal about it, you will highly benefit from it. I hope that you find this exercise helpful and that it will give you a brand-new insight and perspective on how you can improve balance, alignment and connection between body mind and soul in your life.

The benefits of travel for mind and body balance may be the least scientifically proven, but they are my absolutely favourite. Travel is fun! But besides that, there are some surprising side benefits of various getaways like: travel can boost your wellness, and energy levels, it can make you more energized and more productive therefore improve your workflow. Vacations can cut your risk for heart attack.

Travel adventures can give you a natural high and make you happier with your entire life, and finally they can help keep your mind calm and literally help you live longer and happier life.

These are simple but super powerful ideas. And you may say "I already know them all", but knowing is not enough, you have to apply them to see results. Common sense is not always common practice. So in conclusion I can't stress enough how important the body-mind-spirit balance and alignment are. If you'll take time every day and implement even some of these simple tips and ideas you will see an immediate improvement in the overall quality of your life and your happiness. If you underline this with necessity, consistency and determination you will have a recipe for success.

Best of luck and much love,
Jola

ABOUT JOLA PYPNO-CRAPANZANO

Jola is a Certified High Performance CoachTM, founder and CEO of Coaching Journey with Jola.

She has over 30 years of combined experience in working with thousands of very unique groups of people and individuals serving them in many different capacities. First as a tour guide traveling all over the world and translating into 4 languages, then working in the entertainment and hospitality industry as part of the operational management in large publicly traded company in NYC. Finally coaching people initially as a fitness, wellness and lifestyle coach and finally more holistically as Certified High Performance Coach.

Her mission is to help people reach heightened and sustained levels of clarity, energy, courage, productivity and influence and show them that it is possible to live a life of their dreams and be fully engaged, energized and joyful in all areas of their personal and professional lives.

As a coach she is passionate about challenging her clients to reach their highest potential and has the proven ability to help them achieve transformational results. Her direct coaching style is a perfect blend of fun, compassion, tough questions and bold challenges to get her clients desired outcomes and help them move from where they're at to where they really want to be. She offers three different types of coaching services: individual one-on-one sessions, coaching in a small intimate group setting and coaching retreats in exotic destinations around the world.

"The rhythm of the body, the melody of the mind & the harmony of the soul create the symphony of life" B.K.S. Iyengar

A Journey Into The Unknown...

By Jasjit Rai

Getting Kicked Out of My Mind

Inner Voice: "Get out of here."
Me: "What?"
Inner Voice: "Get out of here. Go somewhere else. Anywhere else. It's
time to get out of your head."
Me: "Huh?"
Inner Voice: "You've overstayed your time here."
Me: "What do you mean?"

This was the inner dialogue that showed up 20 years ago. It's rare that I have a clear inner voice speak to me like that! In fact, it might've been the first time I'd ever heard a command.

But I knew exactly what it meant.

My mind is the place where I dream, create, plan, envision, and concoct infinite things I could do and create and experience. It's where I bring in information and turn it into whatever I want, whether it's indulging a curiosity or translating ideas into action in the world.

But apparently the time had come. It wasn't going to serve me anymore in the same way.

Looking back, I now see this happened to serve a higher vision. It needed more of me to show up and it was giving me an instruction to do exactly that!

This wasn't something I'd ever expected. To be told by my inner self to get out of my own mind! Seriously? But when truth speaks, we all know, no matter how crazy it sounds.

Something else had to happen in my narrative.

Yet, no other directions were given to me. No specific suggestions or recommendations were provided.

The Four Realms

I am a follower of intuition, knowing its power to take us far beyond what our minds and thinking patterns allow. I remembered a book, "The Intuitive Way" by Penney Peirce, that talked about four realms we have access to: mental, physical, emotional, and spiritual. Which realm wasn't I using as much I could?

It quickly became evident that the physical realm was my next challenge. I already felt connected to my emotions and spirit.

The body, meanwhile, wasn't given much attention beyond its physical needs.

I'd been operating too much in my head and not enough from my whole self. It felt easier and faster, but I soon learned that this was an illusion. The disconnect from the body meant I wasn't actually picking up and acting on intuition as much as I thought. There was an unconscious censoring that was happening, keeping much of my expression, energy, and power locked within me.

Also, less than a year earlier I had started my own consulting business. This decision was made without a plan or strategy, fully in response to a higher truth that could no longer be ignored.

While on holiday, I'd found myself crying, unable to bear the thought of returning to my job at the time. Even though the job looked good and had all the things one looks for, my soul was slowly dying on the inside. My true yearnings and deeper instincts were hidden under the responsibilities I focused on. My whole self was longing for its fuller expression.

I knew getting another job was not the answer. It was to do what I am designed to do: create a path based on my higher gifts and vision.

Now my new awareness was showing me that the business I'd created was heavily focused on the mental realm too. So the call to the physical became undeniable even though it felt crazy and overwhelming to explore a new direction while my business was in its infancy.

This is how the four realms can be so valuable. They'll show you what's missing to guide you to wholeness. They will provide direction where it's needed the most.

The Search for the Physical

In trust, I began my search for a physical activity.

Intuitive knowledge had begun to arrive more frequently after making the decision to get my business going. One was the realization that working on my own was going to require a whole new level of inner strength and resilience. Being healthy was my responsibility. After all there weren't going be benefits such as "paid sick leave".

I also sensed that running a business meant being able to run a higher level of energy through me.

We can hold a lot of stress and tension in our bodies if we don't have an outlet to let them go. Getting physical would release this, providing me with greater energy for my business.

I'd been feeling stifled at my desk job and needed something more dynamic. What could I do that would ring a greater range of expression? This seemed essential.

Finally, I experienced loneliness in my first months of business. I was used to social stimulation and enjoyed a sense of belonging and connection. These were two of my highest values at the time, so becoming a solo-entrepreneur seemed like the strangest thing to be choosing! I knew being a class where I got to see other people regularly would motivate me.

As I said, intuitive hits just arrived (*or maybe I finally felt free enough to listen*), as if I was being prepared to support myself in ways that I hadn't needed to before.

The journey to find a physical activity that was going to provide all these things that I suddenly required had begun!

Now let me clarify that prior to this, I'd never been a person who exercises regularly. The word "exercise" sounded like a task. I'm much more turned on by "play". I began imagining what would be perfect for me. The two modalities that intrigued me were dance and martial arts, yet neither felt exactly "it".

Looking at what I was drawn to most made this search so much easier.

The Unexpected Gifts of the Body

While on my brief search (so many ideas got eliminated fast), I came across a brochure at my local community centre. It was in black and white and the image on the cover was of a woman's hand and arm that seemed like they were floating in the air. I could feel the energy in the image! My body was already connecting to it.

I read the description and the practice was called Nia. It was described as a blend of dance, martial and healing arts brought together in a seamless non-impact cardio workout to music.

Wow! Dance and martial arts were mentioned, and healing arts…the latter I didn't understand but I knew healing meant energy and connection that goes beyond the physical. It brought in the spiritual realm too! ALL this appealed to me.

Could this be THE class?

The day arrived in February 2000. The class was on a weekend morning.

As life happens, I went to a concert the night before and ended up at an unexpected after-party bringing me home at 4:00 am! You can imagine the temptation the next morning to say I'd go the following week and sleep in instead. But I decided to follow through. I knew that if I didn't, I would likely have another excuse and never go. My inner voice had spoken. A class had been identified. It was no good to back out now!

I managed to get there, a few moments late, missing the introduction, but able to step right into the class as it started.

I don't know how I ended up in the front row, but there I was.

The music came on. The teacher led us with choreography, easy to begin and more complex in parts.

The feelings I began experiencing were incredible. All that I didn't get to express, feel or sense in my daily life and work suddenly FLOODED my awareness.

Some of the steps were easy to follow and some of them I fumbled through. But there was something about this practice that made it so *different* from typical dance or aerobic classes. There was a certain ease, expression, and playfulness that made me feel more "real".

The ability to express my feminine self was the most delicious experience. It was like coming home to myself. The masculine movements and energy were also deeply satisfying, allowing me to access my strength and power. I felt an integration within me that I had never felt before. I walked out of that class feeling 10 feet tall, like I could do ANYTHING! This feeling was new to me.

An Epiphany through Dance

To my amazement, my inner voice spoke to me again!

Here I was trying out this class to get into the physical like I'd been guided. Little did I know I'd been placed at a new fork in my life path.

In less than 10 minutes of starting the class, my inner voice stated, "If you ever want to teach anything physical, this is it."

> *"What?!? Are you kidding me? Teach a dance class! That's nuts. I don't even exercise! I'm not a dancer! I'm not an exercise teacher! This is crazy! Dance and talk and lead a class all at the same time, no way!"*

This was my reaction to the idea I was presented with.

Yes, all this was going on while I did my best to follow the steps, listen to the music, and sense my way into a liberation that I hadn't expected. It's amazing that I didn't yell anything out loud, because inside me there was an explosion of shock!

I continued the class and decided *not* to ignore what I'd been told, but leave the door open for whatever was transpiring beyond my conscious control.

This led me to talk to the teacher after class to express my gratitude and ask why Nia felt so different than other class! She graciously answered, following up with a willingness to tell me more if I was interested.

I made a deal with myself. I'd keep going to class for the next few months. If the voice and feeling didn't go away, I'd consider it. I was hoping that it *would* go away!

Gaining Mastery: Student to Teacher

The feeling never went away. The fear was fully present too. The confusion about doing something so against how I viewed myself was also consistent.

Yet, my inner voice had spoken. My body had responded with absolute power and joy. All my key requirements were met. And on top of that, I KNEW that this connection would expand my life in ways that I would've previously only dreamt about.

I also knew that it would add a new dimension to my work and to my business. I was actually searching for that piece, yet this was not how I expected it to show up!

That summer, I signed up for the training with the Nia founders in the United States that took place in October.

Even attending the training was done with trepidation! Again, I made a deal with myself that I'd only become a teacher if it felt clear after the training. That's how foreign this all felt to me and how scared I was. My body felt like lead when I tried to practice the video material that had been sent to us to practice and play with in advance.

On the last day of the training, we were invited to become teachers. Everything that I'd felt during it was beyond my expectations. It was as if a whole new world had opened up for me. I felt a pull to take on the teacher role.

I wanted more people, especially those apprehensive about exercise or dance classes, to know how fun it could be. If they could just feel the depth of joy, expression, and well-being that was available to them, their health would benefit greatly on all levels.

So with no more stalling, I said "yes". I decided to become a Nia Teacher alongside running my business.

By December of the same year, I taught my first Nia class. A teacher was ill and couldn't make it last minute and gave my number. In a mix of fear and excitement I accepted.

At the end of class, I had the students lie down on the floor for a few moments of relaxation. My own body was bubbling like a volcano on the inside. I'd never felt such powerful sensations.

I landed my own classes as of January the following year and have been teaching ever since, almost 20 years! At the time, I wasn't sure I'd last two.

I eventually completed my Nia Black Belt, being the first teacher to arrive at that level in my city. It was also an honour to be one of 50 international teachers invited to provide input into the newly created Green Belt, the teacher training.

My inner guidance had led me down a path that satisfied what I wanted most in a way I hadn't expected, and it gave me what I had no idea I needed.

It's required a lot of me, but still to this day, I find myself saying over and over, "*Thank you, thank you, thank you,*" as I move and dance through class.

Students often ask if I'd been a dancer before. I joyfully share that I wasn't. It's important for me to remind others that they can be something they never thought was a possibility. Who we naturally are, even if it was never nurtured before, will always come out if we trust ourselves.

The Powerful Body Mind Effect

This new awareness, skill and experience did expand my work and business. I began using it outside the dance studio directly and indirectly. I'd include movement in my corporate workshops and events. I'd offer demonstrations and talks. TV News programs reached out to interview me. A few of my articles got published. My impact had expanded.

The response and reaction were always powerful. People in the non-fitness or dance environments felt like they'd finally been given something real, something they could feel and that brought out their personal power immediately.

A group of teachers from Mexico who were taking an advanced program at the University of British Columbia commented specifically on my 45-minute presentation and demo in their evaluations, even though it was a tiny part of their six-week teacher training program. They saw ways they could far better support their students. They felt free to use their creativity and magic.

Conference attendees who'd chosen my optional workshop felt energized and empowered in 40 minutes on day three of their event where they'd come in already exhausted and unable to take in much more.

I introduced movement into a group presentation during a conference on Spirituality and Sustainability where the visionary Barbara Marx Hubbard spoke. My group eagerly took my direction to create a different kind of presentation than a typical verbal speech, and we were the only ones to receive a standing ovation.

Then there was the talk I did on using body-mind intelligence under the theme of serving clients for a recruitment company. The CEO had just got back from a high level conference where he'd heard a top speaker on Middle East relations. The CEO commented that one of my teachings was exactly what this speaker discussed.

This multi-dimensional approach to learning and transformation was making a difference, one that couldn't have been made without it.

The trick is that you have to fully apply yourself to it. You can't think your way to feeling or sensing. You have to do it! And this holds extra-sensory powers as well as sensory knowing. This is why people feel so alive – their whole being is involved.

This diversity of experience I gained through the mind and body connection is exactly what people are yearning for. People want to feel alive more than anything. Most of what happens on a daily basis dulls this experience significantly. The more we use technology, the more we take attention away from the most sophisticated system...which we inhabit, our bodies. Stress and tension are the norm and they are held in the body. Over-emphasis on the thinking mind is epidemic.

The people who were exposed to the teachings I learned through Nia and through my transformational style of coaching felt liberated by the gift of bringing the physical into their experience. Emotions were felt, spirits woken.

And so, this strange unexpected command given to me by my inner guidance led me to provide exactly what I am most passionate about: transforming people's lives and businesses by bringing their higher visions into reality.

Multidimensional Transformation

As I deepened my practice, I felt more and more called to work one to one with individuals. I wanted people to achieve the transformation they truly desired, not just more information or occasional highs experienced through one-off events.

This is when I moved from consulting to coaching, providing high-level guidance and new tools and approaches to guide them in achieving their bigger visions.

Sensing what stopped people and finding ways to create what they really want became my path. I began to weave together what I was experiencing and learning in the mental, physical, emotional and spiritual realms to do this level of work.

Through this multi-dimensional approach, there was a chance to go deeper and to create shifts that were unachievable and sometimes unfathomable before. New business results and major shifts began to occur for my clients. So much was happening in the process!

Relaxing the nervous system, finding your centre, commanding your will...these happen when you give attention to all of you. And it's so much more fun to feel fully alive and stimulated in healthy grounded ways. This is multidimensional transformation.

An Invitation For You

Now let's talk about you, so what I shared can be applied.

I recommend that you go back and read this chapter again, this time noting the key shifts that you see. What are the main messages for *you*? How can you apply them to create the experiences and results you desire? What realm has been missing in your world?

When is it time to listen more to your inner voice?

Get to know the four realms (mental, physical, emotional, spiritual) and your relationship to each. Use this knowledge to expand your world.

Even if something is scary to you, but your heart or body or spirit is being called, do what it takes to get over the fear. Trust you will be supported, because you will.

Get expert guidance. Going it alone isn't enough. Whether this means joining a program or receiving deeper guidance like coaching or mentoring, for when you really want to move through something or create results, is powerful. Gift this to yourself.

Your bigger vision deserves it and will also require it.

Love,
Jasjit

ABOUT JASJIT RAI

Jasjit Rai birthed her business, Joi Works, in 1999. As a Transformational Coach, Certified Nia Black Belt Teacher, and Personal Stylist, she guides people to bring their bigger Visions into Reality. Jasjit is often described as a catalyst, warrior, and even "little buddha" and mystic in her work. In other words, there are dollops of transformational energetics, spirit, playfulness, precision and deep care for bringing the Higher Self's vision out, along with the most practical actions and business know-how.

"Through a multi-dimensional approach, you can go deeper and create shifts that appeared unachievable before."

THE POWER WITHIN YOU.

By Mike Senior

←—∞—→

I have been a Chiropractor and alkaline health coach for over twenty-eight years now. I began my journey at a young age. I cooked for my parents and friends before I was ten years old. I grew my own vegetables and spent most of my time outdoors. I had many ambitions, wanting to be a chef or a medical doctor. When other kids had models of airplanes, I had plastic models of the human anatomy. When I was fifteen years old, I went to a Chiropractor and at that very moment I knew what I wanted to be when I grew up. Immediately after high school I went to a Chiropractic college and, at 24-years old, finished my degree. These studies led me to the pursuit of health and not disease. I hope the following information helps you as it has helped many others to regain the power you have within you to live long healthy lives.

The fundamental Chiropractic premise is to turn on the power within you to heal yourself. This is accomplished by freeing up subluxations allowing innate intelligence to flow freely. It is then important to be aware of what caused these subluxations to form and your inability to heal. It is caused by our lifestyle choices. These lifestyle choices being chemical, physical, and emotional. The emotional or mental one being the most important.

Early on in my studies and career I realized there was a need for a major paradigm shift. That shift being to make lifestyle choices to improve our health, which will decrease the amount of disease and money spent. Our society today, being heavily influenced by Newtonian science and modern medicine, has us living in fear. The medical profession has nothing to do with increasing our health only curing disease. Almost every day we hear about somebody diagnosed with cancer, diabetes, or cardiovascular disease. If we make any improvements in our lifestyle, we do it for the wrong reasons. We eat right, exercise, and find strategies to prevent diseases out of fear.

In practice this means I don't have to exercise, eat right, or have a strategy for stress, when needed, they will just fix or replace parts of us. The fundamental problem with this model is that we communicate the wrong message to our body. Our unconscious mind doesn't recognise or hear the word no or none. So, if I exercise to reduce the risk of having a heart attack. Our unconscious mind hears heart attack. Where we place our focus that is what we attract, this is the power of attraction.

If we shift our focus on health and a lifestyle in tune with that, health is what we will attract. For example, I eat healthy, exercise and have a strategy for dealing with stress to increase and maintain my health. The power of attraction is very powerful. The one thing important in regards to the power of attraction is not to use the word, want. When you want something, it means you don't have it. You must believe and feel you already have it.

To stay in tune with the theme of this book I want to discuss the emotional side of a good lifestyle. It may be one of the hardest things for people to address in their life. If we don't find some strategies or good spiritual habits, we will be controlled by our emotions. Instead we can control or pick the emotions best suit us. You are the only living organism able to reflect on how you feel and why.

There are many techniques you can use to analyse and experience your emotions. There is meditation, hypnosis, h'oponopo, EFT, or simply reflecting on the day and how you feel and why. There are many more techniques than listed here and you can find some in the other chapters of this book. My experience working with patients is that it's important to find the strategy best suited for you. All of these techniques have one thing in common. We bring to our attention a thought nor feeling. An example would be, "Today I am angry because I didn't get promoted at work this year". Bringing to attention our thoughts or feelings allows us to decide if it's true or there are other versions to our story and maybe a solution. You can also decide whether it's a thought or feeling you want to own. I find that most of the time patients don't even know why they are having a feeling or emotional state until they bring it to their attention. This allows you to clean the feeling that doesn't matter or you don't want to own. Even better yet not to carry your story and feelings around for days, months, and even years.

Living in the present moment is another way of not carrying a story around with you. The thoughts we have in our head are stories from the past or something that may happen in the future. This means you are not living in the present moment. We will never have the past or the future, life is made up of moments. You pass your life in a trance for days, months, even your entire life. But anything you do, be it cooking a meal or going for a run, is more enjoyed when being fully present in the moment. There are ways to regain our presence. One is going to a park or being outside and examining your surroundings. You look at a flower and examine it as if it's the first time you're seeing one. Using most of your senses also turns off the voice in your head. You observe the flower, smell it, feel it, the temperature of the air, and the noises you hear. We have a beautiful universe you need to observe it and be in harmony with it. You know what they say, "don't forget to slow down and smell the roses".

I would like to elaborate a little on the power of meditation which can also be considered a form of hypnosis. We have a ton of programs built into our sub-conscious mind. These have been formed from our childhood experiences, from our parents, and even passed down from generations. An example of such a program would be when we are touched by another person and feel fear or not comfortable. This could have been created from being beaten as a child or physically abused. They are imprinted into our subconscious mind with an associated emotional state. Most of the programs we have are good yet some aren't good or healthy. They were all created for self-survival. To reprogram these, we can use many techniques but I have found that meditation is the most effective method. What you can do is get into a meditative state by yourself, guided by someone, or use an audio recorded source and then imagine the life or day you would like to have. You Imagine it in every detail with all of your senses. You need to associate feelings or emotions to your experience. Associating emotions to your experience is a major key to the reprogramming process. I urge you to try it at least once, it will change your life.

Did you know that you can experience anything you want in your dreams? You can travel to faraway places you have never been before, you can fly like a bird, and even visit people. First of all, our mind doesn't know the difference from an experience in a dream or a waken state until we give it a label. We say, "oh, I was dreaming". You can influence your dreams or even decide what you are going to dream about. One way is meditating just before you go to bed, imagining the life you want to have. Another way is to write down the life and experiences you want onto several sheets of paper. To make it even more powerful, add pictures, colours, and emotional states you want to have. You can have one page of your home and family, one of your job and finances, one of places you want to see, and you can even have pages where you are flying like a bird. There are no limits in our dreams. Just before you go to sleep look through your pages. Influencing your dreams is also good way of reprogramming your unconscious mind.

The last thing I want to point out is the following, firstly that we are either growing emotionally or degrading. There is no in between. And secondly, the stress hormones of cortisol and adrenaline are highly acidic substances. If you are living in a state of fear, anger, or the lack of love for yourself, only you can decide to make the change. No one can do it for you. You can't change someone else, the only person you can change is yourself. Life is a beautiful thing enjoy it and experience it. Love will keep you in harmony with the universe.

Love,
Mike

ABOUT MIKE SENIOR

I'm a Chiropractor and an alkaline health coach. I've been helping people achieve an optimum level of health for over twenty-seven years now. I do this through chiropractic adjustments that free up our innate intelligence flowing through our nervous system. I don't heal you; I stimulate the body to heal itself. These blocks, or subluxations, are caused by three lifestyle choices: chemical, emotional and physical. This is where the alkaline health coaching comes into play. I perform a live and dry blood analysis to determine objectively where you specifically need to make changes in your life. On the chemical side I recommend an alkaline diet, regular fasting, proper hydration and eating raw as feasibly possible. On the emotional side I emphasize finding the proper strategy suitable for you. One needs to achieve love and happiness. There needs to be a cleaning of unwanted thoughts, the sub-conscious mind needs to be reprogrammed. Thus, achieving the life, one chooses, this is done through various techniques. It is probably the hardest area in our lifestyle to address yet not impossible. You take baby steps at first before you start running. Last but not least the physical aspect. One needs to exercise on a regular basis. I recommend people to find something that they enjoy doing. It needs to include exercise for maintaining tone, cardiovascular health and elasticity.

After twenty-seven years of coaching I have come to the realization that people aren't going to implement all of my advice. They usually will do it in stages. The more benefit they find the more they will apply.

 "You can take a horse to water but you can't make them drink it."

COMMUNICATION FOR CONNECTION

by Juanita Viale,
Inspired Marketer & Mindset Coach

"The words we speak is the house we live in." - Rumi

#thewordswespeak
Everything is energy, even the words we speak.

Every word carries an energetic charge either positive or negative and sends out a corresponding vibration. They can raise us up or break us down. They can restore peace or create wars. They can save a life or take one. They can nurture, heal and restore. They can also abuse, cause disease, and drain your energy. They can give us salvation or condemnation. They can educate or manipulate.

The words we hear as a child live in our subconscious. They form our beliefs and the way we view the world. They create our reality and form our dreams, hold our pain and free our inner light.

Words cause emotions that have physical effects on our bodies through our biochemical reactions to them.

Words form the thoughts in our minds and the images we see based on those thoughts. They form the language we speak to each other, and form the dialogue we have with ourselves.

Words hold so much power and relentlessly fill our heads. The quality of all our communication is determined by the quality of our words.

Communication is the exchange and translation of messages.

This exchange is internal, external, spiritual, physical, mental, energetic and biochemical.

The smallest words can have enormous effects like No. Yes. I do. I can. I can't. How? I'm safe, if I had. Our tendency is to remember the painful words that have the capacity to live within our minds for a lifetime.

> *"If you talk to a man in a language he understands it goes to his head, If you talk to him in his language, it goes to his heart."*

#natureofconnection

When we speak about connection we normally are speaking about our connection to others as well to the entity larger than ourselves whether you name it God, the creator, or the universe. There are all types of connection, external, internal, biochemical, neurological, energetic and spiritual with communication happening at all levels, even down to our cells and vibration.

True connection happens when a sent message is received and its meaning is understood. Yet this is the part where disconnection tends to happen because of the gap between the message and its translation. Sometimes the message sent isn't received or completely understood as intended. A connection happens when the message gets through.

External connection which is the type that we most relate to when we speak of connection has so many variables. Our moods, our energy, our history, our pain, our cognitive ability, our personality as well as our relation to the person we are communicating with and everything they are bringing to the conversation or experience. When you consider all these variables it's amazing that we connect at all! But we do, because it is in our nature to connect. Our lives depend on it.

Our connection to our external world is based on our perceived beliefs about it. When we feel lonely, we are disconnecting ourselves from the external environment making us feel separate and isolated. We say "I want to be alone".

Our perceived view of the external environment mirrors how we feel on the inside. When we feel like the world is happening to us instead of for us, this tendency is known as "victim consciousness" such as in Why is this happening to me?

When my second child Taylor was born, she was premature at 8 months with underdeveloped lungs and suffered a massive brain haemorrhage. She barely survived. We were in the hospital 5 ½ months and had 1 week left to go. She was finally out of the neonatal unit and in the gastroenterology unit for general medicine. There were 4 rooms to each section, and we were the only ones there.

I had thought it would be an easy week and anticipated our final leave of the hospital. The last 5 ½ months were the hardest months I ever had in my life, not knowing for the first 3 months if my daughter was going to live or die.

Just when I thought I was done witnessing all the pain and suffering I could bear, something beyond my worst nightmare arrived.

As the hospital was overcrowded in the units for abused children, they brought in two children, one 4-year-old girl and the other a 1-year old baby boy. The little girl had been brutally raped by her mother's boyfriend, and the little boy had cigarette burns and was uncared for. While the little boy was oblivious and calm, it was the little girl who broke me into pieces.

We were separated by a glass partition, her crib up against it with my chair right on the other side. Her face was pressed up to the glass and she screamed all night and all day, screaming her abusers name.

I thought I was in hell.

All I wanted to do was take that little girl in my arms and hold her, but as I wasn't her immediate family, I wasn't allowed. You can imagine the unbearable emotional tundra rolling through my head, and all I could do was ask myself why. Why was this happening to me? Why was I here? Why did I have to witness such horrific damage to a child who was just inches away from my face with tears cemented onto her cheeks as if she had been crying for months.

The pain in my chest grew and I thought I would explode. I kept asking why and then I became still. I sat down, the little girl watching me and then the message washed over me. As I looked around the room, I unexpectedly blurted out loud the answer to my question, I am here because no one else is.

In that moment with my eyes wide open, the little girl looking at me in wonder as I realized my purpose and noticeably feeling the shift in the energy that had just taken place.

I was there because no one was there. Not only was I the mother to my own daughter quietly sleeping in the crib next to me (how she didn't wake up to the screaming I believe was the grace of God), in that moment I needed to be the mother to these two beautiful innocent souls who so desperately needed love and attention.

I started to play with the little girl, taking my daughters toys and using them as puppets. I gave her a doll so that at least she had something to hold on to. I reported everything she said to the investigators and child protective services officers who came in, and basically kept that beautiful child as distracted as possible with loving smiles and play.

By getting still and shifting the focus away from myself (the victim consciousness) which filled my head with so much grief, I was finally able to receive the message, or more appropriately, my call to service. And it was the most profound lesson I have ever learned about my connection to the external environment and to the universe which for me is God.

The reality of our lives reflects our inner dialogue and connection.

During a session with a client of mine who decided to commit to a new path of healing after a lifetime of brokenness, chronic illness and abusive events, she justified her current state of being by saying, "I am damaged."

The inner dialogue that had occupied her conscious and subconscious mind was the deep-rooted belief that she was a damaged person beyond repair, ladened with the hopeless feeling that she would never be whole again or feel better.

After continuous repetition of this thought, I am xxxx (that which you feel), your subconscious will not only believe it as true but search for opportunities in your external world to validate that negative belief. All the choices we make are directly influenced by our subconscious beliefs. Our negative cycles of choices, emotions and circumstances we call our reality.

I went through 8 years of chronic lack of sleep whilst taking care of my disabled daughter at home. Along with checking to see if she was alright, Taylor had to be turned a couple of times through the night since she couldn't turn herself.

As you can imagine, I was completely overridden with fatigue and tiredness. Sometimes family or friends would come over, and empathetically say 'Poor you. Unknowingly, 'Poor you' slipped in through my exhausted mind and sunk in as my belief.

The thought of actually feeling strong and full of energy was tucked away in a faraway corner in my mind. The thought itself was tiring. Eventually, I lost my conscious ability to voice my truth that I was not okay, while keeping up the appearance to others that I was seamlessly managing my life. In actuality, I was drowning in the self-imposed illusion that I had to be superwoman, superwife, and supermom.

As a result, I completely lost connection to myself which later cost me my marriage. By being disconnected with myself, I also disconnected my presence to others.

The words 'Poor me' won.

Even when I used to share my grief and situation with my dear Cuban friend Gladys, she would say Y tu que? (and you what?) because in sharing my stories with her, I was always the one left out of the story. They were about everyone else and their needs or expectations. In my tired state of despair, the feeling that I didn't matter in the story was revealed.

In Cuba they say 'virar la tortilla' which literally means flip the tortilla, or more commonly, turn the page, turn a new leaf, move forward. But it also has a second meaning in that when someone is trying to manipulate or control you, you give it right back so they know you are aware of what they are attempting to do. For me this translated to having the courage to stand firmly in my vulnerability by expressing my truth.

Y tu que? Where are you in your story?

"I AM THAT I AM" - Exodus 3:14

"I am grateful for what I am and have. My thanksgiving is perpetual." - Henry David Thoreau

"I am just a child who has never grown up. I still keep asking the 'how' and 'why' questions. Occasionally I find an answer." Stephen Hawkings

"If I have to, I can do anything. I am strong, I am invincible, I am a Woman."- Helen Ready

Dialogue Detox Exercise:
At the end of your day, journal your experience as a list. Highlight all the negative words you can find.

You will immediately see the quality of your inner dialogue vocabulary.

And now rewrite them in an active positive voice.

Our biochemical and neurological connections are related to all the communication that happens within our bodies microscopically between cells and our physical structures. When we dance, we release the pleasure hormone Dopamine which floods our body and our mood is happy. The same goes for when we are stressed, adrenaline, cortisol and norepinephrine are released to prepare us for the perception of a potential threat.

The foods and drinks we consume also communicate with our bodies. The process of cellular respiration which converts the food you eat into energy for the body is a biochemical reaction that is based on cellular communication. So yes, even your food is speaking to you!

Our energetic connections for many seem mystical and unknown.

We all vibrate a frequency. You can notice when a person is in low energy as well as high energy. Like walking into the Zumba class with the music pumping to raise the energy frequency in the room to motivate people to move and exercise. Or walking into a room just after someone was having an argument where the tension is palpable, or walking into a room when a baby is sleeping, you immediately tune into the calm peaceful energy by becoming quiet.

I always knew about our chakra centres, auras and vibrations, but I'd never paid active attention to it. I just knew they were there and that's all. As my daughter only speaks a few basic words, our communication is heavily reliant on visual, non-verbal communication and energy. I know exactly how she is feeling by her facial expressions, her body position and her vibration. I can tell when she is sick or starting to be sick, when she is sad or tired. The moments when she understands a joke or play is when I am fully attuned to her energy and she reacts because she is attuned to mine. We are fully connected just by our energetic connection and communication.

If I was distracted and not present, her engagement and understanding of our play would be influenced since my energy would be directed elsewhere. This is how subtle and sensitive energetic connections are whether alone or shared. By understanding this subtlety, we can choose to actively place our awareness on how we are feeling, checking in regularly throughout the day

> *"There is always a gap between intention and action."*- Paulo Cohelo

#ConsciousIntentions

When you decide to commit to the transformation of creating and living a positive-led life of wellbeing, you are setting the intention to consciously make better choices based on love instead of fear, anger or pain. When we set intentions, we are saying that we are going to be present and connected within ourselves. This means you will hold these intentions active in your mind and heart as you are confronted by unwanted or unforeseen situations that will challenge you.

It means choosing to stand from the perspective of stillness and wisdom rather than reaction and judgement. It means the willingness to say No to things, people, or situations that don't serve your highest good. It means saying Yes to opportunities that come to you without letting self-doubt convince you otherwise. It means disconnecting from distractions to discover the miracles of taking inspired action, big or small. It means acknowledging the past is the past, appreciating the wisdom learned from it and leaving it there.

It means you are committing to being a new version of yourself from where you are standing right now.

An intention by definition is a thing intended, an aim or plan. In medicine, it means the healing process of a wound as in "the healing of a lesion or fracture without granulation (healing by first intention)."

Our intentions are pathways to healing as they are naturally based in positive growth and expansion. Our conscious state of setting them is providing the resistance free mental environment conducive for this energy to grow and expand within you.

Prayer is similar in that we are acknowledging our intentions and surrendering them to a higher source. Prayer puts us in the heartspace in preparation to receive blessings. Gratitude is the highest form of receivership that helps you get into the vibration of receiving because when you say Thank You, you do so because something was given to you.

Normally when you invite someone over for dinner at your home, you would prepare the table and clean up the room to receive them. The same with conscious intentions, you are preparing the mental room to keep these positive thoughts active within you. However conscious intentions do not just stand alone.

They require one more element, and that is action. A thought without action is just a mere thought.

"Move with no resistance towards the kindest thought involved with action".- Byron Katie

"All good thoughts and ideas mean nothing without action."-Mahatma Gandhi

"Action without thought is empty. Thought without action is blind." - Kwame Nkrumah

"If you spend too much time thinking about a thing, you'll never get it done."-Bruce Lee

So how do we set conscious intentions? With action.

Conscious Intention Exercise:
1. Write down the things that you would like to see unfold in your life and one action you need to take. Perhaps it's a better relationship with your kids and the action could be to be more present with them by committing to putting down your phone when you are with them. Read your intention out loud several times.

2. Prepare your mental space by getting quiet for a few minutes and allowing the stillness to settle in. Close your eyes.

3. In your mind, state your intention and the action you will take. Repeat it several times and be aware of how your body is feeling. If you are feeling unsettled in any area of your body, breathe into it several times. If you are still feeling unsettled go back and rewrite your action. Perhaps your action is too big of a thought for your logical mind at this moment. Write an easier simpler feeling action and return to getting quiet again to try it

for another time.

4. As you repeat the intention in your mind, feeling the energy of your body, start to envision what that would look like and feel and stay in that space for a few minutes.

5. Then just as you were watering a newly planted seed, you are going to let it rest, assured that it is in the best condition to grow and it's planted. It's done. Checked off the list. By doing so you are placing your trust into the universe (you can call this God, higher realm, whatever name or deity you believe in) to align your energy as an open connected channel.

6. Take a deep breath in and let it go slowly. Open your eyes.

7. On your written intention, write down the time you are going to take the action, set a reminder on your phone as if it is an appointment and treat it as such.

8. When the time comes for you to do the action, don't think about it too much, just start moving physically to get you going.

With each day of successfully completing the simple action step, the energy of your conscious intentions will start to gather momentum. You will feel more motivated, confident, and inspired to keep going because you are in alignment with your higher Self. And like with any other skill, the more you repeat it, the easier it feels and becomes a habit, a habit that is rewiring your belief system, changing your life and becoming your new way of being.

"Light and shadow are opposite sides of the same coin. We can illuminate our path or darken our way. It is a matter of choice."- Maya Angelou

#PowerofChoice

There is so much power in your freewill to choose and make decisions. All that power vanishes when your decisions are made out of fear. They are reactive decisions that carry negatively charged energy and are heavily influenced by our imagination. The word we are using in the decision-making process will tilt the scale of the decision by the influential energy of the word.

This is the most widely used example of how this works.

Say you that you are asked to walk on a wooden plank on the floor. You most likely would walk across it with general ease. Now put the same wooden plank between the rooftop of two high-rises and your ease to walk the plank would be greatly affected as your mind would create the image or thought of you falling down. Thoughts like fall to my painful death occupy your mind. And even if you try to win over your imaginative thought by using your willpower, the mental effort you are giving to overcome the fear actually gives the thought of falling to your death more dominant energy.

Basically, you're trying too hard and getting in your own way.

This is known as the law of reverse effort as defined by French psychologist, Émile Coué.

"When the imagination and willpower are in conflict, are antagonistic, it is always the imagination which wins, without any exception."

When you begin to learn how to meditate, the thoughts ramble through your mind and you say to yourself that you just have to force yourself to concentrate and you will arrive to the state of mediation. The feeling is also similar to when you are trying really hard to remember the name of a song when telling your friend about it and then comes to you at night as you're lying in bed. Forcing a smile when you are upset. I'm going to force myself to not eat that cookie.

Words and phrases like force, try harder, Why can't I ...are key terms here, let them be your cue that you are trying too hard. Turn your weight bearing "Shoulds" into "Coulds" that are open with possibility.

The tendency with choice is that when you find yourself in a challenging situation or difficult moment, it is so easy to prescribe to the idea that there is no choice available to you. You feel stuck. But in every moment, you always have the power of choice. You have the power to choose to focus on other things like better thoughts, to direct your attention elsewhere, to get quiet, to ask for help, to get more information, to surrender it to your higher source.

When you find yourself saying 'I had no choice', you are actually reinforcing your old negative thinking patterns because the habit of the old beliefs will convince you to do so. We are wired for comfort, and comfort feels safe and good.

If you want to truly change for the better, adopting a positive vocabulary with the passion of a positive vocabulary snob is essential. Just as you would eat healthy food as part of a healthy lifestyle, you can also develop the skill of using a positive vocabulary full of gratitude, appreciation, love, blessings, gifts and growth and expansion. And like any skill when practiced enough, it then becomes a natural way of being. And yes, this includes when people cut you off when you're driving.

Word Energy Exercise: Absence and Presence
Say it gently or in your mind and think about how each statement feels.
The absence of approval and the presence of trust
The absence of negative thoughts and the presence of possibility
The absence of self-doubt and the presence of support
The absence of resentment and the presence of peace
The absence of darkness and the presence of illumination
The absence of inaction and the presence of flow
The absence of perfectionism and the presence of creativity
The absence of insignificance and the presence of light
The absence of judgment and the presence of appreciation
The absence of distraction and the presence of community
The absence of numbness and the presence of faith
The absence of brokenness and the presence abundance
The absence of disconnection and the presence of love

When communicating for connection, the goal is to feel the energy without judgement, anger or preconceived assumptions. Remember the subconscious brain will believe whatever you tell it regardless if it is true or not. When you make assumptions, you create a story and visions and your subconscious believes it as truth.

But there is a caveat here to remember. When you have a negative experience it's not to say that you are going to justify it by saying to yourself that it's okay when it was something that was aimed to hurt you. You are not trying to trick yourself into positivity by ignoring your pain or by telling yourself it doesn't matter. Feel the pain, acknowledge its presence, deeply breathe into it, hold it and release, and then observe it from a distance knowing that you will feel better. You will feel better because the feeling of wellbeing is important to you. And that forgiveness at some point will be necessary to truly move past it.

Communication for connection requires active listening. This means clearing the thoughts in your head to be fully present when communicating. Actively listening to your body as well when you are speaking to someone or thinking to yourself. You're not listening to respond, but rather listening in order to feel the active energy that is present.

When someone shares a problem or personal story, there is a tendency to want to help them by suggesting a solution in order to fix their problem. But most people share in order to be heard, not for a solution. Sometimes we share our stories because it helps us figure out where we stand in it. Sometimes we share just to not hold the negative experience inside ourselves. If you find yourself interrupting or listening with a response already in your mind than take that as a cue that you are not actively listening.

However, when people repeatedly share their negative stories, they are actually adding momentum to that negative energy and keeping it active in their minds. Have you ever known someone or had a friend that only called you with their problems?

These are the types of people that try to suck you into their misery like energy vampires. Negative thoughts and emotions are addictive by releasing hormones that the body then becomes used to overtime and wants more of, sending the signal to your brain to look for some more negative opportunities. These people aren't present because they are disconnected in the rapture of negativity.

Television programs and movies are made with this in mind to pique your emotions and feed them more of what they crave. Movies and tv series that get bloodier and more violent with each episode...creating the need to watch more. More drama, more pain, more nudity, more chaos, and more things to feed and reinforce the addictive force of negativity. News programs that only report on bad news because they get higher ratings.

Communication with connection is a skill and an awareness that practiced over a period of time, will change your life for the better. Taking stock of the positive people in your life and the activities you participate in, the new words that you will speak and thoughts you will focus on and the discipline to quiet your mind in order to connect to your higher Self will all serve your highest good. Taking action while trusting the process will give you a sense of purpose because you are in alignment with who you really are.

Love,
Juanita

ABOUT JUANITA VIALE

Originally from southern California, Juanita Viale has spent the last 20 years living in Costa Rica and the Côte d'Azur. A former newspaper publisher and co-founder of Ineuf.com, she now serves as an inspired marketing and coaching consultant for entrepreneurs and companies in France, Monaco, London and the Netherlands. She holds a degree in Food Science & Nutrition from San Diego State University and has always been passionate about health, nutrition and wellbeing. She is the mother of two daughters, one of who is completely disabled, a journey that has moulded her agency of presence and unwavering faith.

" I've learned that people will forget what you said, people will forget what you did, but people will never forget how you made them feel." -Maya Angelou

YOU ARE WHAT YOU EAT, YOU ARE WHAT YOU THINK.

By Natasha Volchkova

First of all, I would like to thank my lovely husband - Alexey. Without His wisdom, without his intelligence, without his titanic patience, without his permanent support I would never have become who I am now!

And of course - Mirav Tarkka, who made my dream come true, who recharges me (and all of the authors of this book) daily with her powerful positive energy despite everything, just so you could enjoy my chapter for you.

The connection between mind and body has been known for many years,

> *"In a disordered mind, as in a disordered body, soundness of health is impossible."*
>
> *Marcus Tullius Cicero*
>
> *"To keep our body in good health is a duty ... otherwise we shall not be able to keep our mind strong and clear." Buddha*
>
> *"The body is created by the mind"*
>
> *Friedrich Schiller.*

I would like to welcome you to my very first publication in this unique book, where you find so many different views on ONE subject – the interconnection between the human body and mind. I tried to use the most understandable and obvious examples and explanations for those, who want to achieve unity of body and mind, but do not yet have sufficient information. Both facts from my personal life and scientifically confirmed studies will be given. The idea is to get as close as possible to understanding the interaction system of our body as a single organ without dividing it into separate parts. This is the first step, the starting point. I hope I will succeed in taking you on a journey to a better version of yourself.

We are all used to dividing our body into separate, independently coexisting parts. If we experience a headache, we go to the pharmacy and get medicine, without asking ourselves where the pain came from and why. We temporarily eliminate the discomfort without thinking about the reason for it. Because this is what we do, we eliminate but do not investigate. Most of us do not realize that frequent headaches are caused by dehydration or a lack of magnesium in the body.

If after dinner, we get sleepy and have that tenth cup of coffee so we can keep up with everyone else, we never think to find out why; maybe our body lacks iron? Or maybe gliadin is sensitive to protein, which is part of gluten and causes irritation of internal organs. Our body constantly tries to communicate, gives external signals, a gentle nudge so we would try and figure it out, but we either do not have the possibility (because of lack of time, or lack of information ...) to read, connect seemingly unrelated things, connect inward, merge together - body-mind-soul

For many years now, I have been practicing and helping my clients to live in harmony, be united, listen and recognize signals that our body gives us, trying in this way to restore the natural balance of everything needed for a healthy and happy life, macro and micro elements, the fuel for our body and mind.

Previously, when I did not have this knowledge, did not feel united, did not associate physical ailments with mental imbalance, and vice versa – I felt a little like a dusty bag, forgotten by our Creator in a dark and lonely corner and occasionally people passed by and touched this bag (me) and clouds of dust fell down, and at that moment I felt failure, fear and despair. During my school years, I fought desperately with my body, not allowing it to gain any weight, limiting the necessary nutrients and building materials for the cells that were needed for a young, growing body. The beginning of this psychosis was caused by a visit to a summer camp. I found it a difficult place to endure and repeatedly asked my parents to take me back home, alas they needed to work and I apparently needed to rest in nature but for me it was suffering. At the camp there was a girl who was 1 kg lighter than me. In Russia it is customary to be put on the scales at the beginning of the camp and at the end so they could check they fed you well!

I couldn't deal with this, all my life everyone had been unconsciously damaging me by complimenting me on the fact that I was so thin, slender and pretty... and since my willpower is incredibly strong, I could survive for several days on 1 apple and 30 grams of instant porridge. When I look back now at photographs from that time, I looked very unhealthy. People in the subway used to go out of their way for me, fearing that at the next sharp turn my body would collapse like a house of cards.

Then, as often happens, Bulimia abruptly replaced Anorexia: when you no longer have the energy for anything and the hunger is present, a breakdown occurs, and you start eating without stopping, without any sense of proportion, filling your stomach with everything edible you come across. But the weakened and exhausted organism, unable to digest the entire volume of food that it was suddenly given, rejects it by nausea. For a person who is passionately hungry, but equally passionate about not gaining weight - this is the perfect solution - you eat everything you want, you chew and enjoy, and then just leave everything in the toilet, feeling this incredible lightness in your stomach and memories of the delicious food you had.

But no matter how hard we try - our body was not created to function that way; we cannot deceive our body by trying to trick the mind. And the consequences were not long in coming: teeth began to wear out and deteriorated due to the constant acid that passed through, brittle hair, nails and horrible back pain were all signs of a lack of vitamins and minerals washed out with every nausea attack. The main source of minerals and trace elements entering our body is in the food. We are what we eat and I often add - we are what we think!

Do not let your body suffer, do not deprive it of those vital components that it needs so badly; be in harmony with it, listen to it, respond to its signals. Talk to it, when you are given a clear signal by your body, ask why, what is wrong, what did I eat or drink that caused this signal.

If our body realizes we are trying to take care of it, trying to find the answers to the problem, it will be forever grateful and it will give you the answers you seek, it won't leave you in the dark.

I can confidently say that the body has the ability to heal itself, we only need to let it and not interfere. It is never too late!

Today, the rhythm of life is ten times faster to what it was 40-50 years ago. We get a huge amount of information to process. However, equally it seems, we have less time for ourselves, for solitude and communication with our inner world, to reunite with ourselves. To keep up with this rhythm, the style of nutrition has been simplified and, alas, not for the better. More and more fast-food restaurants are appearing, using products of lesser quality and frequently simply damaging our body.

How often are we told by commercial companies "This is what you need to maintain normal minerals and vitamins in your body", or: "a new formula provides your hair with a healthy look (!) And natural (!) shine ". We're all popping vitamins and pills but not asking ourselves why our hair is not naturally shiny and healthy. Because here's the thing, we should be getting the majority of our vitamins and minerals through food, a supplement can never completely measure up to what we get through the food we eat. And we, being too busy and looking for a fast fix, succumb to advertising, we opt for that quick "healthy" breakfast without checking what is in the box. We quickly glance at the packaging and see "rich in fibre" or "more calcium for strong bones" and often buy things which our body doesn't need... Most store-bought breakfast cereals are simple processed carbohydrates, which are instantly broken down and absorbed into the system, often leading to weight gain, since such carbohydrates should be immediately converted to energy (i.e. sports and active training) but a lot of people go straight to the office instead.

Those of us who understand that this will not benefit the body, will pass the processed cereals and opt for "traditional oatmeal" which takes a little longer to prepare, but will benefit your body ten times more: it takes a lot more energy to digest this kind of breakfast and to break it down into glucose, which is then released very slowly into the system, making it less attractive in order to be stored in fat.

Why doesn't your hair shine without that magic shampoo? Your hair has already been condemned by you. But before you judge yourself and others perhaps think about why you are doing this? What can you change to see things from a different angle? It's not rare to have thin hair but dull and brittle is direct evidence that our hair is lacking in nutrients, vitamins at least - group B. You can also take a blood test for vitamin E and vitamin A.

Calcium, Phosphorus, Potassium... Iron, Copper, Manganese... Did you know that Manganese is present in our body ? It is necessary, albeit in small doses, in the bones, liver, kidneys and pancreas and helps the body to form bones, connective tissues and is involved in fat and carbohydrates metabolism. By maintaining manganese, zinc and copper at the required level in the body, the development of osteoporosis can be prevented. Manganese is found in nuts, in tea, in leafy green vegetables (such as spinach, cabbage, kale). Etc. Zinc, Copper, Cobalt, Iron - all these trace elements play an important role in keeping our body and mind healthy!

Studies at one of the American universities have shown that the use of products that include gluten (namely, the protein that is present in its composition - gliadin) significantly worsens the condition of patients with schizophrenia. And vice versa – the presence subsides with the absence of gliadin in the diet.

Having learned about this, I began to look closely at the behaviour of my hyper- and gluten-free - active daughter at a time when products containing gluten and vice versa were present in her diet. I can say with confidence – if gluten were absent, her behaviour, emotional background and school performance were much more positive than with regular use of products containing gluten.

It is important to clarify here that I am not, and by no means I recommend or insist, an adherent of Orthorexia - a belief in an exceptionally healthy lifestyle without the right to relax – for example by enjoying a warm, deliciously smelling croissant. On the contrary, I consider it normal – our body receives a lot of information from different sources, but just like we filter our intake of information by ignoring spam, the same is necessary when it comes to food. It's ok to have a croissant from time to time, it's an exception to the rule, but when consumed regularly, it will prevent your body from functioning properly.

Here's the science behind it: research has found that the human microbiome (the group of bacteria, yeast and viruses that live in the gut) is critical for more than digesting food. It is the control centre for the entire body. The microbiome is linked to manufacturing vitamins, regulating metabolism and blood sugar, and influencing both genetic expressions and brain chemistry. Isn't that amazing? The gut and the brain are so connected to each other. For every message from the brain to the gut there are nine messages from the gut to the brain. These messages control the brain's response to stress, brain hormone production, the activation of the brain's own immune system, the growth of new brain cells (neurogenesis) and the adaptability of these new cells to learn (neuroplasticity), plus other functions. So, no more doubts – we are what we eat, literally. But here's the good news – our microbiome can begin to change in as little as three days when you change your diet.

When my clients come to see me, during those first moments of communication, I am able to construct a physical and psychological portrait of them. I can determine what they eat, how nervous they are (this can be determined by the condition of the skin of the face, by the shape of their body, overweight or underweight, by the way they communicate, where they look, clench their fists, shakes their knees or bite their nails). There is a reason for everything and an explanation for all behaviour that develops. In order to be able to "read" a person's behaviour and condition, one must be in harmony, in balance with the body, soul and mind. And, when you are and have the capability, to understand the person in front of you, their actions and thoughts - you will be able to avoid many conflicting situations with colleagues, family or friends, that often arise through ignorance and misunderstanding.

Each of us has their own formula for how to be a whole, single organism. And only you can deduce it by trial and error. Don't be afraid of making mistakes, we are all people, we all make them at some point, but without trying, we will never know the truth.

Food and nutrients are only one part of the balance, I would like to talk about another part. As my teacher and founder of the Institute for Integrative Nutrition Joshua Rosenthal called it "Primary Food". Following his theory of "A Happy and Healthy life", you must have more or less a balance between the 12 parts of the various types of Primary food:

Spirituality	Creativity
Finances	Career
Education	Health
Physical Activity	Home cooking
Home Environment	Relationships
Social Life	JOY

Put them in a circle and if you try to connect all the points that you mark as the level of satisfaction for each area (from 1 to 10), at that moment, you will see in which place there is a weakness that needs to be improved, strengthened.

The body also responds to external stimuli when it does (thinks) something (about) that is contrary to its nature. If you listen to Bethany Butzer's TED talk, you will see a great example of this. She studied all her life, pushed herself to win every academic award that she could, 10 years in university and got her PhD in Psychology. She got a job at Harvard Medical School. Bethany was very successful and many people were proud of her. But! She was still not happy. The continuous struggle for perfectionism and victory resulted in depression and therapy. Thanks to this therapy - she began to think about HERSELF! She started yoga, meditation and personal development. Prioritize your health and wellbeing. Stop doing things that don't matter to you and start doing things that do!

The absolute relationship of body and mind:

When the child tries to get out of going to piano practice but his parents make him anyway, the child might endure it one or two times. The next time however the child will start displaying physical symptoms and the parents will fall for it and cancel the lesson. But the parents will not look at the link between the body and the soul, our soul does not lie, it tells our body when it's unhappy. As a parent you should be in balance, whole to distinguish between true resistance or manipulation as younger children always know exactly what they want.

When we grow up, due to external influences, we begin to believe that we cannot have and do what we want. We gradually forget about our innermost desire, our passions, instead we worry about failure and not being able to maintain the standard of living we want.

I often remind my clients: "Remember, you will never know if you do not try", and as said by the Japanese Zen master Dogen Zenji- "life is a continuous mistake".

There is no right or wrong way. Everyone has their own path. Each of us has their own mission. If you learn to slow down and are able to analyse the actions in which you feel joy, pleasure those that nourish and inspire you - you need to see them as a lesson, try to understand how you can implement them into your life on a regular basis , which will bring both moral and material satisfaction. What do you give the world around you? What is the goal - after all, you must admit that everything has a goal? Ask yourself: why are you doing this? Are you happy to get up early in the morning to get to work?

Regardless of the circumstances, if you ask yourself what you truly want, allow your mind and body to feel and experience your question, trust your soul's answers, there will be no barriers, your mind will be free and there will be no obstacles in achieving what you want. The question will no longer be Can I? But how and when can I?

I always wanted to be a doctor. As a child I treated my cuddly toys with care and dedication, they were my patients. I even went as far as shaving my doll because she had to undergo complicated brain surgery. I took it very seriously! But my parents (whom I truly love) unfortunately had neither the means nor the time to allow the development of this passion. As a result, I graduated from the university with a degree in economics, followed by a degree in Art. My husband, who is always by my side, delicately guided me in search of an answer to the question - Who am I? Who am I in this world and how can I contribute to it? I need a purpose in life. Yes, I have a husband and a family - I am grateful for this gift. But I am grateful by nature. I cannot accept the gift and not repay the same. This is my essence and I'm proud of it. So, I started by volunteering. First, I took care of a disabled girl, and even though emotionally it was hard, I felt grateful to be able to give her joy. To take her out of her world and see new things. She holds a very special place in my heart.

Then I went to help at a charity that organizes events for children with Down syndrome and a nursing home. Slowly I approached my vocation - to help. It doesn't matter who, but always, always I tried to come to the rescue, sympathize and inspire hope. I was even given a nickname - Positivist.

My husband, patiently watched all my actions and guided me to discover my profession. I graduated as an Integrative Health Coach, achieving balance in all sections of Primary food: Hobby and Social life; Creativity and Career; Education and Joy, Finances and Health in my job and the rest I get from my family and friends.

It was a long path to reach my mission, but I went with the flow and got there when I was ready.

Of course, we are all human and we are all overwhelmed by external circumstances. Sometimes there is an overload of information and we begin to "crash". This can manifest in different forms, but basically the first indicator is the silencing of your inner voice. The desire to blend in and to swap your cashmere bright red cardigan that sets you apart for a grey coat, because you don't want to be different.

By no means do I want to judge people on this planet, my biggest dream is to inspire as many people as possible to release their inner Self, to reunite their body into a single whole. To "Listen to their gut", their intuition, their inner voice which is almost always right – to not let their mind and reason take over their true self.

Very often our feelings become dull, irritation and anxiety make their way in, you can't cope and you start crowding in because it is so much easier than crowding out.

But, as my doctor once said: "this is a very good sign that your indicators are changing, that the body is adapting to new conditions." And this is absolutely normal and it shouldn't frighten you. You should not feel discouraged and think you are back to square one. Your body and mind need to adapt to these new conditions, to new behaviour, to new thoughts, to new gestures.

Last but not least: nowadays there are so many sources where you can find a lot of different and often – beneficial information about anything you want to know. Be cautious – without professional advice it might be dangerous (for example: everybody is taking Vitamin D, as most of people are deficient in it but it can be harmful so you should consult a medical practitioner).

By reading this book you are on the path to a new way of living. We created it - for you, we lived all of it – for you, so please don't wait till your body gives you a sign – start it right now! I believe in you, so believe in yourself!

With lots of Love and Empathy,
Natalia V.

ABOUT NATASHA VOLCHKOVA

Natasha Volchkova was born in Moscow and graduated in both Economics and Art. After a brief stint in Paris she now lives with her family in Monaco. All this time she never truly gave up on her childhood dream of becoming a doctor however at 33 she realised that medical studies would now be out of reach. Not one to be deterred though she realised that she could still achieve her passion of helping others by taking a slightly different route. She graduated in 2018, from the American school of Nutrition, founded by Joshua Rosenthal - IIN (Institute For Integrative Nutrition), as an Integrative Health Coach, and did a further specialization at the same school in the field of Hormones.

Today she works as a health coach helping others to achieve balance between mind, body and soul.

In her free time, she's an avid sportswoman and continues to develop her professional knowledge.

"In a disordered mind, as in a disordered body, soundness of health is impossible."
Marcus Tullius Cicero

LIFE'S TOOLBOX

By Martina Wojtylova Opava

You know how sometimes you think that everything makes perfect sense? You know exactly what's going to happen and you finally seem to have life under control?

Well, I had this feeling in January 2015 as we came home after a breath-taking holiday in Hawaii. My curly haired husband, two charming babies and me, coming back to the cold Prague winter to face a totally unexpected hardship.

"Where's daddy?", asked my 3-year-old girl. My heart stopped beating for a moment. I couldn't lie. I knew in my gut that I needed to tell them the truth. Despite their tender age, I knew my children would be able to handle it. My husband had cancer.

The first emotion that probably comes to your heart now is – compassion. But I'm not writing this chapter for your empathy. I'm doing this simply to show you my unexpected path in the hope it gives you a powerful energy boost to literally help you MOVE from where you are, to where you want to be.

So, a crisis comes. You feel overwhelmed and insecure. You have no idea where to start and there are thousands of thoughts bouncing around inside your head.

I had a serious panic attack in the car. Parked right in front of the hospital, my love waiting for me inside, the only thing I really wanted to do was run back home to bed and hide under the covers. Perhaps I could go to sleep and wake up when everything was over.

Of course, that wasn't an option. Instead, a ruthless warrior woke up inside of me. This strange new energy pushed me into the highest state of self-discipline. I had no idea I was capable of this. Somehow, I didn't dwell on the negative. I could have walked around like a martyr with a scar on my heart. No. Awakening inside me was a kind & loving Amazon woman with a collection of practical day to day skills that have been helping me ever since. An emotional toolbox.

I put the following tools together for people who are trying hard to find harmony in their busy lives. You don't need to experience a life crisis in order to feel unbalanced and overwhelmed. You don't need to go through anything but daily life to understand my point and the benefits of using this toolbox.

My hope for you is to find this eases the stressors of daily life for you and your loved ones.

TOOL #1 THE ENERGY OF ACCEPTANCE

I'm talking about the pure energy that flows in your veins, beats in your heart and flickers in your stomach when you fully accept yourself. Your whole self. Meaning with all your unique talents and potential but also with your limitations and shortcomings. When you can finally be free and feel you are simply "OK" without trying so hard. When you can feel accepted, even when you suck! When you feel loved, even when you are in the middle of an argument. When you feel you can try everything and anything without the fear of making a fool of yourself. That kind of profound acceptance. But that's just the first level.

Accepting the people closest to us in life is the second level of acceptance. Sometimes this is as hard as accepting yourself. Imagine how many times have you felt embarrassed because of what your siblings, parents, partner, spouse or kids did or didn't do? Imagine the time you had to defend something your closest friend said or did, although you actually knew it wasn't 100% right. Accepting our family, partners, and especially our kids with all of their own flaws can actually be such a relief! It frees our soul and our mind and it stops sucking our inner energy. We stop fighting or defending reality and let it be. It deepens our love for life and people in it. Next time you think about 'your people', stick to the positive acceptance instead of resorting to grumbling over things that are out of your control.

The acceptance of the place we call home. The country, the traditions, the weather and the people. This is the third level of acceptance that can also free our minds and save our inner energy. How often have you complained about your hometown? Is it too dirty, too dangerous, too far away…is it not enough? Change it in your inner dialog to be a place you can fully accept. If you live in a capital city as I do, there are dozens of things I hate about the place, but also hundreds that I love. I have consciously made the decision to create a warm and happy home for me and my family here. I have fully accepted this place with everything it offers and everything it lacks. I spend zero energy on complaining, as I believe this place is worth our acceptance. Accept or change it. It's as simple as that. Complaining is the energetic equivalent of a black hole. Save your energy for more important things, you'll appreciate the reserves when you need them another time.

TOOL #2 YOUR INNER VOICE

Imagine you find a line of clothing where every piece created suits you perfectly. You feel empowered and beautiful in everything you put on. At first, you cannot believe it, but at some point, you give in and start enjoying the fact that you don't have to think about it at all! It just IS what it is, perfect without any effort.

It's the same when you find your inner voice, effortlessly perfect. You don't have to worry about what's coming next, because it's no longer a consideration. Some people call it 'intuition' but I personally tend to mix intuition with my rational thinking and past experience, as it's hard to separate those things. I decided to call this voice my inner "life designer". I want to stay open and unbiased when visualizing my future. I want to feel the sparkle and excitement inside of me when playing with my goals for the future. It's like a vivid dialogue between myself and my "life designer":

ME: "So what am I about to do next?"

DESIGNER: "Well, let me surprise you."

ME: "Ok, I'll stay positive and grateful for everything you throw at me!"

DESIGNER: "Let me see….have you ever..?"

ME: "No, not yet.."

DESIGNER: "So, how about trying something new, so you can learn…"

ME: "Well, I'll try my best."

Every time I sit still and picture this inner dialogue I have to laugh. It's like my private challenge to push myself into the best possible outcomes while staying on track in my life. My inner designer offers challenges on a daily basis and sometimes it's about casual family time and other times it's about presenting my million-dollar idea. I never know what the next day may bring, but since I keep my expectations positive and my attitude gratitude, I mostly find the challenges very amusing and beneficial.

So how did I find the "life designer" inside of me?

I felt so miserable that I stopped looking for one! The same theory as when you're trying to have a baby and as soon as you give up trying, it happens. Let it be. Find some time alone, turn off the world around you and start your own dialogue. How do you feel? What are the emotions coming up? What can you learn from your reactions? Study yourself, observe the formulas you inherited from your parents, cry out your fears, clean your inner dialog and listen! There is a life designer inside ALL of us, it's just waiting for you to hire them.

TOOL # 3: TREE OF HELP

Some trees grow in deserts all alone. Most trees grow in groups and make forests. I used to be a lonely alder until I understood that I couldn't manage without help. I needed my fellow trees to help me survive. Your inner critic probably started screaming: "But I'm special! I'm not just anyone... I'm unique!" Yes, you are. Everyone is. We all possess unique and special qualities and yet we're all part of one collective energy. If we put our ego aside and shut down the inner critic, we can see the beauty in being human, together. Whether it is your family, your project team, your soccer team or just an online community of experts, we naturally seek membership to a group we relate to. You may be a genius but we don't want to celebrate our Nobel Prize alone, do we? Let's stop competing and accept the fact that together we can achieve more than alone.

Here is a step by step guide for growing your own Tree of Help.

Grow and nourish your own Tree of Help so you have enough support in all areas of your life, as well as for your continuous growth and the stability at moments of life crisis. First, take a piece of paper and draw a tree. Draw a regular tree with a wide trunk and several branches. Each branch represents one of your life roles.

For example: my tree has 11 branches: Mother, Wife, Daughter, Friend, Charity Creator, Coach, Entrepreneur, Writer, Boss, Woman, Human being.

Think of all your current life roles and you may even include roles that you wish they become part of your life in the future. For each role, draw one separate branch. Some of the branches (and some of the life roles) may be stronger than the others, that's natural. Now, for each branch you need to think of at least 1 person who you can discuss this area of life with, who you can rely on, who can help you if needed, who is an inspiration as well as a fan of yours. If you have 11 branches like I do, you need 11 people you can turn to for advice, motivation, an honest opinion, a casual chat or a quick confidence boost. Write their names above the branch. You may find a few branches without any name. It took me several years to fill in all the spots with people I love and genuinely want in my life. So do not panic, if there are some empty branches. Take it as a challenge. Filling in these empty spots is an opportunity for unique and purposeful growth.

When you write a name above the branch, try to listen to the inner voice inside you. "Do I truly enjoy having this person in my life? Can I be my true self with all of my ups and downs when I'm around this person? Do they only want what's best for me?" If you hesitate, leave the spot empty for a while and come back to it later. It is important for you to choose these people with care and purpose.

My 11 heroes quickly became a bigger part of my life, my journey, my achievements. Thanks to them, I feel more confident in all of my different roles. They remind me of what is important and motivate me to be better every day. Since I have been working with this tool for almost 5 years now, some of my branches have more than 1 name above it, and that's amazing because the tree gets stronger with each name.

How to use the Tree of help

Two heads know more than one.

Are you looking for a piano teacher for your daughter? Perhaps your mother-branch-person was in a similar situation and can give you advice. Feeling angry after a company meeting? Get it out and write a short text to your job-branch-person. Your baby-sitter got sick? Alert your Mom friend-branch-person. Feeling stuck in life? What about a coffee with your coach?

Communication is the key. Get your emotions out of your body, say it aloud, write it down, share it with your Tree of Help, these people will never judge you, they are here to listen and support you! They are YOUR people and they will always be on YOUR side! (If not, exchange them ☺) You will feel empowered with loads of additional energy after you utilize this amazing tool. Remember, you usually know what to do, how to move forward, you know how to listen to your inner life designer, but sometimes we need a little encouraging kick from people we trust to stop talking and start doing – that's why it's so important to have your own unique Tree of Help.

TOOL # 4: SOUL CLEARING

Forgotten promises, unanswered messages, unresolved issues, hurt or suppressed emotions…so much inner dialog inside our souls! Have you ever imagined how it would feel if you had everything sorted and cleared out and feel confident to look everyone straight in the eye, even yourself? Imagine how light and free that would make you feel!

The first thing we asked the Universe, when my husband and I received the shocking cancer diagnosis, was naturally "What did we do? Why are we being punished?" Of course, now we understand these reactions were just the inherited formulas, probably from our families, that immediately made us feel bad. We started assessing our past and tried to figure out what the reason could have been. But we couldn't find anything alarming enough that would cause such a shift in our lives. The good thing was, we talked. We talked and talked and the more we opened up to each other, the stronger our connection became. It was clear we needed to get rid of all the emotional baggage from the past and start dealing with the present and future. Since then, we never really stopped this process of connection. We check and re-checked our status. There will always be so much work with two young children our busy jobs and all of our other roles in life. So, there we were, with time to talk, to plan, to listen to our inner designers. We came up with a daily evening routine and we called it a Soul clearing. It's a mixture of a gratitude practice, mindfulness, relationship coaching and neutral position. Frankly, I believe that thanks to this routine, all our interconnected family relationships significantly improved.

In the evening, after dinner and baths, after the kids brush their teeth and read stories, before falling asleep, that's the perfect time for Soul Clearing. You can do the clearing together with your children and it will strengthen the loving bond between you. Make your environment soothing, some calming scents or soft music and lie down – all in one bed. Quietly start talking about all the joys and tragedies the day has brought us. Breath in and out, slow your mind, lower your voice, calm down and be there for each other. Do not judge each other, do not tease or make fun, this is a moment when you show respect and support for each other. Anything can be said out loud, anything that bothers us inside.

Saying it out loud in a safe and loving environment immediately starts the healing process. Children are usually very open to this, so please leave your "parenting" or "ego" at the door. No matter how similar you experience, nothing can ever be compared because we are all unique individuals. Listen. Show your loved ones a great deal of tolerance, kindness and understanding.

There may be evenings when you don't feel like sharing your worries or fears, but try your best to find the language your children can understand and be forthright with them even when it's uncomfortable. Many times, my children surprised me with amazing empathy and even offered me a simple solution! Do not underestimate children, without our experience and emotional burden, they can have a very clear view of the situations we are dealing with. Moreover, this daily routine can bring all of you a very harmonizing tool for emotional wellbeing – this is so important in the 21st century.

TOOL # 5: ENERGY MANAGEMENT

You go to the gym, for a run, instead of a nice steak, you order a salad with chicken......and you still feel like you deserve a month off to recharge your batteries?! I know exactly what you're talking about. I've been trying my best to establish and keep a few basic healthy habits for years and I'm just not the type. Honestly, I am too lazy to cook a meal a day ahead, too messy to carry my lunch with me, a snob to not eat from a plastic box and too tired to even think about my diet in general. I eat what I find is the best possible option at that moment on the very spot. Don't get me wrong, I do cook for my family. I prepared daily homemade meals for my husband while he was in a hospital as well. I like salads and fish...I'm just not the kind of regimented fitness guru who regularly exercises, counts calories and follows a dietary plan.

I found that often what others see as an energy source, I found to be my energy leak. I wish I knew this 20 years ago and I wouldn't have wasted so much money on fitness clubs and trainers.

I have several energy resources that I hope can help inspire you to find your own energy boosts and leaks.

First, find what your passion is. I am passionate about coaching, lecturing, writing and the more I do it, the more energized I feel. The more courses pre-booked in my calendar, the healthier I feel. I love exercising in the morning when I know that in 2 hours there will be a group of 8 women I can help with their work-life balance. The awareness of what type of work brings me deep satisfaction boosts my energy and was the key to my successful personal energy management.

Second, plan your family fun. I love our family vacations as we travel, explore new places, discuss all kinds of topics and learn about nature and history together. But it's so much work to get to the fun part! If you are a parent you know what I mean. The only thing we can do to truly enjoy some fun is to plan. I mean a real, hard core planning with plan A, B, C and D somewhere deep inside of you if none of the first 3 works out. To make it easier, when I plan some family fun, I need to take care of 3 basic things: 1. food (where will we have lunch? Is there a place we can buy something to drink?), 2. restrooms (don't laugh, I hate going to parks where there's no option of washing your hands) and 3. fun (are there any playgrounds, how long does the tour take, etc.). If I know these 3 staples, I can fully focus on our kids and enjoy the time together. Find your 3 basic staples and start planning your fun!

Thirdly, nurture your romantic sparkle. The endorphins we receive from a romantic relationship can boost our energy like nothing else. Let's not underestimate the power of love. Before our first child was born, we were both so scared of what was going to happen with our partnership after the baby was born that we made a promise. We'll keep going on dates on a weekly basis. That's a hard thing to do in a long-term relationship. However, it's been 10 years now and there were very few days we both decided to call our date off. "How could you do that to your children?" asked some of our friends. Well, we decided this was crucial in being able to give our kids the best parents we could be. Parents who are full of love and energy. Without occasional baby-sitting we would both go insane very quickly and become the parents we didn't want to. It sounds simple but it makes a bigger impact than you can imagine.

Lastly, plan your own little joys. Chit-chatting with a friend while waiting for kids in front of the school, staying in pyjamas till lunch on

Sundays, making chocolate fondue with fruits for a dessert on a casual Wednesday, buying a grande cappuccino instead of a tall one. There are a million ways of bringing joy into our lives. If you consciously plan them ahead, you can start looking forward to them which immediately pumps up your inner energy. In my case, I love surprising my kids. They are absolutely adorable when they didn't expect anything. Their eyes light up and their amazing smiles and the joy that bursts into a giant hug around my neck...I just love it! Make time to think about joys you can easily bring into your life. You'll see the results right away!

Closure

You have just finished reading my Life's toolbox with the top 5 tools described as, The Energy of Acceptance, Your Inner Voice, Tree of Help, Soul Clearing and Energy Management.

Sometimes you think that you know all the theories, you've heard it all, again and again, but nothing really changes for you? Well, you may leave this book and this chapter gathering dust on your bookshelf OR ...

Take action, I truly hope this chapter will not only inspire you but push you into action so you may create the life you love to live.

I wish you all the very best,

With love,
Martina

About Martina Wojtylova

←∞→

Martina is a successful wellbeing coach, soft skills trainer, founder of the unique Women's Energy Program who currently launched her masterpiece project: Soul Clearing methods for parents & children. In 2019 she was nominated for the "Woman of the year" for her charity work. Martina is known for her positive and high energy attitude and seeks nothing less than an outstanding result in all her projects. She is deeply passionate about empowering women in all their life roles.

Martina is a proud working mama and wife inspiring many women around the world but stays humble and grateful for each day in health and happiness.

"When you find your inner voice, you find your life journey."

ACKNOWLEDGEMENTS & GRATITUDE

←—∞—→

This book is the result of bringing together great minds, vast experience, hard work & enthusiasm, but above all the determination of 22 experts to make the world a better place by improving everyone's quality of life.

The work that each one of the authors, the editor, the publisher, the launch expert has put into this has been extraordinary, and without each one's personal integrity as well as the humbleness to work in a team, "ONE" would have never been born.

Alongside us, there were many others who have contributed to the success of this book.

We would like to take this opportunity to show them gratitude and bless them, as they have all been a blessing for us.

Heidi De Love, our editor

Parul Agrawal, our best-seller launching expert

Deepak Gupta (weformat), our book formatting expert

Avv. Luca Brazzit- our legal council

Sabine Matharu- for business guidance

Mihaela Vlad- for our social media ads management

David J. Ross- for our social media training and advice

Our followers, fans, friends, launching teams and supporters all over the world.

Our families, our children, the people who loved us in the most stressful moments, who have inspired us, who have been our "BIG WHOS".

Ourselves, the authors, who have worked intensively and lovingly to give birth to this book, no matter what.

And finally, our readers, who have picked up this book and are sharing our love, passion and knowledge by reading it.

Thank you all, we couldn't have done any of this without you.

With all our hearts,

Your authors.

GIFTS FROM THE AUTHORS

Olja Aleksic
THE ONE: LEADERSHIP GROOVE COMBO: 2hours of intensive Leadership coaching
+ free membership in Leadership Groove closed community.
Sign up via email: sapfogroove@gmail.com

Shalini Arora Kochhar
Free tarot card reading with a happiness quotient assessment
Contact Shalini via email Shalini.sayss@gmail.com

Carina Bernardino
Free access to: "Connect with your version" meditation.
Grab it here:
https://anchor.fm/carina-bernardino/episodes/Conect-with-your-best-version-eanv4p?
fbclid=IwAR185qCKVveINsyzu7KBViyG_CpVlDilcdFR8qm65g1zYJ3DeIFEeUHvqm4

James & Claire Davis
Free access to the 5 day fitness program
Grab it here:
https://38nacademy.com/online-fitness/5-day-free-40plus-back-to-fitness/

Martine de Petter
Energy is the key to your health - A free One online Introduction to Qi Gong session -
To book an appointment for the online session contact Martine de Petter via email
martine@estarmtc.com

Cristina Drannikow
45 minutes Free coaching-healing session On "how to turn your break up into your
next breakthrough"
Free access to 3 downloadable meditations.
To book please email crisdrannikow@hotmail.com

Udi Gon-Paz
Free 20-minute consultation on nutrition or stress management
To book please email udi@monaco.mc

Amy Gyles
Free access to "Aligning with your destiny" meditation.
Get your copy by emailing AGylesIEA@gmail.com

Nikki H
"Mini Creativity Boost" - a 5-day creativity challenge to connect with and boost your creativity.
To get access, email findyourdelight@gmail.com with "Gift" in the subject line.

Klana
"Pleasure Discovery Session".
To book please visit www.talktoklana.us

Sarah Lines
Free access to the Quantum Alchemy Healing audio
download here https://mailchi.mp/924946bea584/quantumalchemyhealing

Rene Murata
Free access to the CEO VOICE COURSE
To claim please go to http://ceoessence.com/work-with-me/voicebreakdown/ and use the code #ONETHEBOOK

Tatjana Obradovic Tosic
Free 90 minute self-care planning call where we will create a strategy on how to develop and sustain your self-care practice
To book please email whensheleads@gmail.com

Jola Pypno-Crapanzano
Free access to the "Five to Thrive" 5 day challenge; tips and strategies how to reach that next level in life everyone wants, desires and deserves.
To join the challenge visit:
https://www.coachingjourneywithjola.com/offers/Phb8Ba2P

Jasjit Rai
Free access to my guide with 3 potent yet simple ways on how you can bring multi-dimensional awareness to your daily life and live your bigger vision.
To grab your copy please email info@joiworks.com with ONE the book in the subject line.

Mike Senior
Free access to "Panayama training" video guide + workbook.
To get your copy please email: seniorchiropratica@gmail.com

Mirav Tarkka
"Power Of Warrior" wonder woman activation meditation.
To access please visit:
https://anchor.fm/onebodymindsoul/episodes/Power-Of-Warrior-Wonder-woman-Activation-Meditation-eabi5k

Elena Berezina Velema
Free access to a one hour personal development coaching online or by telephone.
Reserve your time slot at elena.velema@gmail.com

Juanita Viale
Inspire & Rewire Mindset Coaching Session
Group coaching session working on creating a new inner dialogue with inspired
positive language and some fun exercises to rewire our mindset!
Please email at madameviale@gmail.com

Natalia Volchkova
Free copy of the "New life" guidance session
Get your copy by emailing natalie13a@gmail.com."

Martina Wojtylova Opava
Bonus tool # 6 – free copy of: Soul clearing for children 3+ how to start your child's
mental growth
Get yours by emailing martina.opava@dailyenergy.cz

Manufactured by Amazon.ca
Bolton, ON

14261589R00164